Assessing Writing Across the Curriculum
Diverse Approaches and Practices

Perspectives on Writing: Theory, Research, Practice

Kathleen Blake Yancey and Brian Huot,
series editors

volume 1:
Assessing Writing Across the Curriculum: Diverse Approaches and Practices
edited by Kathleen Blake Yancey and Brian Huot, 1997

Assessing Writing Across the Curriculum
Diverse Approaches and Practices

edited by

Kathleen Blake Yancey
University of North Carolina–Charlotte

Brian Huot
University of Louisville

Ablex Publishing Corporation
Greenwich, Connecticut
London, England

Printed in the United States of America

Library of Congress Cataloging-in-Publication Data

Assessing writing across the curriculum : diverse approaches and
    practices / [edited by] Kathleen Blake Yancey & Brian Huot.
        p.   cm. — (perspectives on writing)
    Includes bibliographical references and index.
    ISBN 1-56750-312-8 (cloth). — ISBN 1-56750-313-6 (paper)
    1. English language—Rhetoric—Study and teaching.
    2. Interdisciplinary approach in education. 3. English language-
    -Ability testing. 4. Academic writing—Evaluation. I. Yancey,
    Kathleen Blake, 1950–   . II. Huot, Brian A. III. Series.
    PE1404.A875 1997
    808'.042'07—DC21   96–52285
                                                       CIP

Ablex Publishing Corporation   Published in the U.K. and Europe by:
P.O. Box 5297   JAI Press Ltd.
55 Old Post Road #2   38 Tavistock Street
Greenwich, CT 06831   Covent Garden
                                     London WC2E 7PB
                                     England

Contents

Preface

.

The WAC Archives Revisited

Toby Fulwiler

Art Young

The current interest in qualitatively assessing writing-across-the-curriculum (WAC) programs is a natural and welcome evolution in the writing process movement. Portfolios, for example, have long been a useful and respectful way to assess student writing in composition classes, dating at least from the work of Ken Macrorie, Don Murray, and Jim Moffet in the mid-1960s. We remember assessing writing students with portfolios in the mid-1970s. However, in the early days of WAC, neither of us tried to convince colleagues in other disciplines to follow our lead. It wasn't until Peter Elbow and Pat Belanoff published their ideas about using portfolios for whole program assessment in the early 1980s that we realized the wider possibilities of portfolio assessment throughout the curriculum.

With the benefit of hindsight, it's clear that WAC also evolved from the writing-process movement, with the earliest programs at Beaver College (PA), Central College (IO), and Michigan Technological University dating to the mid-1970s. Although the evolution of process writing from English classes into classes across the curriculum now seems logical and even inevitable, publicity surrounding these early WAC programs caused something of a revolutionary stir; you could feel it at over-enrolled CCCC workshops and could read it in professional journals. By 1983, more than one third of American colleges and universities reported having WAC programs (Huber & Young, 1986).

Although the general idea of WAC soon became widespread nationally, the local conditions that gave rise to WAC programs were always quite specific. For instance, WAC started at Michigan Technological University (MTU) in response to the perceived institutional problem that graduating seniors were good engineers but poor communicators. Anecdotal stories carried a disproportionate amount of weight in those early years.

One story we both remember vividly from the spring of 1977 is the time Art received a call from a professor in biology complaining that a senior had just turned in a poorly written laboratory report—yet she had received a B+

from Art in English 101. His question: How could students be good writers in English and poor writers in biology? To help answer the question, we talked to the student in question, and found out that she was, in fact, a good student with a 3.0 GPA in her biology major; however, she had no experience writing biology reports nor any guidance for doing so. Nor, apparently, had she realized that clarity and correctness counted in writing outside of English classes.

Meanwhile, simplistic solutions to cure the perceived undergraduate literacy were on the horizon. The Dean of Engineering, for instance, favored a writing competency test for all junior engineering majors, with those who failed taking remedial English until they passed. He was serious, but we considered a rising junior writing examination more of a hindrance than a help in developing students' long-term literacy skills. The president, the provost, alumni, and recruiters had similar stories as well as a variety of fix-it solutions: raise admissions standards, test and track all first-year students, attach dual grades to every student paper—one for writing, one for content. And, everybody looked to the Humanities Department for leadership.

These incidents and others like them crystallized things for us: (a) The young biology major would have passed easily a junior level competency test, but would still have turned in the poor report to her biology professor the next year—passing a test was never a problem for her; (b) many students did not write much outside of English—and when they did, they did not take it seriously; and (c) some instructors were assigning writing—to test and measure rather than rethink and revise—so that accomplished writers did fine, but weak writers got little help. What we needed was a program that would specifically help inexperienced writers and, at the same time, satisfy faculty and administrators that something was being done (Fulwiler & Young, 1982).

In the summer of 1977, Toby, a new assistant professor and newly appointed Director of Freshman Composition, attended an NEH summer institute, "Writing in the Humanities," at Rutgers University to learn more about the composition field in general and how to be a more knowledgeable director of first-year writing courses in particular. As it happened, the primary mission of the three-week seminar was to introduce the ideas of James Britton, Nancy Martin, and the London School of Education—"writing across the curriculum"—to humanities instructors in the United States. Institute leaders included Lee Odell, Dixie Goswami, and Robert Parker. Janet Emig was also at Rutgers that summer, beginning the New Jersey Writing Project; she read a prepublication draft of "Writing as a Mode of Learning" to seminar participants in July. For 3 weeks "writing to learn" was the major agenda in a program that included reading and discussing the ideas of Emig, Britton, Martin, Moffet, Macrorie, Elbow, Schaughnessey, and Kinneavy.

Though Art sent Toby to Rutgers to learn about directing first-year composition, he came back with writing-across-the-curriculum. That October, Toby and Robert Jones held the first interdisciplinary writing workshop for 16 MTU faculty on the screened porch of the Keweenaw Mountain Lodge, 40 miles north of campus.. There was no budget for these first workshops, so each MTU department sponsored one person for two days' meals and one night's lodging. Participants experimented with freewriting and journals, multiple-draft assignments, and peer writing groups—all concepts modeled at the Rutgers Institute.

MTU adapted the British secondary schools model to fit the needs of university-level technical education. We believed that the Britton model of promoting writing-to-learn in the lower grades would promote the same at the higher levels as well, and—at least as far as we took it—we believe we were right. We ran campus-wide workshops—two days during the semesters, four days in the summers—which got many people talking writing and sharing writing-process pedagogy. Early WAC participants included faculty we believed to be among the best and the brightest—or at least the best and most flexible—who offered to introduce more writing to their students in more helpful ways across the curriculum. By the early 1980s, more than a dozen tenure-track humanities department faculty were working in one way or another on the project, co-leading workshops, consulting with academic departments, presenting WAC ideas at professional conferences and in professional journals—work that created a strong sense of purpose among our small community of scholars. Though we didn't know it at the time, the main work of our professional lives had begun.

Across campus, the word-of-mouth reputation of our writing workshops was very good; eventually we secured the help of the new provost in obtaining a five-year, quarter-million-dollar grant from General Motors to transform the MTU campus. He also helped us secure new faculty positions in the Humanities Department; we hired instructors who were committed to a process model of teaching writing and reading, able to collaborate in developing and, increasingly, assessing the WAC program. We hired faculty to participate in program development, not just to fill every gap in the literary canon or conduct traditional literary research. Our primary purpose was to break the long-standing tradition of tenured faculty devoting full energies to literary enterprises while adjuncts and graduate students attended to composition.

During the late 1970s and 1980s, we recruited Randy Freisinger, Diana George, Peter Schiff, Beth Flynn, Bruce Petersen, Carol Berkencotter, James Kalmbach, Jack Jobst, and Cindy Selfe—all of whom now have national reputations in some way connected with their early WAC work. We published *Language Connections: Writing and Reading Across the Curriculum* (1982) in which 14 of us collaborated to disseminate our model of WAC broadly within the profession. Later, we published *Writing across the Disciplines: Research into Practice* (1986) to explain our attempts to assess our WAC program. This book was authored by nine humanities faculty and five faculty from other departments at MTU.

We would like to boast that we did transform the MTU campus, but in truth, that didn't happen—or at least it didn't happen in ways we could successfully measure or demonstrate. We hoped the research that went into *Writing Across the Disciplines* would show the world that our program worked; instead it showed only that our program needed more carefully designed assessment strategies.

We did, however, transform the Humanities Department—the collection of 35 English, foreign languages, speech, philosophy, music, theater instructors responsible for virtually all communication and humanities education for 6,000 undergraduate students. This departmental commitment to WAC transformed the Humanities Department from a service department to a scholarly department in less than a decade. By 1986 MTU had a Masters Degree in Technical Communications and by 1989 a full Ph.D. program.

From the start, we felt assessment pressure from without and within. Was what we were doing working? What did "working" mean? Were faculty members across the curriculum using more writing in their teaching? Were students becoming more confident and skillful writers? The General Motors grant helped most by providing released time for humanities faculty to research and write about the WAC program—all of the later work focusing on assessment. We became obsessed by assessment and recruited faculty better trained in composition studies than either of us—both with straight literature Ph.D.'s. With these new faculty, we formed a research team that included two experimental psychologists, two empirical composition researchers, and a psycholinguist. All seven of us met each week to examine and assess the WAC program. We focused on "formative" assessment in hopes of making discoveries to help us understand the impact of our program and to suggest possibilities for strengthening and improving what we were doing.

Lee Odell visited MTU and advised us that, because of the amorphous and multidimensional program, we should adopt a multiple measures model to include numerous assessment strategies, from statistical to interview, quantitative to qualitative. We handed out pre- and postworkshop surveys to measure faculty attitudes toward writing; yes, we could demonstrate that they changed in positive ways, but we could not demonstrate the same for the writing abilities of our undergraduates. We attempted to measure writing samples of entering first-year students and compare those with samples written by graduating seniors; yes, the seniors wrote better, though we couldn't prove our program made the difference. We used journals in one section of a math class, quizzes in another, and both sections took the same final examination; no, there were no differences in their exam scores—though we noted that those keeping journals did as well as those taking quizzes. In the end, however, we had no more proof than Toby's anecdotal piece, "How Well Does Writing Across the Curriculum Work" (1984). Aside from individual stories ("the writing changed my life" or "the writing made no difference") and blatantly raw numbers (276 faculty took part in 14 workshops over 5 years), we could not demonstrate conclusively that students were writing better *because* of our program.

All along we knew, too, about the dark side of the program: the people who left the workshop fired up, but who cooled quickly amid the realities of four-course teaching loads on the quarter system; people who tried peer evaluation once, stumbled, and didn't try it again; people who were alarmed that something as formless as expressive writing could help in the writing of technical reports, but who never attended a workshop to find out its academic uses. We learned that what most worked against full institutional commitment to WAC was the institutional reward system itself, which measured professional worth by research and scholarship rather than thoughtful time spent on teaching.

The greatest, most measurable success from those formative WAC years was perhaps the transformation made on those who practiced and researched these techniques, especially on workshop leaders like ourselves who internalized them. The value of tutoring on the tutor first, the tutee second has never been more apparent than in the development of WAC programs.

At this writing, teaching is the center of our professional lives, mainly because of WAC. Both of us have come to believe that WAC programs do make a difference, hard as that difference is to demonstrate; we believe that the effort to develop university-wide WAC programs has had a powerful and positive effect on English departments as well, pulling together diverse individuals in a common effort; and we believe that WAC ideas have had perhaps their greatest influence on individual instructors like us. According to Toby:

> In the end, what I've learned to trust most is my own experience with my own students whom I can observe and listen to and challenge, about whom I can say something real and specific and have evidence in their writing that demonstrates—if not proves—that something thinking and writing changed for the better.
>
> And so, for me, WAC assessment, too, comes down to smaller and more personal units. I learn most watching and interacting with individual teachers and individual students and trying to learn what makes a difference, what doesn't, in their thinking and writing.

Art puts most of his energy now into using writing to teach his literature classes and into coordinating Clemson University's WAC program:

I regularly teach courses in British Romantic and Victorian literature, making them interactive and writing intensive. We write daily, to each other and to people outside our classroom, keeping our writing in portfolios. And I'm using classroom-based research techniques to look very carefully at how WAC affects the learning of both me and my students. So "assessment" in this sense is integral to my teaching on a daily basis.

In addition to integrating assessment as a natural part of my teaching process, I'm involved at Clemson in assessing general education, assessing education in the major, assessing our WAC program—it's all part of the same picture, right? We call our program C—communication across the curriculum—AC, not WAC, to include oral and visual and multimedia and etc. So while keeping writing at the center of the WAC enterprise, I'm looking at how to more fully integrate student talk and student stories into the curriculum.

The audience for WAC programs, and hence for WAC program assessment, has always been mixed: The students, the faculty, the administrators, the program leaders, and everybody else in the world at large want WAC to work. They want people to be better thinkers and writers. It's because this audience is so vast, varied, and interested that the idea of WAC programs continues to be a major reform movement in higher education.

It's only natural that over time researchers will learn how best to assess these programs. Both our experience and our instincts tell us that the stories of individual students and teachers, as illustrated in this volume, will yield the most information and the best results.

REFERENCES

Fulwiler, T. (1984). How well does writing across the curriculum work? *College English, 46*, 113-125.

Fulwiler, T., & Young, A. (Eds.) (1982). *Language connections*. Urbana, IL: NCTE.

Huber, B., &Young, A. (1986). Report on the 1983-84 survey of the English sample. *ADE Bulletin, 84*, 45-46.

Young, A., & Fulwiler, T. (Eds.) (1986). *Writing across the disciplines: Research into practice*. Portsmouth, NH: Boynton/Cook.

Chapter 1

.

Assumptions About Assessing WAC Programs: Some Axioms, Some Observations, Some Context

Kathleen Blake Yancey
Brian Huot

Assessment is a funny term. It sounds formal and institutional. It frequently generates fear and anxiety, and it's not something most people seem to want to do—voluntarily or otherwise. To say that you are being assessed, we concede, sounds too much like being victimized by oppressive actions associated with arbitrary and inefficient governmental edicts, or by the mandates of faceless educational management: actions that in both cases are at best irrelevant; at worst, quite simply bad, detrimental to the teaching and learning we work so hard to promote. As the contributors to this volume suggest, however, assessment can be defined differently: It can help us—as students, teachers, and administrators— learn about what we are doing well and about how we might do better—quite specifically, by using assessment to create and maintain writing-across-the curriculum (WAC) programs. The purpose of this text then, is to show how to conduct such learning-based assessment.

This introductionary essay discusses ways that assessment can enhance WAC programs, in three movements. First, this chapter focuses on a set of grounding assumptions for the programs described and recommended in the following chapters. Second, on the basis of the arguments within this text, the introduction offers several, more general observations about how assessment is currently being constructed and about how it links with other educational movements. Finally, the introduction does what readers typically expect it to do: briefly preview the chapters within.

Generally, the following discussion relies on a single, overriding assumption: that assessment is an important and valuable component both

7

of program management and of an effective educational environment. Like the contributors, we believe that, when done well, academic assessment can be exactly what we expect of and hope for all things academic: an opportunity to learn something worth learning. To assess—in this sense of the word—we seek to understand: ideally, to understand on its own terms a product, performance, artifact, or program. Why do we undertake such a task? For any of several reasons: to investigate questions for which there are no clear answers (i.e., to learn something); to applaud successful efforts and to define what the phrase "successful efforts" means, particularly in a given context, perhaps so that we can replicate and/or extend the success; to identify and enhance what we do well and to improve that which needs improvement. There are many good reasons to assess—reasons that do not presuppose inadequacy, insufficiency, or even budget cuts. Rather, they presuppose that investigating what we do helps us appreciate it more fully, perhaps even do it better.

At its best, assessment is about learning. What we see in this volume are rich and extended discussions about learning—about how institutions have changed their missions, about how faculty have changed their teaching, and about how students have changed both what they have learned and how they have learned. These discussions present many lessons and many approaches, from interviewing faculty and sitting in on their classes to collecting work from students to bringing in outside experts. Still, despite this diversity, these approaches share some common assumptions.

GROUNDING ASSUMPTIONS

First, WAC program assessment focuses on the big picture. Although the work of individual students is always at the heart of education, program assessment typically shifts its focus from individual students to whole classes, sets of classes or programs, and/or groups of students. Its perspective is thus larger rather than smaller. Moreover, unlike in a classroom situation where each student's work is typically assessed often throughout the term, program assessment relies on sampling: A subset of the population is, typically, used to represent the whole. Because the validity (i.e., the truthfulness or accuracy) of an assessment measure is judged partly by its ability to measure what it purports to measure, program assessment does exactly what it says: focuses on the program. In other words, program assessment, unlike classroom assessment, addresses the total nature of the program rather than its individual components. This is consistent with the purpose of an assessment that seeks to provide information about an entire network or system that constitutes any program.

Second, WAC program assessment is similar to research in that it typi-

cally relies on a question or set of guiding questions that motivate inquiry. The creation of the questions that articulate the purpose of the assessment is in some ways the most challenging and important part of the program assessment. What this means, in the first instance, is that we have to resist the temptation to think automatically in terms of methods and materials. Because both methods and materials are concrete and inform our daily teaching lives, there is an almost natural tendency to say, "Let's examine these papers," before we know why we are collecting them or what we might be examining in them. Instead, we advocate a contextualized, purposeful use of methods and materials in which both the mode of inquiry and data— interview or observation or a review of sets of student texts, for instance— are selected because they provide the best vehicle for answering the assessment questions, which of course were determined first. WAC program assessment is inquiry driven.

Crafting the assessment questions will take some time and can also be the trickiest part of the assessment. It's not uncommon that the kinds of questions we'd like to ask, such as "Are our students becoming life-long learners?", aren't easily answered. Ambitious questions like this do, however, provide an excellent place to start articulating what it is that we can more easily determine: Who, for instance, are our students? What do we mean by life-long learning? How would this habit of mind show itself? How might we document it? What timeframe would be large enough to address this claim: one year, five, 10? Thus, even initial questions that in their unwieldiness and vagueness cannot guide an assessment can provide two other services: (a) they help raise other good questions; and (b) they lead to questions that can be used.

And a fine point here: guiding questions fall into three (sometimes interlocking) categories: short, medium, and long term. First, there are questions that can be answered pretty readily, such as those dealing with the number of students in writing-intensive courses, the number of faculty teaching these courses, the kinds of writing students are asked to compose, and so on. By itself, this information doesn't tell us very much, but it does help provide a context for what is occurring at a particular institution, especially when it is relativized in some way, for example, to the number of such students in years past, or to the number of students per writing-intensive class, to the kinds of writing previously included and so on. As important, such data can help us discern patterns such as whether or not students continue to meet their writing-intensive requirements with the same courses; whether or not a larger number of faculty are teaching such courses; and so on. Second, there are questions that will take some time to answer: middle-range questions. Suppose we want to know about WAC from the students' perspective, and suppose we decide to elicit this information from surveys or interviews. Developing the questions we want to ask the students is a key component, and then we need to determine how the information will be collected, how it will be reviewed and analyzed, and how it will be used to enhance learning: through contact with teachers, through reviewing the curriculum, and so on. These processes will take more time than simply accessing numbers from an existing data bank or identifying kinds of writings from a set of syllabi. Third, there is the long-term effort: the longitudinal study of students across the college years or spanning the college and career/graduate/professional school years, or the intensive ethnographic work with faculty in their classes.

These three categories of questions are not mutually exclusive or incompatible; in many (if not most) cases they work together. Moreover, different kinds of questions tend to recommend different kinds of data, thus permitting us to "triangulate" the results of an assessment, i.e., to see a program through the lenses provided by different kind of data, so that we understand it from multiple perspectives. In all cases, the needs of the institution will dictate which questions are most appropriate and the patterns they might form.

Third, WAC program assessment also begins with an explicit understanding about the nature of writing. Writing is not a set of discrete skills that lend themselves to the kind of atomized testing that we see in multiple-choice tests, but rather is a way of learning and performing that is philosophical and epistemological as well as behavioral in nature. Writing thus cannot be represented or measured in multiple-choice instruments that disregard context. Through writing, students learn to explore, analyze, critique, argue, and negotiate, and they learn to talk about all this in the language of rhetoric. (And yes, we hope they learn to copy edit.) In sum, writing is a way of learning, and it is increasingly understood to operate within disciplinary boundaries. In all cases, it is also a way of performing that carries with it high stakes: on essay examinations, in papers of various kinds, within a resume or on a graduate school application.

Fourth, as suggested earlier, WAC program assessment relies on diverse methods. The chapters in this book provide a wealth of methods to draw on, and, in most discussions the methods are multimodal, i.e., various methods are brought together to answer the designated questions. In the language of *Fourth Generation Evaluation* (Guba & Lincoln, 1989) and Total Quality Management, such methodological diversity usually means that the perspectives of various stakeholders—like those of students, faculty, administrators and legislators—will be taken into account. The assumption here (like the assumption governing the triangulation of data) is that a single perspective provides a too-narrow window into the program and that to develop a more accurate and rich picture, multiple perspectives are desirable, even perhaps necessary.

Fifth, WAC program assessment focuses on learning and teaching and on how the two interact so as to chart that interaction in order to understand how to enhance it. Accordingly, WAC program assessment is as much about faculty development—about how faculty develop and monitor their teaching and about how their understanding of learning changes—as it is about student development. Ideally, because both faculty and students participate in learning, it is about the development of both.

The exact focus of an specific program assessment depends on the specific program being evaluated and its institutional and evaluative context. The validity of specific assessment depends, in part, on the impact of the decisions made because of the assessment. Consequently, WAC program assessment takes its results and uses them to inform and improve the curriculum so that teaching and learning are enhanced. In this sense, then, WAC program assessment is always formative—regardless of its genesis, its institutional setting, or its political context. It is assessment that focuses on the ongoing development and improvement of a program rather than a summative, final statement of value. As Sue McLeod and Rich Haswell suggest, however, different audiences will find different components of an assessment plan useful. Some will need to report out to the public whereas some will want to apply some results to their teaching immediately. Some, like Paul Prior, Gail Hawisher, and the team at University of Illinois, will want to link assessment with a formal research agenda. The point, however, is that the results are valuable and valid to the extent that they can and are used to inform the program.

In order to be useful, such an assessment also needs to embody three characteristics: It needs to be regular, systematic, and coherent. A regular program of assessment is one that is ongoing and that can be counted on to provide information to the institution. Ideally, as new programs are introduced and/or new components of existing programs designed, an assessment component is built into the design so that ongoing assessment is integral. A coherent, systematic program of assessment is one whose parts fit into and within its larger institutional context, and whose development over time reflects the emerging concerns of faculty, students, and the culture at large. It stands in contrast to the scattershot assessment, the kind (we all know this variety) provoked by crisis, completed without regard to the larger rhetorical situation, and then left untended until the next crisis occurs.

SOME OBSERVATIONS

As we have reviewed these chapters and worked with the contributors and talked about current practices, we have been reminded of what Donald Schon claims in "The Study of Organizations." He identifies managers, like those responsible for WAC Programs, as causal inquirers and talks about both the value and the practical effects of such inquiry.

Organizational inquirers are concerned with pattern causality that combines cause by reason with efficient cause. The causal inferences made by organizational practitioners are contained in episodes of inquiry, in the Deweyean sense of that term. Their investigations aim directly at interventions, and their interventions are experiments that test, in the most decisive sense available to them, the adequacy of their causal stories. (p. 96)

As causal inquirers, we offer the following observations about the current state of program assessment so as to set a general context for the articles to follow.

1. As a mode of inquiry, assessment is increasingly collaborative and democratic. In the past, program assessment was often designed, managed, and delivered by experts (often by experts without teaching experience); today, however, it is understood as a curricular task—one that all members of the university share and learn from.
2. Like any task, program assessment is a rhetorical enterprise. This means that there is an "exigence," a need to know, which could be motivated by an accreditation visit or by an individual faculty member's interest in modifying her teaching. The exigence, of course, also narrows useful methods: The ethnography of a single teacher is unlikely, by itself, to satisfy an accrediting agency. Similarly, because program assessment is rhetorical, there is an audience, perhaps multiple audiences, and they too shape what is learned and how it is presented. Furthermore, as the rhetorical nature of program assessment is increasingly understood, and as faith in objectivist measures and positivism more generally declines, models that are more constructivist in nature will continue to proliferate, models that are appropriate to the needs of particular institutions.
3. Much of the learning produced in the name of assessment is very subtle in nature. Through attention to detail, through pulling the details together and discovering patterns, through discussion with others, and through inquiry, tentative theses are articulated; these provide the basis for the next inquiry. If the potential is rich, the processes here are, admittedly, slow.
4. Program assessment is linked, directly or otherwise, to reformist agendas. In some cases, like the one described by Marty Townsend, the agenda is explicit (and in that case, linked to general education). In other cases, as described by Chris Thaiss and Terry Zawacki specifically and by Barbara Walvoord more generally, the agenda can be very implicit. Nonetheless, as Fulwiler and Young suggest in the Preface, from the start WAC was motivated by reform. That reform took the form of curricular innovation and faculty rejuvenation—and specifically at Michigan Tech, it took this form as an alternative to testing. To this day

(some two decades later), reform is still motivating WAC, and assessment is understood as an important vehicle in achieving this reform.

THE CHAPTERS WITHIN

Barbara Walvoord opens the first set of chapters; these focus on informal, formative WAC assessments. In Chapter 2, Walvoord outlines the guiding assumptions that motivate different models of WAC, from a leader-directed model to faculty-owned models. As she demonstrates, each brings with it specific aims and agendas, and, likewise, different forms of assessment. Given that different models make different assumptions, it makes sense that the questions posed, the inquiry made, would be different one to the next. In "Documenting Excellence in Teaching and Learning in WAC Programs," Joyce Kinkead uses a heuristic approach to WAC assessment, showing us in general the kinds of questions we might consider as we develop an assessment plan. Particularly valuable in her chapter is the discussion of how students can be involved in the assessment process, not just as objects of our teaching, but as participant observers and contributors to the curriculum. In Chapter 4, Cindy Selfe focuses on the agency that makes an assessment possible (especially in a postmodern world) and on a variety of formative assessment methods and questions that we might want to consider. In locating her argument this way (i.e., in bringing theory to assessment), Selfe likewise links the inquiry of assessment to larger epistemological issues: to what and how we know—and to political issues—to the social action that is change. Brian Huot, in "Beyond Accountability: Reading with Faculty as Partners Across the Disciplines," also focuses on formative assessment, i.e., on the kinds of change that can be motivated by intensive and collaborative work with faculty as they focus on student work. His emphasis underscores the importance of involving and working with faculty from the disciplines to assess WAC programs. Finally, Chris Thaiss and Terry Zawacki continue this emphasis on informal and formative assessment with their discussion of what they have learned from a WAC portfolio exemption requirement. As they narrate, they inform us regarding what goes on inside their institution as well as how that links with what goes on outside, and they have brought this knowledge to their faculty development efforts.

The next set of chapters discuss more formal efforts to assess WAC; often these too are formative. Larry Beason and Laurel Darrow discuss an interview procedure that provides a window into a program from the students' perspective. This chapter shows how such a process might be conducted, how the analysis might be made, and what it might show. In Chapter 8, Anne Herrington and Charlie Moran approach WAC assessment from a perspective that is specific to their institution, using case studies to show how change can be effected when faculty are trusted. Their lesson shows us that encouragement and resources, as well as assessment, can motivate long-term, substantial change. In Chapter 9, Meg Morgan talks about another systematic approach modeled on the principles of Total Quality Management. Morgan's model is also based on trust: In all the stakeholders of a process and product, and in the outcome of the assessment process they create. In "Integrating WAC into General Education: An Assessment Case Study," Martha Townsend guides us through another systematic approach: an external review. For this review, considerable preparation was made in the form of constituting various committees, collecting considerable data, analyzing the data, and generating questions. The external review is not the answer, but rather a response to a careful self-study that sets the stage for curricular enhancement and greater support to enact it. In Chapter 11, Chris Farris and Ray Smith take a systematic approach that focuses on the individual teacher. Their discussion highlights the tension that can occur between the objectives of a WAC director and a WAC teacher. They also show how the instructor's objectives should guide the inquiry. Prior, Hawisher, Gruber, and MacLaughlin make a similar argument, this one connecting research and assessment, which here are seen as natural allies. The kinds of questions that guide researchers are often the same ones used for an assessment. This chapter shows how each can inform the other. What to do with these (i.e., who is interested in these results) is the question discussed in Chapter 12. Sue McLeod and Rich Haswell consider the rhetorical situation framing an assessment. They distinguish between reporting in and reporting out and review what kinds of information are most useful to different stakeholders. The volume concludes with a more theoretical and historical look at WAC assessment by Michael Williamson. He explains the larger political and historical context that has governed assessment and outlines its assumptions. He then moves to explain what is needed now—as we move forward.

SOME CONCLUDING THOUGHTS

The modern, and postmodern, history of writing instruction is fueled by knowledgeable teachers who invite others to participate with them in making students the center of learning. Central to that act is assessing our own work with those students. The writers here have been true to that central thesis at their own institutions, and, in their contributions here, they issue the same invitation: to join with them in understanding what it is that we do to and with others in the academy. It is only through that understanding that we will all learn.

Chapter 2

·

From Conduit to Customer: The Role of WAC Faculty in WAC Assessment

Barbara E. Walvoord

Writing-across-the-curriculum (WAC) programs construct assessment in many different ways, and with many different meanings. It is, therefore, important to be conscious of the implications of various kinds of WAC assessment and to choose among them knowingly and deliberately. In thinking back over my 25 years as a WAC director and assessor and while reading the literature on WAC assessment, I am amazed by the shifting roles that faculty members play in WAC assessment and by the fact that I've never read a thorough analysis of these roles and their implications. I believe a careful consideration of these roles is crucial to any WAC program that embarks on assessment.

Faculty play seven roles in WAC assessment. The fact that they all begin with "C" shows, I believe, that configurations of the cosmos confirm their correctness: *Conduit, Convert, Changer, Case, Creator, Collaborator, and Client–Customer*.

There is a general progression in these roles from least empowered to most empowered roles for faculty. However, I do not want to judge which role is "best," because different ones will be most appropriate for different purposes. The roles are not mutually exclusive, nor always found in "pure" form. However, analyzing them separately can make us more aware of the fundamental assumptions underlying our assessment and keep us from being naive or from making choices that embody assumptions we do not want.

I will concentrate on faculty roles because, though student learning is the goal of WAC programs, faculty have usually been WAC's immediate audience their change its immediate goal, and their loyalty is its lifeblood. For each type of faculty role, I will suggest what we are assessing, why we are assessing it, the implications of those choices, and where each might be most and least useful. At the end of the chapter, I illustrate how vario* types might be combined in an institution's WAC assessment program.

I define as "assessment" any study, whether it is called "research" or "assessment," that seeks to determine the outcomes of WAC. For this analysis, I'll draw on the WAC literature and on my own experience at three institutions where I've been WAC director and at several hundred more where I've been a consultant, assessor, or workshop leader over the last 25 years.

CONDUIT

One role for faculty in WAC assessment is the Conduit. In Conduit studies, the assessor seeks to know whether, as a result of a WAC experience, identifiable WAC beliefs or strategies come out the other end. Questionnaires, syllabi, assignments, and classroom observation by students or researchers are the usual data. These studies assume that the greater the percentage of faculty who are practicing WAC strategies or beliefs, the more successful the program.

This model is based on the foundationalist assumption that there is a reality out there, and that the assessor's job is to find it: Are the folks REALLY using WAC? Eblen (1983) notes that "self reports may blend respondents' beliefs and intentions with actual practice" (p. 347). In the Conduit study, that is bad. The goal is to determine actual practice, untainted by faculty beliefs and intentions. Thus, syllabi and assignment sheets, classroom observation by outsiders, or questionnaires to students about classroom practices are regarded as stronger data than faculty self-report or as being necessary to validate faculty self-report.

One published example of a conduit study is Smithson and Sorrentino's 1987 investigation of 13 of the 18 faculty who had attended a workshop at Virginia Polytechnic Institute and State University. The faculty indicated their agreement, on a Likert scale, with WAC principles and classroom practices that the authors of the test had formulated (e.g., "Writing cannot be used to teach concepts in the subject disciplines but only to test if concepts have been learned" p. 338). This survey was administered four times in a pre-post test design: (a) before the workshop; (b) immediately after the workshop; (c) after 10 weeks; and (d) after 5 years. At the 10-week and 5-year points, 10 of the faculty also responded in writing to queries such as "Did you continue to use writing to teach your subject?" and "If you use fewer methods now than you did during your first quarter after the workshop, which ones have you dropped and how soon after the workshop did you stop using them?" (Note also that WAC is defined as "methods"— bounded entities to be counted.) The authors found that, even 5 years after the workshop, the faculty reported using more of the writing strategies than they had before the workshop. (Note the implication: the longer the time, the greater the success.) In addition, this study used student reports to corroborate faculty self-reports. Two hundred thirty-eight students in 10 class-es reported their teachers' use of methods the assessors had defined, such as "shared his/her writing with the class" and "used peer evaluation of drafts" (p. 340). Eighty-six percent of the students stated that the teacher provided for peer evaluation of drafts.[1]

Conduit assessment offers several advantages for this purpose. First, the results of such studies, taken within their paradigm, suggest that asses-sors can find identifiable WAC strategies and beliefs after a faculty mem-ber's WAC experience. Second, it produces quantifiable data that can be easily and quickly communicated to a broad spectrum of internal and exter-nal audiences. Such a paradigm is familiar and powerful for the media, the business and governmental communities, and often for educators as well. Third, if conducted by questionnaire to faculty, Conduit studies are relative-ly easy and cheap to perform. The faculty have a limited role and need not be asked for significant time involvement.

However, in its pure form, the Conduit model has limitations that may be more or less serious depending on one's goals. (In pointing out these lim-itations, I'm analyzing the Conduit paradigm, not necessarily criticizing the studies I've mentioned.) In Conduit studies, the assessor defines what counts as WAC beliefs and strategies; the *assessor's* voice dominates. If fac-ulty are quoted, it's within strictly limited frames. If faculty are not using WAC strategies, readers do not learn why, or what faculty are doing instead. It's a yes or no distinction: Faculty either do or do not adhere to what the assessors define as WAC—which is the presumed goal.

The assessor is assumed to be the neutral, objective collector of data. Assessors typically do not describe their own roles, interests, stances, or political contexts for the study. Much current thinking in WAC and other fields challenges the assumption of "objectivity" in an assessor or researcher; accordingly, if WAC programs assume this "objective" role for the assessor, they will want to acknowledge that fact and know their reasons for choosing the paradigm.

Further, when the assessors, not the faculty respondents, define WAC strategies or beliefs, two dangers arise. One is that the questions will mean different things to the responders than the assessor thought they would. On a Likert-scale question, it is hard to state a belief in such a way as to gather reliable and valid information about whether people actually hold that belief. You would think strategies such as "journals" would be easier to test than beliefs, but they, too, have danger. In a forthcoming study of WAC out-comes, my colleagues and I found that the word "journal," for example, might be quite differently interpreted, even by faculty who had attended

---

[1] Other published Conduit studies are Goetz (1990), Kalmbach and Gorman (1986 Hughes-Weiner and Jenson-Chekalla (1991), and Braine (1990).

workshops where journals were heavily emphasized. Further, our data suggest that faculty are not always very sure, or very concerned about, which teaching strategies would be classified as WAC and which would not. The faculty who come to WAC may be involved, as well, in other kinds of growth experiences, and they sometimes don't even remember whether an idea came to them from a WAC source or some other source. Conduit assessment tends to ignore all this.

A second danger of having the assessor define WAC is that WAC classroom strategies may not be the most enduring or important outcomes of WAC. My and my colleagues' forthcoming study suggests that WAC faculty constantly change their classroom *strategies* anyway—both before and after WAC workshops. The more enduring outcomes, and the ones many faculty state are most important, may be philosophies of teaching and learning, general guidelines for classroom practice, or a model of the learning community experienced in a WAC workshop or writing response group. These qualities are harder, however, to measure than observable teaching strategies.

In addition to silencing the faculty and giving the assessor the privilege of defining WAC and of being the "objective" data collector, Conduit studies also imply a "training" model. For example, the WAC program "trains" faculty to do something that the leaders and researchers assume to be good. The more of it that faculty do and the longer they continue to do it after the WAC training, the more successful WAC is.

The issue of faculty change is problematic in Conduit assessment. Faculty are supposed to change once, when they come into WAC, but then stop changing, or at least not change beyond the boundaries of what the assessors would define as WAC beliefs and practices. The Conduit paradigm implicitly assumes that if faculty are not doing WAC, they have backslid, resisted, or stood still. Whether they might have developed something better than the assessor's version of WAC, given their situations, is not entertained. Conduit research also does not fully acknowledge that a set of pedagogical practices and philosophies might work better in one situation than in another.

A final issue in Conduit assessment—as in every other kind of assessment—is how do we know that WAC is "good." In every type of assessment, I've seen cases where WAC was merely *assumed* to be good. But when the assessors try to demonstrate that WAC is good, their mode of doing so may affect, and be affected by, the role that faculty play in assessment. Conduit studies, in accord with their foundationalist assumptions, typically define "good" as that which results in measurable student learning. The strategies, not the teacher, are assumed to be the cause of the learning. Thus, if the strategies result in student learning, then teachers who adopt the strategies should be producing student learning.

Conduit studies typically measure student learning directly or indirectly: (a) They may directly measure student learning in the classrooms of the faculty who are being assessed or (b) They may measure faculty behavior that the research literature suggests will result in student learning.

As regards the first option, direct measurement of student learning, the field is littered with corpses (see Klaus, 1982; Young & Fulwiler, 1986, for the difficulties; see MacDonald & Cooper, 1992, for a more successful example). A variation is to measure students' *perceptions* of their own learning (see Marsalla, Hilgers, & McLaren, 1992).

Indirect measures, measuring teacher behavior, depend on a research literature that establishes the efficacy of WAC strategies. Then, if one's own faculty can be shown to be following those strategies, one can reasonably assume that student learning is occurring. Attempts to establish student learning as a result of WAC strategies per se have been very mixed, thus leading Ackerman, in 1993, to state that research on student outcomes had yet to show conclusively that WAC practices enhance student learning. However, a broader body of education literature is useful here. That body of research strongly suggests that student "involvement" is the key to student learning, and that having students engage interactively with each other, with the teacher, and with the subject, in modes such as writing, enhances student learning (Angelo, 1993; Astin, 1985; Chickering & Gamson, 1987; Kurfiss, 1987). On the basis of this research, the National Center for Educational Statistics (1995) has recently suggested that, instead of trying in every case to measure student learning directly, assessors may measure the faculty behaviors that this national body of research suggests will enhance student learning.

Conduit assessment, then, may simply assume WAC teaching strategies to be good, or it may try to establish that they are good because they result in student learning, measured either directly or indirectly. Either way, the faculty member's role is that of Conduit. The assessor's gaze is fixed on measurable student learning or faculty behaviors that result in learning. The strategies are assumed to be the key to the learning. The faculty member is a conduit for the WAC strategies.

In my own WAC program, I have used Conduit studies for particular goals and audiences. But, I always want to be aware of their limitations: lack of power and authority for the faculty member, the absence of the faculty member's voice, the dominance of the "objective" voice of the researcher, the foundationalist assumptions, the "training model," the assumption that WAC is the only catalyst for change, the issue of faculty change itself (i.e., its meaning, its value, and its role in WAC outcomes), and the problematic definition of "good." The Conduit paradigm can be modified in actual practice to transcend or minimize some of these limitations, or the Conduit model can be combined with other models in an assessment program. The end this article shows an example of such combining.

CONVERT

The Convert role places more emphasis on the richness of the faculty member's lived experience, and it changes the basis of authority for claims that WAC is "good." Fundamentalist Christian religion is the analogy: The *preacher* may talk about the benefits of salvation or publish surveys about how many folks adhere to the religion, but nothing can match the power of the *convert herself*, who stands up in the congregation and testifies, "I was a sinner, and now I am saved."

Published examples of WAC "testimonial" literature, authored by discipline faculty, appear in disciplinary journals (search ERIC under "writing instruction," "higher education," and the name of the discipline) and within various edited collections (e.g., Fulwiler & Young, Eds., 1990; Parker & Goodkin, 1987; Griffin, Ed., 1982; Thaiss, Ed., 1983). Testimonials published for a wider audience are the tip of the iceberg; the underwater base is the wealth of information from local sources: campus WAC newsletters, local and regional conferences, campus WAC assessment reports, and WAC workshop brochures ("Former participants say…").

The usual aim of Convert assessment is to persuade unbelievers or to help other faculty implement WAC. Faculty testimonial accounts are sometimes cast in a "how to" frame: here's the classroom strategy I use, here's how to do it, and here are its results. They are sometimes cast in a narrative frame: here's what happened to me as a result of the workshop. Faculty authors may present actual classroom assignment sheets, syllabi, student work, or student evaluations, which are used as concrete models or, as in Conduit assessment, as evidence to back up the speaker's self-report. The faculty member's own persuasiveness and passion, or evidence of student learning in his or her own classroom, are typically the basis of the speaker's claim that WAC is "good."

Sometimes faculty converts report struggle, disappointment, change, adaptation, or abandonment of WAC strategies. These are similar to the religious convert's description of past sins: A necessary part of the genre, to be followed by accounts of how faculty eventually saw the light, adopted WAC strategies, and how well these work in the classroom.

I am not saying that Convert accounts are false or that genre influence is wrong. The influence of genre is always present in discourse. Some faculty *do* experience WAC as a kind of conversion experience that *does* change their practices and beliefs, as my and my colleagues' forthcoming study demonstrates. Further, testimonials can powerfully move an audience as conduit studies rarely can. They allow the hearer to identify with the testifier as a person "like me." Such stories can transfix a board of trustees, a Rotary Club, and many other kinds of internal and external audiences. The "how to" element can be both useful and persuasive to other faculty. The testifier role may be the first opportunity for a faculty member to speak publicly on behalf of WAC, thus leading to further, more complex leadership roles. Convert accounts give faculty a voice. Convert accounts probably merit a place in every WAC program's assessment mix; I have used them in my own WAC programs.

However, to construct assessment around the degree to which someone is converted is to fall into some of the same assumptions as the Conduit role: the faculty member should ideally follow "our" model; the workshop or other WAC experience is the one important point of significant change, and after that, we hope the WAC faculty will stay on the true road and not backslide. The "testifier" role can be powerful for faculty in assessment, but can also be a limited one. WAC assessors who use it need to be aware of its limitations.

CHANGER

WAC assessors can move away from the "our model" limitations of the Conduit and Convert studies by focusing on faculty change and WAC's impact on change, without trying to define what kind of change it should be. Through questionnaire or interview, the assessor asks faculty open-ended questions about change and about WAC's role in spurring change. Change itself, rather than "our model" or specific beliefs and strategies, now becomes the implied goal of a WAC program and the object of its assessment. The faculty member is cast as "Changer." The frequent goal of such assessment is to demonstrate that the WAC program has produced beneficial results; the typical audiences are administrators and funders.

One published Changer study is Eble and McKeachie (1985). During the late 1970s and the 1980s, the Bush foundation supported faculty development, including a number of WAC programs at 24 institutions of higher education in Minnesota and North and South Dakota. Eble and McKeachie asked, via questionnaires, a random sample of faculty at these institutions: "Did [the faculty development program] have an effect on teaching?" Of 455 faculty, 383 responded; 78% of those replied "Yes." In Kalmbach and Gorman's 1986 study at Michigan Technological University, 82% of the 90 respondents said their teaching of writing had improved since the workshop. The definitions of "effect" and "improve" were left to the faculty members. (See Beaver & Deal [1990] for another "changer" study.)

Changer studies allow freedom for faculty interpretation of WAC and of effective classroom strategies. The faculty member is given the power to define what "change" is and whether WAC has spurred change. I've used Changer studies for reporting to my administrators and Board that X% of the faculty who have been through a WAC workshop reported they ha "changed their teaching in some way." It works, politically, if the administrators, board members, or other audiences see change as a valid goal.

The Changer model may still be foundationalist, however, and audiences may ask for confirming evidence that these changes REALLY occurred. Like the Conduit model, the Changer model may devalue faculty voices as "self-report."

The Changer model also reifies change for its own sake. What about the faculty member who was doing much of this from the beginning, and so reports little change? Does she count as a "failure" in the assessment? Or what about the faculty member who has another style and philosophy worked out, who is effective with it in the classroom, and who decides not to change it? And how about the possibility that change could be for the worse?

Further, a "did you or didn't you change?" questionnaire, like the "did you or didn't you use WAC?" Conduit questionnaire, may fail to provide rich detail about the complexity of classrooms and faculty lives.

CASE

To discover in more detail what is happening in the classroom and to get away from questionnaire or testimonial, one can go into the classroom for direct observation. A growing number of WAC case studies are doing just that. The "case study" *research method* can be broader than assessment per se (although it can contribute to assessment), and it can be broader than the faculty role I have called "Case." In the Case role, the faculty member remains the object of the assessor's gaze. The case often focuses on problems or difficulties, not on testimony of success. Assessors may use cases to explore troubling issues and to inform program improvement.

The Case role, like the Convert role, highlights the faculty member's lived experience. However, the faculty member's role may still be quite limited. When Pulitzer Prize-winning journalist and teacher Don Murray agreed to have his composing practices observed as a case study by Berkenkotter (1983), he wrote an end piece to Berkenkotter's report, which he entitled "Response of a Laboratory Rat." Just so. Unlike Berkenkotter's study, many WAC classroom case studies don't give the rat a chance to speak. The assessor's is the voice of authority: Observed details and quotations from the teacher are framed to support the assessor's conclusions. Despite their seeming candor about classroom realities, case studies can still privilege the voice of the outside assessor, silence the teacher, and resemble the Conduit and Convert paradigms in which the assessor knows best and in which change is desired only in the direction the assessor defines.

Some recent published case assessments have cast the faculty in two roles: (a) "resistor" to WAC ideas or (b) well-intentioned but unsuccessful.

In one "resistor" case study, Swilky (1992) followed two faculty during the semester after a WAC workshop. She details the suggestions she gave them and notes ways in which they either "resisted" or "adopted" what she calls "my ideas." Her practice of referring to the teachers by their first names casts them as research subjects, not professionals whose words are being cited by a colleague. She points out the dissonance between what "Robert," the teacher, has stated as a goal and what she, the researcher, perceives actually happens: "By maintaining this approach to responding to student texts, Robert works against his goal of assisting students...." (p. 58).

However, "*Robert's*" views on this perceived dissonance are absent. Did he *intend* to work against his own goal? Has his goal changed? What was his reasoning? The researcher uses quotations from Robert's letters to her to illustrate what she calls "both positive and negative resistance." Positive resistance she defines as "productive responses that question the agendas that reformers impose on others"; negative resistance is "unproductive opposition" (p. 51). But the judgments about positive and negative are the researcher's. Swilky acknowledges the possibility of positive resistance and concludes that "different determinants, including personality, assumptions, beliefs, and institutional conditions, affect teachers' decisions about pedagogical priorities." However, she explores these determinants not from the teacher's point of view, but from her own view. She does not question the value or rightness of the ideas she gives to the teachers. The article is strangely split, in this way, with a nod to the teachers' concerns, but within a dominant paradigm of researcher-controlled WAC orthodoxy against which teachers are counted as "resisters." Because "my ideas" still form the goal, the assessor's emphasis is on whether "my ideas" are adopted or not, rather than on the teacher's own goals and theories, the teacher's ongoing growth and change, career patterns, or ways of interpreting the data.[2] While WAC literature about student learning increasingly acknowledges the productivity or at least the legitimacy of learners' resistance to received authority (Chase, 1988; Mortensen & Kirsch, 1993; Trimbur, 1989), in "resistance" studies there is little acknowledgment that in a WAC workshop, WAC is the received authority, and "resistance" to authority may be an appropriate, even desirable, stance for a teacher–learner.

Several other published case studies highlight not so much the teacher as resistor, but the ways in which teachers' good intentions for writing may go awry in the classroom. Marshall (1984) investigates two high school classrooms—one in science, one in social studies—where the teachers deliberately tried to use writing for learning and themselves had led in-service workshops for their colleagues about using writing. The social studies

---

[2] Similar in many ways is Deborah Swanson-Owens' (1986) case study of two high school teachers with whom she worked for a semester on a project to use writing.

teacher, Marshall concludes, mainly accomplished his goals. In the science class, however, students' ways of handling the assignment subverted the teacher's goals. The focus of the study is on "how successful were [the teachers] in meeting their objectives?" (p. 168). The objectives, then, are supposedly the teachers', as interpreted by the researcher. But the judgments about success are Marshall's. The teachers' voices, their judgments about their success—or about his judgment—do not enter; nor do student voices, except in short quotes framed by the researcher. Despite the seemingly detailed analysis of the classroom, the teacher is silenced; the outside assessor is in control.

Johnstone (1994) details a college geology class where the teacher, though a strong advocate of WAC among his colleagues, does not achieve his learning goals because, the researcher judges, he does not integrate journals effectively into his class but keeps them peripheral, relying mainly on lecture and multiple-choice testing. The responsibility for the classroom failure is placed squarely on the teacher, but his voice is oddly absent. We do not learn from his perspective his rationale for doing what he did or even whether he concurred with the researcher's judgment.

Case studies of how WAC is used by teachers in the classroom are useful to assist in program planning, to share with faculty in workshops, and to make WAC programs humble and realistic after listening to Convert stories. However, Case assessment may fail to focus squarely or fully on why the teachers did what they did, from their point of view. It casts them as resistors or as well-meaning, by the assessor's judgment. Their voices, judgments, reasons, and conclusions are often still missing. They are still the object of the assessor's gaze. The assessment does not present the teachers richly to us as creators of meaning, as people who are struggling in often skillful ways to realize their own goals, and to juggle multiple constraints in the classroom. This more powerful teacher role emerges in the "Creator" model.

CREATOR

In the next three types of assessment (Creator, Collaborator, and Client–Customer), both the faculty member and the assessor assume quite different roles than any we have discussed so far. These roles may challenge some fundamental assumptions that WAC assessors have usually made.

In the Creator role, the faculty member is regarded by the assessor not as an implementor of assessor-defined WAC activities, but as a creator who will make something new, perhaps unexpected, from WAC, and who has the right to do so without judgment by the assessor. Such studies may use case study research methods, but the faculty role is quite different from what I have called the Case.

A model for understanding teachers in the Creator role is provided by Carneson (1994), who studied elementary and secondary school teachers in Britain. In his diagram, teachers are shown working among many diverse and even conflicting forces. At the base of the diagram is the teacher's accountability to the self, to professional colleagues, school management, students, parents, friends, family, and community. The teacher then moves through a "framing matrix" composed of many different perspectives and theories of teaching, not just those of a particular project like WAC. Finally, in the classroom, with all its constraints and stimuli, teachers try to maximize control over elements that are in turn controlling them.

Carneson's model is similar in spirit to the view of teachers proposed by Hargreaves (1988), who also works in K–12. Research suggests, Hargreaves notes, that learning is enhanced by student involvement—by what might broadly be called the interactive classroom. Yet most teaching is "transmission" teaching that relies on lecture and keeps the student passive. Most current theories about why transmission teaching is so widespread are "psychologistic," says Hargreaves—that is, they blame teachers' personal qualities or lack of competence. On that basis, proposed remedies are to select better teachers and to train them better. But Hargreaves counters with what he calls a "sociological" explanation for the dominance of "transmission" teaching.

> The framework I want to propose rests upon a regard for the importance of the active, interpreting self in social interaction; for the way it perceives, makes sense of and works upon the actions of others and the situation in which it finds itself; the way it pursues goals and tries to maximize its own (often competing) interests; the way it pursues these things by combining or competing with other selves; the way it adjusts to circumstances while still trying to fulfil or retrieve its own purposes—and so forth. In this view, teachers, like other people, are not just bundles of skill, competence and technique; they are creators of meaning, interpreters of the world and all it asks of them. They are people striving for purpose and meaning in circumstances that are usually much less than ideal and which call for constant adjustment, adaptation, and redefinition. Once we adopt this view of teachers or of any other human being, our starting question is no longer why do teachers fail to do X [as in WAC "resistor" studies], but why do they do Y. What purpose does doing Y fulfil for them? Our interest, then, is in how teachers manage to cope with, adapt to and reconstruct their circumstances; it is in what they achieve, not what they fail to achieve (p. 216).

Hargreaves' theory of teacher change is made more explicit later in his article:

> All teaching takes place in a context of opportunity and constraint. Teaching strategies involve attempts at realizing educational goals by taking advantage

of appropriate opportunities and coping with, adjusting to, or redefining the constraints. (p. 219)

To Hargreaves' notion that teachers seek to realize educational goals, Raymond, Butt, and Townsend (1992) add the teacher's goal of creating a self:

> The process of teacher development has to be understood in relation to personal sources, influences, issues and contexts. While changes in status and institutional mandates provide both possibilities for, and limitations to, ...development, there is also a deeper, more personal struggle to carve a... self.... Professional development is, in this sense, an enactment of a long process of creating self, of making and living out the consequences of a biography. (p. 149)

This Creator model represents an important shift from Swilky's and Swanson-Owens' focus on "resistance" and the causes of resistance to WAC. The Creator model focuses on assessing why the teacher does what she or he does. It recognizes that teachers often have very sensible reasons for decisions and are motivated by multiple, powerful forces and loyalties. There's a recognition that teachers are deeply rooted in their own pasts and that they have philosophies, outlooks, and investments that shape their use of new ideas. The assessor attempts to illuminate the reasons, goals, and principles that guide teachers' actions and development. In the pure form of Creator assessment, the assessor gives up the sole right to judge what is "good" in the teacher's situation because the goal of assessment is to research teacher behavior and rationale, not to pass judgment on it.

Once an assessor shifts to a view of the faculty member as creator, then a collaboration—rather than a subject–object relationship—becomes possible. So Creator and Collaborator roles tend to appear together. The next part of my discussion discusses both of them.

COLLABORATOR

In Collaborator assessment, the assessor not only views the faculty member as Creator, but also collaborates with the faculty member in establishing the goals, methods, models, and/or uses of the assessment itself.

One version of the Creator–Collaborator role is provided by Guba and Lincoln's (1989) "fourth generation evaluation." Such evaluation eschews the foundationalist assumptions we noted as characteristic of conduit and convert research, in favor of a social constructivist paradigm. Evaluation is "created through an interactive process that includes the evaluator...as well as the many stakeholders" (p. 8). The evaluator and the other stakeholders collaborate to create the meaning of the evaluation. To ensure effective action based on the evaluation, Guba and Lincoln recommend "negotiation" to arrive at a course of action on which multiple stakeholders can agree (p. 10). This is very different from the Conduit, Convert, and Case paradigms where the assessor defines what is "WAC" and what is "good." Creator and Collaborator studies may use the methods of the "case study," but they transcend the Case role for faculty as I have defined it.

McCarthy and Fishman's collaborative work provides a published example of the faculty member as Creator and Collaborator. In several articles published over several years, McCarthy, a writing specialist, and Fishman, a philosopher significantly influenced by WAC, examine Fishman's teaching as it grows and changes over several years (Abbott, Bartlet, Fishman, & Honda, 1992; Fishman, 1985, 1989, 1993; Fishman & McCarthy, 1992, 1995, 1996; McCarthy, 1991; McCarthy & Fishman, 1991, in press). What emerges is the story of a teacher's journey whose outcome the writing specialist does not pretend to know or control, but for which she, and their interaction, provide a rich resource.[3] McCarthy the researcher watches keenly and collects data as this fascinating development unfolds. Each collaborator learns from the other. Readers of their accounts learn the complexity of the human journey, share Fishman's reasoning about his classes, and come to understand how he balances conflicting needs, adapts ideas he reads or hears, seizes opportunities, juggles constraints, shapes goals and changes them, combines paradigms and philosophies, but always insists on his own right to determine what is "good" for him and his classroom. The assessment is his.

It's true that only Fishman's class is studied, not McCarthy's, so it's not a completely reciprocal exchange of roles. Further, McCarthy's voice as the framer, explainer, and outside investigator is dominant in some of their pieces. They struggle with issues of equality and authority in their collaboration, as they admit. But their study goes as far as any I know within WAC literature to approach the Creator–Collaborator model.

Another study where teachers' voices enter as coauthors, and their growth, rather than their resistance or conversion, become the focus, is a 1991 study of four college classrooms by me and McCarthy and our college-level teacher–collaborators from four disciplines. The teachers, all former WAC workshop participants, collaborated with McCarthy and me, the outside researchers, to study the "difficulties" that arose in their classrooms where WAC workshop ideas were being implemented in various ways. The point of the study is not "resistance" in the teachers, but the mutual efforts of teacher and outside researcher to learn what was happening in the class-

---

[3] Models for such collaboration are described by McCarthy and Walvoord (1988) and by Cole and Knowles (1993).

rooms and to make pedagogical changes of the teachers' own choosing. Our study suggests that WAC methods discussed in a workshop may work more or less well in actual classrooms and that classroom research is one way for the teacher to gain fuller insight on which further pedagogical changes can be based. In the biology classroom, for instance, Anderson (the teacher), and I (the outside researcher) trace over 4 years Anderson's pedagogical changes and the subsequent rise in the quality of students' scientific experiments and reports.[4]

My own work, then, and that of McCarthy, Fishman, Anderson, and other colleagues moves along a continuum toward assessing not the adoption of particular WAC-defined agendas, but rather more generally how teachers change over time, what factors influence those changes, and how particular events such as a WAC workshop fit into personal journeys, into broader institutional contexts, and into career-long growth patterns—that is, why teachers do Y, not why they fail to do X. The work increasingly privileges faculty voices and relies on collaboration with faculty for the creation of knowledge.

If we translate the Creator–Collaborator roles into campus assessment, perhaps the most difficult aspect for WAC programs is the loss of "our model" or "our ideas" as the standard against which faculty behavior is measured. The Creator and Collaborator roles require that faculty themselves shape the standard. If assessment is determining whether a program is meeting its goals, then the goal of a WAC program must be not to operationalize WAC as WAC assessors understand it, but to assist faculty members in their own growth as they understand it. WAC leaders provide a certain kind of expertise; faculty provide other kinds. WAC leaders may take a facilitative role, managing the WAC budget, planning workshops and other aspects, but faculty must be acknowledged as full partners in the overall endeavor. WAC leaders may suggest new ideas, but faculty members themselves are the final arbiters of whether these ideas will "work" for them or not. WAC leaders may be facilitators of the growth process, but faculty must grow in their own direction. Assessment in such a program, then, seeks to determine whether faculty-directed, faculty-owned growth has resulted from WAC's activities.

"Yes," you might say, "but isn't there good growth and bad growth? Isn't teaching with WAC better than teaching without WAC?" Yes, perhaps, for some or many situations. But the assessor can't finally determine that. In this situation, the assessor begins with the commitment to a faculty-owned WAC: The only effective WAC is WAC that the teacher has made her own,

---

[4] For another study that attempts to present WAC faculty members' experiences from the "Creator/Collaborator" perspective, see my and my co-authors' 1997 NCTE study *In the Long Run: A Study of Faculty in Three Writing-Across-The-Curriculum Programs.*

and the only effective changes in teaching are the changes that the teacher herself has constructed. Results of this kind of assessment are stories of growth and change, presented without assessor judgment, often told by multiple voices. The difficulty, of course, is that such results are difficult to present in meaningful ways to the Rotary Club or the Podunk City News, or even sometimes to one's own colleagues and administrators. So, like the other roles, this one also may be softened, adapted, or combined with others.

CLIENT–CUSTOMER

Related to the collaborator role is the Client–Customer. In this role, the faculty member is clearly in charge of deciding what is needed. The faculty member comes to WAC for expertise or services, but is assumed to be free to use the advice or service in whatever way she or he sees fit. If service to the Client–Customer is the goal of WAC, then assessment of WAC outcomes would measure not adherence to "our ideas" or growth defined by "our" models, but rather whether or not the Client–Customer believes WAC has contributed to whatever he or she needed. WAC assessment measures how WAC succeeds as a consultant.

One force that will drive this role in the future is the student outcomes assessment that faculty and institutions now must conduct for accrediting agencies, legislatures, and boards. In the past, WAC leaders have needed to do assessment in order to justify their budget requests and defend their right to exist or their plans for new initiatives. But the faculty who were being assessed had no particular stake in how the evaluation turned out. In most disciplines, faculty did not usually have to submit to rigorous assessment of their own teaching, certainly not in terms of student outcomes. (Disciplines that prepare students for licensure are the exception.) As that changes, faculty will seek help in assessing student learning. With new urgency, they will want to know the outcomes of their classroom strategies, including but not limited to WAC strategies. Departments and programs such as General Education will need to document student outcomes.

They may ask WAC to help with this assessment. After all, WAC programs and workshops have traditionally offered help with assigning grades and with classroom research. The potential of WAC strategies for contemporary assessment is illustrated by Thomas Angelo and K. Patricia Cross's *Classroom Assessment* (1993), a widely used publication. WAC proponents will find much that is familiar, particularly the "one-minute paper" and other forms of informal writing. WAC has called these strategies "journals" or "expressive writing" and has focused on their use as "writing to learn." Cross and Angelo recommend some of the same strategies but focus on their utility for assessment, that is, for telling the teacher how well learning is progressing.

Another example of WAC's potential for assessment is how my colleagues and I in 1985 began showing teachers in the disciplines how to use Primary Trait Analysis (PTA), which was developed for the National Assessment of Educational Progress and described by Richard Lloyd-Jones (1977) in the literature that composition specialists read. In my and my colleagues' 1991 study of teaching and student learning in four disciplines, PTA functioned as a research tool. But now the potential of PTA for contemporary assessment is becoming more clear. Not only can teachers use PTA to assess student learning in their classrooms, but departments and institutions can use it in their assessment processes. Other WAC leaders and I are beginning to do workshops and consulting under the "assessment" flag, not the "WAC" flag. For example, as WAC director on my own campus, I have been asked to work with one of the branch campuses to help them assess student learning in their General Education program. That job feels very much like a consultancy to me. It is clear that they are requesting my services; they are the Clients–Customers. It is THEY who have to figure out how to assess General Education in their college, and it is THEY who will be held accountable by the administration, the accrediting agency, and the board for doing so.[5]

It seems to me that the strength of this Client–Customer role is the power it gives to faculty. There are limitations and challenges as well, however. One limitation may be that the client's framework does not fully utilize what WAC has to offer. A too-narrow focus on assessment as product, for example, may blur WAC's important insights into the role of writing in discovery. The client's agenda may not include the kind of thoroughgoing transformation of the academy that WAC's vision has often embodied.

Another limitation is that, as in the Creator–Collaborator roles, WAC gives up power to the faculty member. Once again, WAC leaders will be tempted to say, "Yes, but isn't teaching with WAC actually better than teaching without WAC?" and they will have to answer, "Perhaps, but it's the faculty member who must determine that, who must create meaning from what we offer."

One challenge of the Client–Customer role is to define WAC's own role in this new relationship. Will WAC be co-opted by faculty or departments who want WAC to collaborate in showing success? More broadly, Guba and Lincoln (1989) discuss the close relationship that often exists between assessor and assessed. How can assessment be best constructed to help WAC handle that relationship?

---

[5] The strategies I and my colleagues are developing for assessment are further explored in a monograph manuscript by me and Virginia Johnson Anderson, tentatively titled Using the Grading Process for Assessment.

The Creator, Collaborator, and Client–Customer roles, then, represent a radically new approach for WAC. They bring their own benefits and limitations and their own uses and challenges.

COMBINING FACULTY ROLES IN A CAMPUS WAC ASSESSMENT PROGRAM: A CASE STUDY

To illustrate how various kinds of WAC assessment, with varied faculty roles, can be combined by a single WAC program, I will describe the program I know best: the one I directed at the University of Cincinnati (UC) from 1991 to 1996. Equally complex stories of WAC assessment could be told about other campuses. Two that can be followed over a period of time through published works include Michigan Technological University (Flynn, Jones, Shoos, & Barna, 1990; Fulwiler, 1981, 1984, 1988; Fulwiler & Young, 1982, 1990) and the University of Hawaii at Manoa (see the bibliography in Hilgers, Bayer, Berghi, & Tanguchi, 1995). These programs have constructed WAC in complex and multivocal ways, combining the faculty roles I have discussed and integrating multiple points of view.

In fall of 1991, I was hired as director of a 3-year-old WAC program funded on year-by-year "one-time" funds out of the provost's office. Its primary activity had been workshops for faculty. End-of-workshop freewrites by faculty had shown high faculty satisfaction, but little other assessment had been done. The legislature and board were sharply reducing the university's funding and were highly critical of how undergraduate education was being conducted. As I saw it, the program needed four things immediately: (a) as the new director, I needed to establish good rapport with the faculty who had attended workshops and who now were the "heart" of the WAC program; (b) UC's WAC needed to collect outcome evidence that could be used in a campaign for permanent funding, or even just to ensure the year-by-year funding, especially if we got a new provost; (c) UC's WAC could prove its usefulness by providing the president with ammunition in his effort to prove to the legislature, board, and media that UC was working hard on undergraduate education and making some changes; and (d) I needed to do all this with limited time, staff, and money.

Because we thought change was a valued goal for us and for other audiences, the WAC Committee and I designed a simple yes or no question in the Changer mode: "Did you make any changes in your teaching as a result of the workshop?" A second question asked, "What changes did you make?" To avoid taking total control of the definition of changes, we left the second question open-ended for the first half of our sample. From those first answers we composed a list of strategies such as "added more writing to the course" and "sequenced assignments in a different way." The second half of our sample were given this list of strategies and were asked to mark the ones they had used. Thus, this part of the questionnaire was Conduit research, asking faculty whether they had used WAC strategies the assessors named, but with a twist: We had given faculty some power to define the strategies we would name. We queried 117 people—89% of the workshopped faculty still on campus—so we had a good sample size. Ninty-nine percent of the faculty queried answered that they had made some changes. The most frequent change they reported was to add more writing. We used that information widely and with good effect for internal and external audiences.

Further, the committee and I used a method of administering the questionnaire that helped us strengthen our evidence within the foundationalist paradigm, to gather some of the richness of faculty experience, and to help me get to know the WAC faculty. We invited all the workshopped faculty to lunch-time discussion groups of six to eight people. We asked them to bring syllabi or course materials for a discussion of what WAC had meant to them and what they would suggest for WAC's future. At these lunches, faculty filled out the questionnaire and then just talked about their WAC experiences. Faculty who did not come to the lunch groups we contacted by phone. These discussions yielded several things. First, we could argue that the syllabi and course materials, as well as the experience of talking about one's use of WAC before a group of colleagues, some of whom might know something about one's teaching, would serve to curtail exaggeration or wishful thinking in the "self-report" questionnaire about changes. Second, we got a list of converts and testifiers, that is, faculty who had benefitted from WAC and who were good at talking about the benefits to faculty colleagues. We later invited these faculty to testify in the media, in our own WAC newsletter, and as presenters at future faculty workshops. We also identified faculty who would help us with various WAC projects. Third, people really did share with us their problems and disappointments as well as what had worked well for them, thus helping to improve our program.

Finally, these conversations made us increasingly dissatisfied with the limitations of the Conduit, Convert, and Changer modes and stimulated us to think about how to conduct assessment in which the faculty members played more powerful roles. We began to read and to discuss other modes. The result was a study of WAC faculty on three campuses reported in the forthcoming book by me, Hunt, Dowling, and McMahon. In that book, we try to move toward the Creator and Collaborator roles. But, after all this, in my fifth year at UC, a public relations consultant hired by the university to help publicize its work came to interview me about WAC. It was hard to make the three-campus study, with its qualitative results, its rich faculty voices, and its complex outcomes of WAC, seem usable to him. He wanted numbers. So I went back to the 99% of faculty who had changed their teaching after a WAC workshop. Aha! said his face, now we're getting somewhere.

I think this story illustrates my point that an individual WAC program might mix the faculty roles and research paradigms, choosing whichever meets both the needs of one's audiences and one's own personal and professional integrity.

I also want to emphasize integrity. Integrity is a tough issue in a postmodern world and within a social constructivist paradigm. I believe, however, that it is important to work out the ethical implications of one's assessment. At UC, we used several paradigms and faculty roles, depending on the needs of our program and our audiences: Ya want numbers, I give ya numbers; ya want stories, I give ya stories. But we have tried to follow the "rules" of each paradigm, never to falsify data, always to be candid about what we see as strengths and weaknesses of our data, and always to respect the rights and needs of our faculty and students, even in, or perhaps especially in, paradigms where they play circumscribed roles.

One thing is very clear to me: WAC assessment is becoming more complex, more varied, and more self-aware. As WAC programs face a complex and challenging future,[6] WAC assessors need to think carefully about how they construct faculty roles in their assessment and about what those faculty roles imply for WAC's mission, its goals, its identity, and its relationships with the faculty colleagues who from WAC's beginning have been its heart and its life.

REFERENCES

Abbott, M.M., Bartlet, P.W., Fishman, S.M., & Honda, C. (1992). Interchange: A conversation among the disciplines. In A.Herrington & C. Moran (Eds.), *Writing, teaching, and learning in the disciplines* (pp. 103–118). New York: MLA.

Ackerman, J. (1993). The promise of writing to learn. *Written Communication, 10,* 334–370.

Angelo, T.A. (1993). A teacher's dozen: Fourteen general, research-based principles for improving higher learning in our classrooms. *AAHE Bulletin, 45*(8), 3–13.

Angelo, T.A. & Cross, K.P. (1993). *Classroom Assessment Techniques.* 2nd ed. San Francisco: Jossey-Bass.

Astin, A. (1985). *Achieving educational excellence.* San Francisco: Jossey-Bass.

Beaver, J. F., & Deal, N. (1990). *Writing across the entire curriculum: A status report on faculty attitudes.* Paper presented at the annual meeting of the Northeastern Educational Research Assn., Ellenville, NY, October 31 through November 2.

Berkenkotter, C., & Murray, D. (1983). Decisions and revisions: The planning strategies of a publishing writer, and response of a laboratory rat—or, being protocoled. *College Composition and Communication, 34,* 156–172.

---

[6] See my 1996 essay on the Future of WAC.

Braine, G. (1990). Writing across the curriculum: A case study of faculty practices at a research university. ERIC ED 324 680.

Carneson, J. (1994). Investigating the evolution of classroom practice. In H. Constable, S. Farrow, & J. Norton (Eds.), *Change in classroom practice* (pp. 101–112). London and Washington DC: Falmer Press.

Chase, G. (1988). Accommodation, resistance and the politics of students writing. *College Composition and Communication, 39,* 13–22.

Chickering, A. W., & Gamson, Z. F. (1987). Seven principles for good practice in undergraduate education. *AAHE Bulletin, 39*(7), 3–7.

Cole, A. L., & Knowles, J.G. (1993). Teacher development partnership research: A focus on methods and issues. *American Educational Research Journal, 30,* 473–495.

Constable, H. (1994). Introduction: Change in classroom practice: The need to know. In H. Constable, S. Farrow, & J. Norton (Eds.), *Change in classroom practice* (pp. 1–10). London and Washington, DC: Falmer Press.

Eble, K. E., & McKeachie, W. J. (1985). *Improving undergraduate education through faculty development.* San Francisco: Jossey-Bass.

Eblen, C. (1983). Writing across the curriculum: A survey of university faculty views and classroom practices. *Research in the Teaching of English, 17,* 343–348.

Fishman, S. M. (1985). Writing-to-learn in philosophy. *Teaching Philosophy, 8,* 331–334.

Fishman, S. M. (1989). Writing and philosophy. *Teaching Philosophy, 12,* 361–374.

Fishman, S. M. (1993). Explicating our tacit tradition: John Dewey and composition studies. *College Composition and Communication, 44,* 315–330.

Fishman, S. M., & McCarthy, L. P. (1992). Is expressivism dead? Reconsidering its romantic roots and its relation to social construction. *College English, 54,* 647–661.

Fishman, S. M., & McCarthy, L. P. (1995). Community in the expressivist classroom: Juggling liberal and communitarian visions. *College English, 57,* 62–81.

Fishman, S.M., & McCarthy, L.P. (1996). Teaching for student change: A Deweyan alternative to radical pedagogy. *College Compostion and Communication, 47,* 342–366.

Flynn, E., Jones, R. W., with Diane Shoos and Bruce Barna (1990). Michigan technological university. In T. Fulwiler & A. Young (Eds.), *Programs that work* (pp. 163–180). Portsmouth, NH: Boynton/Cook.

Fulwiler, T. (1981). Showing not telling in a writing across the curriculum workshop. *College English, 43,* 55–63.

Fulwiler, T. (1984). How well does writing across the curriculum work? *College English, 46,* 113–126.

Fulwiler, T. (1988). Evaluating writing across the curriculum programs. In S. McLeod (Ed.), *Strengthening programs for writing across the curriculum* (pp. 61–76). San Francisco: Jossey-Bass.

Fulwiler, T., & Young, A. (Eds.) (1982). *Language connections: Writing and reading across the curriculum.* Urbana, IL: National Council of Teachers of English.

Fulwiler, T., & Young, A. (Eds.) (1990). *Programs that work.* Portsmouth, NH: Heinemann, Boynton/Cook.

Goetz, D. (1990). *Evaluation of writing-across-the-curriculum programs.* Paper presented at the annual meeting of the American Psychological Assn., Boston, August 10–14. ERIC ED 328 917.

Griffin, C. W. (Ed.) (1982). *Teaching writing in all disciplines.* New Directions for Teaching and Learning No. 12. San Francisco: Jossey-Bass.

Guba, E. G., & Lincoln, Y. S. (1989). *Fourth generation evaluation.* Newbury Park, CA: Sage.

Hargreaves, A. (1988). Teaching quality: A sociological analysis. *Curriculum Studies, 20,* 211–231.

Hilgers, T. L., Bayer, A. S., Stitt-Bergh, M., & Taniguchi, M. (1995). Doing more than "thinning out the herd": How eighty-two college seniors perceived writing-intensive classes. *Research in the Teaching of English, 29,* 59–87.

Hughes-Weiner, G., & Jensen-Chekalla, S. K. (1991). Organizing a WAC evaluation project: Implications for program planning. In L. C. Stanley & J. Ambron (Eds.), *Writing across the curriculum in community colleges.* New Directions for Community Colleges No. 73. San Francisco: Jossey-Bass.

Johnstone, A. C. (1994). In B. Johnstone & V. Balester (Rev. Eds.) (1994). *Uses for journal keeping: An ethnography of writing in a university science class.* Norwood, NJ: Ablex.

Kalmbach, J. R. & Gorman, M. E. (1986). Surveying classroom practices: How teachers teach writing. In A. Young & T. Fulwiler (Eds.), *Writing across the disciplines* (pp. 68–85). Monmouth, NJ: Boynton/Cook.

Klaus, C. (1982, Spring). Research on writing courses: A cautionary essay. *Freshman English News, 11,* 3–14.

Kurfiss, J. (1987). *Critical thinking.* ASHE-ERIC Higher Education Report. Washington, DC: The George Washington University, School of Education and Human Development.

Lloyd-Jones, R. (1977). Primary trait scoring. In C. Cooper & L. Odell (Eds.), *Evaluating writing: Describing, measuring, judging* (pp. 33–66). Urbana, IL: National Council of Teachers of English.

MacDonald, S. P., & Cooper, C. R. (1992). Contributions of academic and dialogic journals to writing about literature. In A. Herrington & C. Moran (Eds.), *Writing, teaching, and learning in the disciplines* (pp. 137–155). New York: MLA.

Marsalla, J., Hilgers, T. L., & McLaren, C. (1992). How students handle writing assignments: A study of eighteen responses in six disciplines. In A. Herrington & C. Moran (Eds.), *Writing, teaching, and learning in the disciplines* (pp. 174–190). New York: MLA.

Marshall, J. D. (1984). Process and product: Case studies of writing in two content areas. In A. Applebee (Ed.), *Contexts for learning to write: Studies of secondary school instruction* (pp. 149–168). Norwood, NJ: Ablex.

McCarthy, L. (1991). *Multiple realities and multiple voices in ethnographic texts.* Paper presented at the annual Conference on College Composition and Communication, Boston, March 21–23. ERIC ED 332210. *Research in Education* Oct. 1991.

McCarthy, L. P., & Fishman, S. M. (1991). Boundary conversations: Conflicting ways of knowing in philosophy and interdisciplinary research. *Research in the Teaching of English, 25,* 419–468.

McCarthy, L. P., & Fishman, S. M. (In Press). A text for many voices: Representing diversity in reports of naturalistic research. In G. E. Kirsch & P. Mortensen (Eds.), *More than data: Ethics and representation in qualitative studies of literacy.* National Council of Teachers of English.

McCarthy, L. P., & Walvoord, B. E. (1988). Models for collaborative research in writing across the curriculum. In S. H. McLeod (Ed.), *Strengthening programs for writing across the curriculum* (pp. 77–89). New Directions for Teaching and Learning No. 36. San Francisco: Jossey-Bass.

Mortensen, P., & Kirsch, G. E. (1993). On authority in the study of writing. *College Composition and Communication, 44,* 556–572.

National Center for Education Statistics (1995). *College student learning: Identifying college graduates' essential skills in writing, speech and listening, and critical thinking.* Washington, DC: U.S. Department of Education.

Parker, R., & Goodkin, V. (1987). *The consequences of writing: Enhancing learning in the disciplines.* Montclair, NJ: Boynton/Cook.

Raymond, D., Butt, R., & Townsend, D. (1992). Contexts for teacher development: Insights from teachers' stories. In A. Hargreaves & M. G. Fullan (Eds.), *Understanding teacher development* (pp.143–161). New York: Teachers College Press.

Smithson, I., & Sorrentino, P. (1987). Writing across the curriculum: An assessment. *Journal of Teaching Writing, 6,* 325–342.

Swanson-Owens, D. (1986). Identifying natural sources of resistance: A case study of implementing writing across the curriculum. *Research in the Teaching of English, 20,* 69–97.

Swilky, J. (1992). Reconsidering faculty resistance to writing reform. *WPA: Writing Program Administration, 16,* 50–60.

Thaiss, C. (Ed.) (1983). *Writing to learn: Essays and reflections on writing across the curriculum.* Dubuque, IA: Kendall-Hunt.

Trimbur, J. (1989). Consensus and difference in collaborative learning. *College English, 51,* 602–616.

Walvoord, B. E. (1996). The future of writing across the curriculum. *College English, 58,* 58–79.

Walvoord, B. E., & Anderson, V. J. In preparation. *Using the grading process for assessment* (working title).

Walvoord, B. E., Hunt, L., Dowling, H. Fil, Jr., & McMahon, J. (1997). In the long run: A study of faculty in three writing-across-the-curriculum programs. Urbana, IL: National Council of Teachers of English.

Walvoord, B. E., & Dowling, H. Fil, Jr., with J. Breihan, V. Johnson Gazzam, C. E. Henderson, G. B. Hopkins, B. Mallonee, & S. McNelis (1990). The Baltimore area consortium. In T. Fulwiler & A. Young (Eds.), Programs that work (pp. 273–286). Portsmouth, NH: Boynton/Cook.

Walvoord, B. E., & McCarthy, L. P., with V. Johnson-Anderson, J. R. Breihan, S. Miller-Robison, and A. K. Sherman (1991). Thinking and writing in college. Urbana: National Council of Teachers of English.

Young, A., & Fulwiler, T. (Eds.) (1986). Writing across the disciplines: Research into practice. Montclair, NJ: Boynton-Cook.

Chapter 3

.

Documenting Excellence in Teaching and Learning in WAC Programs

Joyce Kinkead

Increasingly, the constituents of higher education institutions call for accountability. National reports recommend that we involve students more in learning, emphasize values in the curriculum, and demonstrate that students are learning as a result of four or more plus years of postsecondary education. Typically, one area most frequently targeted in these accountability and assessment conversations is writing. As state committees, institutional boards, central administrators, and accreditation agencies turn to compositionists for answers about how best to assess the growth in writing of our students, we need to be able to provide some answers or at least explain the complexities of the question. By knowing the questions to ask and the answers to seek, the often disparate groups that come together to enter the dialogue about assessment can begin at a common point.

In meetings with our general education reform task force at Utah State University (a committee that I chair and that includes highly regarded faculty members from across the campus), whenever the conversation turns toward *assessment*, all of us tend to look to Jim, a professor from the College of Education who joined the group as the "assessment expert." Perhaps no single word—with the possible exception of *grammar*—strikes as much fear in the hearts of composition teachers and, in fact, almost any faculty as does assessment. Why? Although we have expertise in evaluating individual student work on a day-to-day basis, marking essays and holding face-to-face conferences with writers, the image provoked by "assessment" includes descriptors such as vague, large-scale, unwieldy, expensive, and unpredictable. No wonder we run for cover. Assessment seems to have taken on mythic proportions.

It does not have to be that way. This chapter describes some of the directions that a conversation about assessment among faculty might take, acknowledging that the possibilities I list are only a few of the options available and that many of the decisions made about the assessment of writing must take into account institutional context. Finally, I will draw on specific illustrations, especially of students' involvement in assessment as researchers.

WHO CARES ABOUT ASSESSMENT?

The first logical question to ask about assessment is: Who cares? Who are the stakeholders? Potential audiences for assessment include students, teachers, administrators (e.g., writing program or WAC director, department head, dean, provost, president), institutional governing boards, legislators, and state offices of higher education. Other groups external to the campus consist of parents of students, alumni, feeder schools (both secondary and 2-year colleges), donors, and the public—especially those in the immediate community.

Placing the question of assessment of writing in a rhetorical arena, as we see in Figure 3.1, we ask not only who is the audience for the data, but *why do they care* about these results? Administrators, for instance, care for several reasons. First, they care about responding to the calls for increasing accountability of higher education (see, especially, *Strong Foundations, Integrity in the College Curriculum,* and *An American Imperative*). Assessment is also a vital component of the popular strategic planning and total quality management (TQM) initiatives: Administrators are, after all, responsible for long-range planning, goal-setting, and institutional image. At programmatic and institutional levels, accreditation is a primary concern. Most accrediting agencies want information on how students' writing has improved midway and at the end of undergraduate studies. The standards for the Northwest Association of Schools and Colleges, for instance, address composition in this way:

> If the institution has some kind of required writing course or an emphasis on writing across the curriculum, what evidence is there that students are better writers after having been exposed to the course or curriculum? How are these judgments rendered? If student writing improves, do students appear to retain this newly acquired proficiency? If so, why so, and if not, why not. What changes are planned as a result as a result of the assessment exercise? (p. 59)

To meet accreditation needs, an institution may choose to realign resources to improve instruction in important competency areas, such as writing.

Faculty care—or should care—about assessment of writing for any number of reasons. At the most basic level, teachers usually prefer knowing if their instruction is effective and why. No doubt, there is a sense of pride involved in teaching well. Another objective is to learn whether or not the students' writing continues to develop as they progress through the college

WHO IS ASSESSED?	Individual student	Group of students	Individual teacher	Peer colleague	Department or program	College	University or institution
WHAT IS ASSESSED?	how students conceptualize task of writing	how group writing works	how writing is integrated in a content-area course	attitudes toward writing (student or faculty)	student outcomes	how a dept addresses WAC	how university addresses WAC
WHERE: LOCUS OF EVALUATION	individual student	groups of students	teacher	class with multiple sections or a core curriculum	department	college	institution or alumni
WHO IS THE AUDIENCE?	students—to understand purpose of WAC	program administrator	department head or dean	colleagues in same institution or other	• public • alumni • donors	governing board	legislators
WHY: PURPOSE	to improve student learning	to improve the ways groups of students function with writing tasks	to improve the ways in which teachers integrate writing in the discipline	to make decisions for tenure, promotion, awards	to form a coherent departmental approach to WAC to share teaching stories with colleagues	to assess employer satisfaction to share success stories with public	ACCREDITATION accountability realign resources development—$$$

Figure 3.1.

years. As Erika Lindemann notes, "writing is a skill that requires development over a lengthy period of time but atrophies quickly." (p. 22) Of course,
faculty often measure their own success by how well their students gain
access into prestigious graduate schools and professions in which competency in writing plays a major part.

WPAs[1] have a dramatic stake in caring about assessment. Too often
underfunded, writing programs may benefit from internal and external
financial support. For the WPA, this means that an articulate document on
how well students are currently being instructed in writing and how that
scenario might be improved could result in funding being redistributed to
writing programs, including WAC Programs. For instance, if an institutional goal is to increase retention, then data from a writing center demonstrating success in that arena could help obtain additional monies.

In taking a proactive stance vis-a-vis assessment, the WPA may position
the writing program favorably for new monies, perhaps from development
efforts in, say, a capital campaign in which a university declares excellent
undergraduate education its most important priority and targets course
development, professorships, and scholarships for donor support. The
results might be an endowed chair in rhetoric, scholarships for students
majoring in writing, support for writing tutors across the curriculum, and
backing for a regional conference on portfolios. Although it may seem odd to
look to the public for financial support, many state universities have moved
from "state-supported" to "state-assisted" in the increasing privatization of
public institutions. A development campaign may enhance an institution's
image during a time when many universities need to apply spit and polish
to tarnished facades in order to regain public trust.

Reporting on the writing program can take many forms, as Sue McLeod
and Rich Haswell explain more fully in Chapter 13. Qualitative assessments
help get "the teaching story" to the public. Understanding the American cit-
izens' response to human interest stories, many university public relations
staff look for inspirational anecdotes about how public institutions care for
their students. For instance, Jane Q. Public may be impressed to find that
in many writing programs individualized conferences between teacher and
writer take place on assignments—an example of the tremendous workload
of the teacher who cares about writing. Parents especially appreciate this
kind of one-on-one attention to their children as a concrete example of what
their tuition dollar buys, in contrast to the anonymity of typical large-enrollment lower-division courses.

Students care about assessment of writing, mainly because they want to
ensure that they receive the skills necessary for life after college. A WAC

---

[1] When I use WPA, I refer to writing program administrators in a generic sense and include
ctors of writing programs, WAC programs, and writing centers.

HOW IS ASSESSMENT DONE?	one-minute paper or half-sheet response (Angelo & Cross)	interviews	self-evaluation form; audiotape of conference	colleague observation	surveys	syllabi analysis	exit interviews
WHEN DOES ASSESSMENT OCCUR?	beginning of term/mid-term/ end-of-term	decision	dept	curriculum review	response to alumni surveys	general education reform;	reaction to receiving grant support

Figure 3.2.

Program that articulates its overarching goals for the undergraduate experience communicates to students the importance and complexity of good writing. Explaining the college curriculum graphically and visually helps novice students understand the purposes and goals of department and university-wide programs. For instance, students often perceive their general education courses as something they must "get through" so that they can move on to their major courses. If an administrator of the general and liberal studies program were to map a curriculum so it is apparent where skills and concepts are likely to reappear, then aims and connections would be more clear to both students and faculty. For students, this should result in increased motivation in the foundation courses. For faculty, it means understanding how courses feed into and out of each other and promotes faculty dialogue about these connections. Take, for instance, a writing course that forms a general education requirement; if a curriculum grid illustrates that the principles learned in that entry class will reappear in the student's sociology major in five required courses ranging from demography to medical sociology, then the student is more likely to foresee the applied nature of the course. In a general education program that emphasizes good communication skills, the mapping of oral and written requirements in upper-division courses provides reinforcement. In the figure opposite, the writing is mapped in just such a way and appears in many of the core and distribution courses of a sample University Studies program (Figure 3.2).

Students may also care about how another stakeholder feels the university succeeds at teaching writing: the employer. How satisfied are employers with the communication skills of their workers, especially writing? Typically, knowledge of subject matter and good communication skills are cited by this employers as imperative to success in the workplace (e.g., Astin, 1991, 1993; Bok, 1990; Bowen, 1977; Gaudiani, 1994). A savvy WPA may create an advisory board with members of this constituency to increase attention to the role of writing in the curriculum.

DOCUMENTING EXCELLENCE AND IMPROVING INSTRUCTION

WPAs should have common cause with others on campus whose goal is the reform of instruction. Assessment of writing can be integrated with efforts to evaluate such reform efforts. An approach of documenting excellence that I have found particularly useful is to bring in stellar undergraduate and graduate students as researchers. These students come from a number of academic venues, most notably from courses that focus on the theory and practice of WAC, from thesis projects, and from our Rhetoric Associates Program. (In the Rhetoric Associates Program, a decentralized WAC tutoring approach, faculty request tutors to work with writing assignments in the context of a specific class.)

For example, Alan Rhees, a masters-level student in a seminar on WAC, conducted a case study of collaborative writing groups in a large anthropology class and isolated characteristics of successful cooperative groups. He investigated how group writing works: how tasks are assigned, how leaders are formed, and how shirkers are punished. The faculty member who teaches the class and believes in the importance of writing, but who did not want to evaluate 90 term papers, divided the class into groups of five, and as a result he graded fewer than 20 final papers. Drawing on Rhees' work, the professor articulated the qualities to students, thereafter incorporating them into an extended syllabus. This study not only gave the teacher concrete suggestions for improving instruction, but also the researcher and the teacher collaborated on an article published in a higher education journal (Lancy, Rhees, & Kinkead, 1994). Thus, another goal of involving students as researchers is to help them write studies of publishable quality.

As we analyze our own WAC program, several questions present themselves: How is writing integrated in a specific discipline? What guides faculty to join the WAC movement? What are faculty attitudes toward WAC? What are successful practices of WAC? Of particular note on our campus is the approach taken by the Department of History toward writing. In 1989, the acting department head requested a presentation on writing to his faculty, an invitation based primarily on conversations over lunch and an interest in student outcomes. Many of the history faculty attended this one informal hour-long session. From the discussion on WAC philosophy and questions about specific applications to history, the faculty immediately began experimenting with various techniques in their classrooms and sharing that information. Within 3 years notable changes in a majority of history professors' attitudes and pedagogical approaches to writing had occurred, including the drafting of a policy statement.

Two separate case studies in years 4 and 5 of the department's involvement in WAC were conducted by students. Fishburn (1994), a graduate student, selected two sections of History 499, the senior seminar capstone required for graduation, to study. Students were interviewed to assess their perceptions of themselves as historians and their attitudes about writing after completion of this writing-intensive course. She also interviewed the two faculty members teaching the course to chart the development of their innovations regarding writing. One teacher, Dr. Jones,

> sees a dramatic improvement in student writing and learning since WAC methods have been implemented.... "I've seen what it can do to the extent that we've had to re-norm because the class performance has gone way up. The students will say things like 'you saved me in my Political Science class

because without the training on how to write essays, how to think critically about a document, I never would have gotten that." (p. 18)

The teachers noted that not all faculty had jumped on the WAC band-wagon and even went so far as to say that there is a gap between students who major in American history and those who major in British history because one group of teachers employs more writing in its courses.

Walker (1995), an undergraduate, used Fishburn's work to increase our knowledge base about the changes that occurred in this department. Her study reveals that over 5 years, faculty, disenchanted with the "traditional term paper as the primary expression of student writing [and] ... the lack of opportunity for revision," turned increasingly to multiple drafts of peer-reviewed essays based on primary documents. As the policy guide for *Writing Across the Curriculum in the Department of History* (a handbook that includes departmental syllabi) notes, "This method allows for writing on many different occasions, as opposed to last minute cramming, provides feedback from four or five different individuals with direction from the instructor, and teaches the student not only how to identify 'good' writing, but how to describe it." (p. 1)

Walker is one of 23 Rhetoric Associates (RAs) from the class of 1994, all of whom were assigned to analyze the writing conventions within their majors. Kristi, a natural resources major, identified two types of writing gen-res in her essay, "Spotted Owls and the Written Word." Karen, an English major, dissected the different tones, stances, and documentation styles among the subdisciplines of English—literary criticism, creative writing, and technical writing—in her essay "You Say Tomato." Students learn in researching their own disciplines that distinctive differences exist in how information is gathered, compiled, and created. Professors often do not explicitly discuss "issues related to the functions and methods of writing in different disciplines" (Hilger, Bayer, Stitt-Bergh, & Taniguchi, 1995, p. 81). The RAs come to understand disciplinary "accents"—as Karen puts it—but they also trigger faculty to make explicit their philosophies of writing's role, during interviews. A rather subversive approach to increasing the turf and interest in WAC, students-as-researchers offers a nonthreatening but knowledgeable way to acquire information. As important, the case studies then produce conversations about writing across the campus .

Besides producing case studies, the RAs help us gauge the efficacy of writing instruction in the classes that use them as tutors (classes=32 annu-ally) by reporting on meetings with the teachers involved and gathering syl-labi with writing assignments. RAs can help faculty understand when instructions to class members are confusing, unclear, or insufficient. Likewise, RAs nominate excellent assignments for inclusion in our monthly "Writing & Speaking at USU," a brief newsletter that goes to all faculty and includes two model assignments. The RAs meet with approximately 1,600 students annually (USU student enrollment = 20,000) to confer on their writing and to offer a reader's perspective. From these interviews, we learn that students still tend toward the "midnight wonder" approach to writing rather than multiple drafts. The students with whom RAs work provide feedback twice during the term on the RAs' performance as well as the clarity of the assignment. Although this is informal data gathering, these "one-minute" responses written on index cards provide important information to the RA, the RA supervisor, and the faculty member teaching the class.

ATTITUDES TOWARD WRITING

Besides the writing itself and process of writing, attitudes toward writing form another influential aspect of any WAC Program. I would suggest that attitudes to monitor include those of students, faculty, and administrators; doing so will result in an overall picture of the effort of an entire university toward WAC. Take, for example, how faculty perceive writing in the disciplines. According to Hilger et al. (1995), faculty can be surprisingly naive about disciplinary writing conventions: "It is only through experience with their students-as-writers that professors come to learn that good writing in their own field is in some ways quite different from good writing in, say, physics or history" (pp. 80–81). If the faculty outside departments of English believe that writing should be taken care of in a single department, then efforts at curriculum reform to integrate writing in the various disciplines may not meet with much success. Surveying the faculty on such issues helps WAC administrators know where to start in development workshops.

Two students who were also in the RA program—Browning and Obray (1995)—undertook a case study to trace attitudes toward writing in the sciences as their undergraduate honors thesis. Although these pre-med students took some flak for not doing "real" science as their capstone project, they thought that they could have a lasting impact on the College of Science through their research. As their abstract notes, they took on an ambitious task:

> This research is an attempt to understand the role of writing in undergraduate science education, including the development of writing's current role in scientific education, the present nature of writing in the scientific disciplines, and its value. With this understanding, we feel it is possible to successfully improve the communication skills of undergraduate students in the scientific disciplines, which, in turn, will benefit both the scientific community and society itself. A case study of undergraduate writing in the sciences was conducted at Utah State University, both to assess the present attitude of faculty toward this subject and to investigate practical approaches to disciplinary writing instruction. (p. 1)

After gaining permission of the dean, Jon and Susan distributed surveys to 126 faculty; 70 were returned. Their three primary research questions focused on finding out how well students write, whose responsibility it is to teach writing to science majors, and how the writing skills of students in the college could be improved. They also asked faculty to define "adequate writing skills" in order to judge consistency of terms. Most faculty thought that high school, core writing classes, and the student were significantly responsible for the acquisition of writing skills. Most thought that the department and graduate school were not very responsible (p. 16). In fact, faculty suggested higher admission standards as the preferred remedy. They believed that if peer tutors were to be used, then only science majors would be effective. The information gathered by these two honors students will help determine what route to follow in formulating a plan for WAC in Science.

It is also helpful for the WAC administrator to know how specific departments address WAC. Although this kind of assessment may take place in informal conversations with colleagues or department heads, it is also possible to accomplish this in other ways, such as reading departmental syllabi or guidebooks, especially the philosophy statement or "what we believe." Our Political Science Department, for instance, publishes a guide for undergraduates where it articulates its stance on the importance of good communication skills:

> Most political science courses require extensive reading and writing, and some of our courses require research and oral participation. Your ability to read carefully, synthesize the information you have read, and effectively analyze it with clarity and persuasiveness will be challenged again and again in essay examinations, paper assignments, and sometimes in oral presentations.... Be prepared to meet this expectation.

Analyzing undergraduate handbooks, guides, and syllabi is facilitated when there are common gathering points for such documents, such as departmental archives, general education administrator's office, or a decentralized tutoring program. Understanding departmental writing priorities builds to a larger question of understanding the institutional priority and responsibility toward writing.

WHO AND HOW?

Another way to talk about assessment is to consider the *locus of evaluation*: individual student, groups of students, a core curriculum, one multiple-section class, a teacher, a department, a college, an institution, or alumni. This is a necessary question in order to determine appropriate instruments.

DATA SOURCES	Formative	Summative
One-minute paper	At end of each class meeting	
Chain Notes	When problem arises	
Opinion Polls	At course's beginning to assess attitudes	
Electronic Mail Feedback	Mid-term	
Student-generated Instrument	Mid-term, end of term	
Learning Logs or Dialogic Journals	After each writing assignment	End of term
Annotated Portfolios	End of course	Capstone seminar
Audio- or videotape	During conferences on writing tasks	Five-year timespan of archival footage
Quality Circle	Weekly	
Student Management Team	Weekly	Meeting w/prof every 2 weeks
Undergraduate Teaching Fellows or TAs	Weekly or as needed	Summary conference
Standard Student Evaluation Forms		End of course
Teaching Portfolio or Dossier	Pre-tenure	Tenure and/or Promotion Teaching Awards
Student research project	Student management teams	• Individual student project • Group of students (e.g., team, class) • Thesis/dissertation
Senior Exit Interviews		Effectiveness of general education as well as major
Workload Document		Policy statement
Program Review	WPA Consultant Evaluators	Accreditation Team
Telephone survey of alumni	In preparation for fund-raising drive	
Institutional Information Office		SCH generated (student credit hours)
Center for Teaching Excellence		Pinpointing master teachers

Figure 3.3. Data Sources

How the assessment is done may be the question that arises first in any discussion, but actually it is the one question to be delayed—at least until purpose and audience are specified. The instruments used should be appropriate to the goals or objectives being assessed. For instance, if teachers want to know how well the students have understood the material presented in a single class period, then the one-minute paper or half-sheet response (Angelo & Cross, 1993) would seem appropriate. Perhaps teachers want to know what knowledge and communication skills students bring to a class on day one; in this case, a survey or diagnostic writing might fit the situation. (A summary of data sources is included in Figure 3.3.)

In contrast, an assessment given to students on graduation that focuses on discipline-specific concepts and communication skills might be an exit interview to discover strengths and weaknesses of a program or an oral exam to assess whether or not students can articulate major principles (see Hilger et al., 1995; Light, 1992). Our College of Science instituted oral exit interviews of randomly selected graduating seniors to test the ability of students to discuss major concepts in the discipline. They found that students rarely were able to see the "big picture," as the Dean put it, that they had not moved to synthesis. As a result, science departments are reviewing and revising their curricula, investigating active learning methods, and adding more cross-disciplinary communication. Too often, students rightly complain that they do not see the connections among and between courses. Explicit maps explaining a department's approach may help students see the often invisible webbing of a curriculum. Likewise, if clear-cut goals for cross-curricular writing were implemented, then faculty in other disciplines might not hear the query, "Does spelling count?"

SUMMARY

The goal in assessing writing at both micro or macro levels is to achieve a good description. In addition, assessment is an opportunity to learn and then document what we do well. What I hope I have suggested here is: (a) there are many ways to assess the use and effectiveness of writing in the curriculum and (b) that partners in the process may come from our own student population. This article includes only a few of the possibilities for inviting students to partner with us. Making decisions locally about assessment in the context of the institutional mission will, no doubt, produce further appropriate options. The basis for sound assessment lies in a conversation of colleagues who begin by asking simple questions: What is assessed? Who is assessed? When does assessment occur? How is assessment done? What is the locus of assessment? Who is the audience for assessment results? Why is assessment needed?

Within these various scenarios (accreditation, strategic planning, employer surveys, and case studies), there lies a powerful platform not only for creating WAC Programs but also for fostering them.

REFERENCES

Accreditation Handbook. (1994). Commission on Colleges. Northwest Association of Schools and Colleges.

An American imperative: Higher expectations for higher education. (1993). Wingspread Group on Higher Education, Johnson Foundation.

Angelo, T. A., & Cross, K. P. (1993). *Classroom assessment techniques: A handbook for college teachers* (2nd ed.). San Francisco: Jossey-Bass.

Astin, A. W. (1991). *Assessment for excellence: The philosophy and practice of assessment and evaluation in higher education*. New York: Macmillan.

Astin, A. W. (1993). *What matters in college? Four critical years revisited*. San Francisco: Jossey-Bass.

Bean, J. C. (1994). Evaluating teachers in writing-across-the-curriculum programs. In C. Hult (Ed.), *Evaluating teachers of writing*. Urbana, IL: NCTE.

Belenky, M. F., Clinchy, B. M., Goldberger, N. R., & Tarule, J. M. (1986). *Women's ways of knowing: The development of self, voice, and mind*. New York: Basic Books.

Bok, D. (1990). *Universities and the future of America*. Durham, NC: Duke University Press.

Bowen, H. R. (1977). *Investment in learning*. San Francisco: Jossey-Bass.

Boyer, E. L. (1990). *Scholarship reconsidered: Priorities of the professoriate*. Carnegie Foundation: Princeton University Press.

Browning, S., & Obray, J. (1995). *Writing in science*. Honors thesis. Utah State University.

Cerbin, W. Documenting excellence in teaching. (1991, October). *Teaching Professor*, 2–3.

Edgerton, R., Hutchings, P., & Quinlan, K. (1991). *The teaching portfolio: Capturing the scholarship in teaching*. Washington, DC: AAHE.

Educational Testing Service and The College Board. (1991). The academic profile: Assessing general education. Princeton, NJ.

Evaluating teaching: Purposes, methods, and policies. (1982). Committee on the Evaluation and Improvement of Teaching and The Instructional Development Board: University of Washington. [Copies available through Center for Instructional Development and Research, 206-543-6588.]

Fishburn. S. M. (1994). *Becoming a historian: The role of writing across the curriculum methods in the development of professional identity*. Unpublished manuscript. Utah State University.

Gaudiani, C. L. (1994). For a new world, a new curriculum. *Educational Record, 75*, 20–29.

Golin, S. (1990). Four arguments for peer collaboration & student interviewing: The master faculty program. *AAHE Bulletin, 43*(4), 9–10.

A *handbook for student management teams*. (1992). Teaching Excellence Center, University of Wisconsin at Platteville and Office of Teaching Effectiveness, University of Colorado at Denver. [Available from David Zierath at UW-P, 608-342-1798.]

Hilger, T. L., Bayer, A. S., Stitt-Bergh, M., & Taniguchi, M. (1995). Doing more than "thinning out the herd": How eighty-two college seniors perceived their writing-intensive classes. *Research in Teaching English*. 29(1), 59–88.

Integrity in the college curriculum: A report to the academic community. (1985). Washington, DC: Association of American Colleges.

Katz, J., & Henry, M. (1988). *Turning professors into teachers: A new approach to faculty development and student learning*. New York: Macmillan.

Lancy, D. F., Rhees, A., & Kinkead, J. A. (1994). A sense of community: Collaboration in a large anthropology class. *College Teaching, 42*, 102–106.

Light, R. J. (1992). *The Harvard assessment seminars: Second report, Explorations with students and faculty about teaching, learning, and student life*. Cambridge: Harvard.

Lindemann, E. (1995). *A rhetoric for writing teachers* (3rd ed). New York: Oxford.

Political Science Major Undergraduate Handbook. (1994). Utah State University.

Seldin, P. (1991). *The teaching portfolio: A practical guide to improved performance and promotion/tenure decisions*. Bolton, MA: Anker.

Smagorinsky, P. (1991). *Expressions: Multiple intelligences in the English class*. Urbana, IL: National Council of Teachers of English.

Sommers, N. (1980). Revision strategies of student writers and experienced adult writers. *College Composition and Communication*, 31, 378–388.

Strong foundations: Twelve principles for effective general education programs. (1994). Washington, DC: Association for American Colleges.

Teaching performance memo. (1992). Committee on Teacher Evaluation. Department of English, Utah State University.

Walker, R. W. (1995). Writing in the discipline of history: Evaluating the student paper. In A. Freer & J. Kinkead (Eds.), *You say tomato...: Essays from the rhetoric associates program* (pp. 32–41). Logan, UT: Utah State University.

Weimer, M., Parrett, J. L., & Kerns, M. M. (1992). *How am I teaching? Forms and activities for acquiring instructional input*. Madison, WI: Magna, 1988. [Sixth printing, 1992.]

White, E. M. (1992). *Assigning, responding, evaluating: A writing teacher's guide* (2nd ed.). New York: St. Martin's.

Writing across the curriculum in the Department of History. (1993). Utah State University.

Chapter 4

.

Contextual Evaluation in WAC Programs: Theory, Issues, and Strategies for Teachers

Cynthia L. Selfe

Drawing on the work of scholars in assessment and evaluation (Huot & Williamson, 1997; Moss, 1994; Berlak, Newmann, Adams, Archbald, Burgess, Raven, & Romberg, 1992; Guba & Lincoln, 1989; Davis, Scriven, & Thomas, 1981), this chapter describes a contextual model for evaluating writing-across-the-curriculum (WAC) programs and discusses why such a model is important, particularly for teachers as major participants and stakeholders within such programs. In the article, a model of contextual assessment is defined for WAC programs in terms of assumptions, purpose, timing and duration, methodology, and ways in which it reflects and enacts relationships of power. For teachers within WAC programs, this model offers a productive—and all too rare—vision of agency within complex social systems. This notion of agency is explored in detail, particularly as it relates to Donald Schön's (1987) concept of reflective professional practice and Anthony Giddens' (1979) theory of human agency and social structuration. Finally, the article provides some principles to guide ongoing contextual evaluation projects and offers some ideas generated by WAC practitioners about how to conduct such efforts.

During the last decade, a great deal of attention has been focused on the challenges involved in evaluating—on a large scale and in practical ways—the many WAC programs that have been started in high school, two-year college, and university settings (cf., Young & Fulwiler, 1986; White, 1985; Fulwiler, 1988; Hartzog, 1986). These efforts have been encouraged—to varying degrees and in different situations—by the growing professionalization of composition studies as an academic specialty, the social pressures of accountability associated with tightening fiscal situations, the movement toward national standards, and the growing distrust of higher educational institutions as responsible social agents. In general, the faculty carrying out these large-scale program evaluations have come to recognize the value of conducting local, site-based assessments that involve teachers in the design, analysis, and interpretation of data from multiple perspectives and using multiple methods of inquiry (Young & Fulwiler, 1989).

These practical experiences of WAC evaluation, when coupled with recent scholarship in assessment theory, can help teacher–researchers identify the outlines of an emerging model of contextual program assessment for WAC efforts that differs in important ways from conventional assessment approaches. As this chapter suggests, this emergent assessment model is nontraditional in terms of its assumptions about who should design and participate in assessment projects; in its devaluation of traditional, positivist constructs of reliability and validity; in its recognition of social contexts and the constructed nature of knowledge; and in the value it places on the social–educational action that grows out of assessment processes. Although the model draws heavily from more recent practice, scholarly thinking, and theoretical perspectives that have come to influence assessment theory and psychometrics—particularly social constructivism, postmodern theory, and poststructuralist theory—elements of the nontraditional approach can also be traced to earlier discussions of formative evaluation (Davis, Scriven, & Thomas, 1981)—localized, ongoing assessments of program effectiveness, performed by teacher–researchers within a program, and aimed at immediate improvement of teaching practices and curricula.

Several terms have been used to describe this alternative set of approaches to program evaluation: contextual assessment (Berlak et al., 1992), responsive constructivist evaluation (Guba & Lincoln, 1989), and assessment based on the "enlightenment model" (Moss, 1994), among just a few of them. These terms refer, in common, to efforts that recognize effective evaluation as a complex, ongoing "sociopolitical process" (p. 19) drawing heavily on the locally situated knowledge of teachers as major "stakeholders" (Guba & Lincoln, 1989, p. 11); that locate the impetus for data collection and analysis in the every day efforts of practicing teachers (Davis, Scriven, & Thomas, 1980); that support a local, decentralized approach to decision making in evaluation efforts, thus placing power in the hands of those individuals most immediately affected by those decisions" (Berlak et al., 1992, p. 3); and that tie curricular and educational change directly to ongoing efforts of teachers who assess their own practices and the performances of students.

Importantly for teachers, as this chapter suggests, the characteristics and values this new model of contextual assessment embraces can offer WAC instructors, researchers, writing center tutors, and program directors (referred to, hereafter, as WAC practitioners) increasingly sophisticated insights into their roles as agents for productive change within educational and cultural systems. This is especially so when the discussion of contextual models for WAC program evaluation is linked to Donald Schön's (1987) concept of reflective professional practice and Anthony Giddens' (1979) theory of human agency and social structuration. In this chapter, the contextual model of program assessment will first be described generally in relation to the evaluation of WAC programs, and then linked to these two relevant theories—reflective teaching (Schön, 1987) and social structuration (Giddens, 1979)—with the goal of providing teachers a productive way of conceiving of their roles as change agents within WAC programs.

SOME BACKGROUND AND DISCUSSION BY WAC PRACTITIONERS

At the 1994 meeting of Conference on College Composition and Communication, in a workshop entitled "WAC and Program Assessment: Multiple Realities, Multiple Solutions," chaired by Kathleen Blake Yancey, WAC specialists and practitioners discussed the challenges involved in conducting large-scale evaluations of WAC programs and the subtle ways in which such evaluations can shape and inform the attitudes that both faculty and students have toward writing and writing programs.

One group at this gathering focused its discussion on nontraditional techniques of observation and evaluation that teacher–researchers could identify locally and use on an ongoing basis to support their own monitoring and improvement of the WAC programs in which they were working. The participants contrasted these locally determined strategies of ongoing assessment and adjustment with more formal and conventional evaluation efforts—efforts that tended to be larger in scale, that were often designed and carried out by outside consultants, that rested on measurements of statistical reliability and validity, that were described in formal reports to school or institutional administrators, and that occurred only at major milestones in a program's history.[1]

The discussion these teacher–researchers had at this meeting mirrored, in an important and immediate way, recent discussions of assessment practice and theory occurring among groups of professionals who share the fields of educational evaluation and composition studies, especially those individuals who focus on the large-scale assessment of writing programs. In particular, these discussions have begun to identify an emergent model of ongoing contextual program assessment that contrasts sharply with more tradition-

---

[1] I am indebted to Brian Huot and Kathleen Yancey for the sound advice they offered for revising the initial draft of this manuscript and the direction they generously provided for my additional reading in assessment literature.

al models of program assessment and evaluation, but that could have value when applied specifically to the large-scale evaluation of WAC programs.

Traditionally, as these scholars note, conventional methods for assessment and evaluation have been heavily influenced by intellectual and historical ties to the project of science and the related assumptions of positivism (Guba & Lincoln, 1989; Moss, 1994; Berlak et al., 1992; Huot & Williamson, 1997). Given this framework, conventional assessment methods rely on a common set of practices and assumptions. First among these is the assumption that education is most efficient and effectively carried out through a centralized authority (e.g., principal, a school board, an institution, a state or national education agency) that determines curricular direction, delegates responsibility, and assumes control of educational decision making. Following from this assumption is a reliance on standardized tests that allow centralized authorities to efficiently and accurately measure and then compare the performance of individual students, teachers, and programs (Berlak et al., 1992). In such a model, as Berlak notes, assessment efforts become a

> means of maintaining centralized control, providing those higher up in the educational bureaucracy (central office administrators, school board members, state educational officials, legislators, etc.) with relative rankings of organizational units (classrooms, schools, districts, etc.) and or students and teachers. (p. 5)

Program-evaluation efforts based on this traditional model subscribe to the assumption that standardized assessment measures are scientific instruments that can be constructed so that they are value neutral and—with proper attention to the constructs of validity and reliability—can identify a truth that "transcends social context and history" (Berlak et al., 1992, p. 13). According to this model, program evaluation and assessment are "unidirectional" (p. 19), initiated by a central authority and conducted by psychometric experts; teachers and students are the objects of assessment techniques rather than active participants in—or shapers of—such projects. Hence, as Huot and Williamson (1997) note,

> To control testing [and, I would add, to control program assessment] is to control education, to control what will be valued and taught within the schools. Crucial decisions concerning assessment are often made by regulatory agencies and political and educational policy makers based on practical and political concerns of cost, efficiency and public opinion. (p. 2)

In contrast to the conventional model of program assessment based on the values associated with science and positivism, a more recent model of assessment—called in this chapter *contextual assessment* (Berlak et al., 1992, p. 12)—assumes that evaluation is a sociopolitical process that should be shaped actively by major stakeholders. This model, which is readily adaptable to WAC program practices, acknowledges teachers as major stakeholders in writing programs and assessment efforts, individuals who have a particularly penetrating local knowledge of—and a vested interest in—the results of program evaluation (Guba & Lincoln, 1989).

This contextual approach to program evaluation and assessment is also congruent with WAC practices and program values because it acknowledges that evaluation involves a "continuous, recursive, and divergent process because its 'findings' are created social constructions that are subject to reconstruction" and, hence, must be "continuously recycled and updated" (Guba & Lincoln, 1989, p. 263). Given the process-based nature of this model, then, a project of program assessment "cannot be fully designed in advance" (p. 263) because its shape depends on active input and information from teachers and other major stakeholders.

The contextual model also recognizes—again in congruence with recent WAC theory and practice—that the data gathered in evaluations and the results of such evaluations (indeed, that program evaluation efforts themselves) represent social constructions of truth rather than irrefutable scientific findings (Guba & Lincoln, 1989). All findings, according to this model, are interpreted hermeneutically by program participants so as to arrive at temporary conclusions and recommendations. As Guba and Lincoln describe it, "evaluation thus implemented simultaneously aids understanding and clarifies the nature of needed action" (p. 264) in the future. Thus, action deriving from such findings is tied directly to instructional approaches and curricular change carried out by teachers and administrators involved in the process of writing program assessment—another approach familiar to WAC practitioners. Within this participatory model, the teacher—as a major stakeholder within a program—is a "political collaborator, a stage manager, a reality shaper, and a change agent" (Guba & Lincoln, 1989, p. 264).

Basing WAC evaluation efforts, then, on a contextual evaluation model makes sense in that it assumes faculty will shape WAC programs actively and on an ongoing basis, not only after major formal program evaluations that occur at milestone points of a program's history, but also *at the point of enactment*—as such efforts unfold on a daily basis within particular writing assignments designed by individual teachers with specific instructional goals in mind, within classrooms that house differing populations of students, within the social communities of writing centers and in the presence of writing coaches with various agenda, and within the curricula of discipline-based courses in various departments. In this framework, contextual evaluation can provide faculty and staff with a dynamic sense of their own agency as professionals and as a basis for encouraging and acting on their own reflective teaching practices.

THEORETICAL LENSES ON THE PROFESSIONAL
AGENCY OF TEACHERS

In a practical sense, most WAC practitioners, and indeed most teachers of writing, can identify immediately with the primary characteristics of the contextual evaluation model—the kind of ongoing participatory effort that practitioners engage in to determine how effective various WAC instructional materials are, how particular instructional efforts are being received by different writers, or how much students are writing and learning about writing. Indeed, in this sense, the intellectual impetus for contextual evaluation efforts is closely related to the professional impetus that gives rise to reflective teaching habits (Schön, 1987): Educators who want to do a better job of teaching begin observing their own teaching as it happens, monitor the results of this teaching in terms of student response and behavior, and shape future teaching and curricular efforts on the basis of this self-reflective monitoring.

As Donald Schön (1987) notes in his discussion of reflective practice, the habit of systematically monitoring one's own professional effectiveness involves the continual "application of theories and techniques" to "instrumental problems of practice" and the subsequent analysis of performance and consequence. This habit of reflective practice is characteristic of competent practitioners in a wide range of disciplines, Schön continues, and especially of professional educators well versed in the art of teaching. These individuals engage in a kind of "rule-governed inquiry" that requires a constant routine of "data gathering, inference, and hypothesis testing" about what goes on in classroom and other instructional situations (p. 34). For writing teachers, as Louise Phelps (1991) points out, this notion is hardly strange. Writing teachers regularly and systematically observe their own instruction as it unfolds in the course of an assignment or in the course of a class; analyze the effects of this instruction on students by reading students' assignments, discuss writing tasks with students, listen in on the conversations of writing groups, compare current performance with past performances, or talk with other teachers; and modify instruction to improve its effectiveness in terms of explicit, or implicit, instructional goals. Because this kind of reflective practice—or ongoing self evaluation—involves careful observation and data gathering, analysis, and assessment of findings, Phelps (1991) points out that it is "a form of thinking that closely parallels academic research methods" (p. 873), especially when such research is conducted within, and acknowledges, site-based contexts and locally derived, practically based questions of relevance to teaching professionals.

If the process of reflection/observation, analysis/evaluation, and classroom/program change has credence at a practical level, however, it may be harder to understand within the context of some social theories that have come to inform the research efforts of composition specialists during the last 5 years. Indeed, as Carl Herndl (1993) points out, at least one major strand of contemporary composition theory (comprised of poststructuralist theories of language, the sociology of science, and ethnography) has served to focus the profession's research efforts on *description, explanation, and analysis* of the "relations among rhetoric, knowledge, and society" (p. 349) rather than on making change in an active sense.

Research based on such theoretical approaches, as Herndl (1993) notes, leaves little room for the concept of purposeful action undertaken by effective social agents who utilize their situated knowledge effectively. In the case of WAC programs, these agents are typically teachers, administrators, tutors, and students. Their inability to act rests theoretically on a reliance of a "pessimistic and mechanical model of social reproduction associated with orthodox Marxism—one which envisions ideology and domination as the homogenous and all-powerful determinant of cultural and institutional practice." These structuralist models, adds Herndl, have "both theoretical and practical limitations. The theory of structure and determination doesn't allow for change and reduces the individual to a function or bearer of structural meaning" (p. 352), thus rendering the idea of purposeful human agency and the related notion of productive social action, suspect and problematic.

As a counterbalance to this tendency, Herndl suggests a closer look at the related concepts of resistance and human agency, especially as these terms are articulated in the social theory of Anthony Giddens. Giddens, reacting against social systems theories and linguistic theories of the 20th century which fail to provide a robust theory of human action, takes on the project of describing how human beings function as effective agents within complex social systems—how they make choices to enact change and undertake productive programs of action even within social systems that seem highly structured and overdetermined. In this project, Giddens objects, for example, to the explanations of social theorists such as Durkheim, Parsons, Marx, and Althusser whose work, he claims, locates human beings within complex webs of historical–social–economic systems that prescribe their action in overly narrow terms. These theories, according to Giddens, portray humans as subjects constituted almost entirely by complex systemic effects within rigidly structured social fields that leave little room for human agency. For related reasons, he also objects to the work of language theorists—among them, Lacan, Sassure, Culler, Wittgenstein, Derrida, and Ricoeur—who conceive of an increasingly "de-centered subject" constituted only through the "discourse of the Other" and a resulting "mistrust of consciousness or 'subjectivity.'" The work of these scholars, Giddens suggests, portrays human consciousness as a "fractured and fragile set of processes" (p. 38), one that furthers the "conceptual disappearance of the subject"

(p. 44) and renders suspect the concept of humans as effective social agents.

These theories, as Giddens explains, share a "blindness to the everyday fact that all social agents have an understanding, practical and discursive, of the conditions of their action" (p. 112). Social institutions, he adds, "do not just work 'behind the backs' of social actors who produce and reproduce them." Rather, he continues, "every competent member of every society knows a great deal about the institutions of that society," and the nature of this knowledge is not simply "incidental to the operation of society, but is necessarily involved in it" (p. 71). Human beings, Giddens observes, are involved on a continual basis in the "reflexive monitoring" (p. 25) of their conduct within social contexts. This monitoring—which happens at both conscious and unconscious levels—enables individuals to make choices and then to intervene in "the ongoing process of events-in-the-world." (p. 55). Social agents, for example, recognize that they are "only one among others in a society" and are, thus, "bounded in specific ways, that connect with the 'situated' character of actors' activities." Within this theoretical framework, the social structures and systemic formations that constitute a society can be understood as "both the medium and the outcome" (p. 69) of human practices.

The concept of human agency that Giddens' theory provides is useful for WAC teachers, administrators, tutors, and students who believe that they can act with purpose and effectiveness in the classroom, and within programs of assessment that recognize the richness of site-based contexts, the importance of local knowledge, and the importance of linking evaluation and educational change. And such a contextual model is also congruent with the observations of writing program directors like Louise Phelps (1991) who have maintained that teaching professionals can, and should, undertake systematic programs of inquiry, analysis, and improvement within writing programs. Taken together, the concepts of reflective practice and social agency provide WAC practitioners an extended framework for understanding the value of contextual assessments of WAC programs as efforts that support teachers as they actively shape and change the social structures within which they work.

SOME PRINCIPLES OF FORMATIVE EVALUATION

Giddens' theory of social structuration is not only useful in explaining how teachers, as human agents, understand and act meaningfully within their social circumstances. It can also suggest key principles for structuring the contextual evaluation of WAC programs. This type of work is definitely needed. Although sustained discussions of contextual evaluation methods— and related approaches—continue to occur in the literature of measurement and evaluation (Guba & Lincoln, 1989; Berlak et al., 1992; Moss 1994; Huot & Williamson, 1997), relatively little has been written about how the principles of such a model could be applied to the assessment of WAC programs within real social situations, the complex settings of institutions, the environments of WAC classrooms. Among the principles that can be derived for this purpose are the following:

Principle 1:

WAC programs exist only as they are constituted by individual participants ("stakeholders" in Guba & Lincoln's terms) and their actions. Given this involvement and investment in social structures, and the power relations operative within such structures, these same individuals should design and carry out program evaluation projects. In this way, the most active participants in a program can get at questions that concern them directly. The people who make up a system know best where the system is weakest and needs the most improvement.

At one level, a reading of Giddens social theory helps us recognize that WAC programs are social formations that exist not in and of themselves, but rather as they are continually, and historically, constituted through the actions of ensembled human agents—not only individuals directly involved in the programs themselves (e.g., program directors, teachers in various disciplines, students, and Writing Center coaches), but also individuals whose actions affect the WAC effort at more of a remove (e.g., teachers who are not participating directly in a WAC Program, university administrators, legislators, parents, state education officers, professional journal editors, scholars in other locations who write about WAC, and many others).

Given the complexity of social formations contained with a WAC Program, contextual evaluation efforts will help provide the most useful information when they are designed and enacted locally, by groups of WAC Program participants who have some personal knowledge of—and stake in finding out—what is happening in a particular situation: for example, why individual students perform as they do on a particular writing assignment series; how students perceive writing and its value to their career; what writing assignments teachers design and what written responses their assignments generate; how writing center coaches respond to students who need help in a particular class; how university administrators form their perceptions of WAC program performance and WAC program needs.

If Giddens is correct, the individual agents involved in creating a particular social formation have the deepest and most penetrating understanding of its workings—although this understanding may not always be accessible on a conscious level. As the next principle articulates, the methodologies of reflective teaching practice (Schön, 1987; Phelps, 1991) and contextual program assessment (Guba & Lincoln, 1989; Berlak et al., 1992)—given that they involve participants in generating questions and concerns, carrying evaluation projects, and analyzing results—can make such understandings increasingly accessible at the level of consciousness and, thus, begin to take advantage of the intimate knowledge that social agents have of the situations within which they operate.

Principle 2:

Contextual assessments of WAC programs should involve participants in sharing and discussing findings with each other. Knowledge of social systems often resides at an unconscious—or tacit—level, and individuals can help each other make such knowledge available at a conscious and discursive level.

Although participants have a naturally deep understanding of WAC programs as social formations, and are thus able to take purposeful action within these programs, this understanding is not always based on consciously accessible information. Much of what individuals know about such programs, for example, is based on tacit understandings and observations—as Giddens notes, on experience, habit, and convention—that are not available in discursive form to the conscious mind. WAC faculty, for example, may know a great deal about how to create writing assignments that accomplish an unstated set of professional goals in a particular discipline, but this understanding remains tied to a set of unconscious understandings: how practicing professionals react in certain common situations; what communication skills and communication styles are expected of professionals; what registers and vocabulary are commonly used in various professional situations; how supervisors, other professionals, and the public react to professional communications; which issues are sensitive, or even taboo, in a given profession, etc. Based on a complex set of unconscious social understandings, such information is not always immediately or readily available to individuals involved in formative evaluation projects or those conducting such evaluation projects, even though it might have important bearings on a curricular program or the particular evaluation question under consideration.

For this reason, it may be useful to involve WAC participants in evaluation groups or teams that discuss the information gathered during contextual evaluation efforts. Such a setting may help individuals articulate the reasons for—and the circumstances of—their actions by providing corroborating or disconfirming insights from other people's perspectives. These teams, for example, may provide opportunities for teachers, students, and administrators in a WAC program to examine some of the choices they are making and articulating for both themselves and others why they act as they do within a particular situation. More particularly, they may indicate why students interpret and perform a writing assignment in a particular way, why a teacher chooses to ask for certain formal elements in a biology lab report, why a program administrator chooses to incorporate a writing-intensive engineering course at the sophomore rather than the junior level. The observation, evaluation, and analysis of the human and social dynamics within these situations can enrich the understanding that participants have of their own and others' actions within the program, and, thus, of the program itself.

Principle 3:

Contextual evaluation efforts should mirror, at programmatic levels, the reflexive monitoring of individuals at personal levels—both are aimed at making decisions about improvement. In a WAC program such improvement should have a relationship to curricular change.

The interpreted findings of contextual evaluation efforts should be tied directly to action designed to serve students, teachers, administrators, and other legitimate stakeholders in WAC programs—action that improves WAC programs themselves. This critical examination of evaluation results—in the context of program improvement—is congruent with the recognition that teachers and other WAC practitioners act as effective social agents. It is also is a necessary step for ongoing curricular development within a WAC program.

This process of tying assessment findings directly to curricular and programmatic change has strong support from the literature of both practitioner inquiry and program assessment. Referring to the work of Lawrence Stenhouse (1985) on practical inquiry and its relation to curriculum development, Phelps writes,

> ...the curriculum itself should be thought of as a great research project, the medium in which practitioners together experiment with hypotheses about teaching and learning. In that light, practical inquiry becomes indispensable as a means for the community to discover more about what is going on, to develop new information and interpretations as they are needed for further decision-making. Simply reflecting on personal practices and sharing them with each other is not enough. The community needs to study itself: its students, choices and their impacts, structures, conceptual bases, contexts within the university and elsewhere... (1991, p. 880)

Indeed, the importance of such work may be particularly demonstrable in WAC programs where new methodologies and courses continue to emerge as teachers from multiple disciplines work together to reach an understanding regarding curricular practice. In such environments, which are often multiply constructed by the instructional values of several disciplines and decentered in terms of their departmental location, the project of contextual assessment may be more important in identifying curricular direction and effectiveness.

STRATEGIES FOR GATHERING DATA IN CONTEXTUAL EVALUATION EFFORTS

This chapter has covered, in principle, the concepts that contextual evaluation efforts may be most effective because they grow organically out of the questions and concerns of program participants, and that such evaluations are best conducted by these same people as part of an ongoing program of social action. However, principles that help give a *general* shape to the evaluation projects that WAC practitioners undertake provide little assistance in terms of *specific* strategies that teachers, students, and writing center tutors can use to gather information and that can lead to program improvement.

Although suggestions about the specific strategies used to gather contextual data are often best identified by participants within individual WAC programs—by those social agents whose activities constitute a WAC program and who, thus, have the deepest possible familiarity with the social structures of that program—they can also emerge, fruitfully, from discussions that involve participants from different programs. Such public discussions can also lead to an expanded conscious understanding of social formations and the possibilities for agency within WAC programs—one that may be more robust than the conscious understanding of individual participants. This kind of productive discussion occurred at the CCCC session mentioned earlier—"WAC and Program Assessment: Multiple Realities, Multiple Solutions." At that gathering, participants talked about the challenges associated with conducting WAC evaluation efforts and compiled a list of possible strategies for gathering data and artifacts from WAC programs as they unfold at the point of enactment.

As the WAC practitioners noted, the artifacts and data gathered in contextually based assessment projects can yield valuable information about how individuals perceive and act on the social conditions within which they operate at a given time and in given situation. The document of a writing assignment, for example, tells not only about a particular faculty member's expectations for his or her students in a WAC program, but also about the particular writing skills that the faculty member thinks is important for students to learn as professionals in a discipline, and the evaluation criteria that the faculty member has identified for successful writing. An assignment provides additional information on the professional values inherent in a discipline, the technical skills required for a particular task, and the social conditions surrounding the practice of a profession, among many other things.

Given these characteristics, the materials gathered for contextual assessment projects can yield not only short-term evaluation and program improvement, but can also point to long-term evaluation and curricular improvement. Frequently, in fact, long-term assessment efforts are difficult to undertake precisely because the smaller bits of information that comprise the rich history of a program have been lost gradually over the years and are difficult to recapture. Faculty, for example, may fail to gather early baseline (and ongoing) information about various efforts or fail to save various artifacts generated in their classes (e.g., student papers, assignments, faculty stories, syllabi) that could help provide a rich social and historical picture of WAC efforts at an institution.

Among the specific evaluation strategies that the WAC practitioners identified in the CCCC WAC Program Assessment session are those in the following list. It is important to note that no one program will find all of these contextual strategies useful. Individual programs and participants will have to gauge the usefulness of particular items on their own understanding of the programs within which they work.

- **Collect benchmark information before a WAC program begins.** Before beginning a WAC program or *before* implementing a new phase of a program, survey students and faculty about the numbers of writing assignments they get or give in various disciplines; the kind, length, and variety of writing assignments common in various disciplines; the frequency and duration of writing assignments in various disciplines; and the audiences and purposes of writing assignments in various disciplines. Gather information on the attitudes of students, faculty, and other stakeholders toward writing and writing instruction (both before and after graduation), and their experiences with writing and with writing instruction. Collect information on students' performance on writing tasks and the kinds of writing that they do in connection with various classes. Collect completed writing assignments, course syllabi, goal statements, student evaluations, writing portfolios, and peer-group commentary on papers all before the WAC program is begun.

  WAC participants beginning such benchmarking projects may want to refer to Brian Huot's (1992) useful contribution on inventorying writing programs.
- **Collect students' and parents' stories and histories about writing practices, assignments, successes, failures, attitudes, and experiences.** As a WAC program proceeds, gather students' and parents' stories about writing experiences. Focus not only on written literacy practices in formal academic settings, but also on those that occur in the home, in peer groups, in the dorm, and in various disciplines. Ask about the writing instruction that goes on in these different settings. Use audiotape or videotape; consider transcribing the most useful comments.

- **Collect faculty members' stories and histories about writing and WAC instruction.** As a WAC program proceeds, ask faculty about memorable students and the writing challenges that they have faced; the attitudes toward written communication that various groups of students have brought with them to the classroom; designing and evaluating written assignments, and grading and responding. Have teachers talk about the WAC assignments they have introduced in their classes, the process they went through to integrate writing into their syllabus, the responses they have had from peers and/or administrators to their WAC efforts, and how they, themselves, learned to write. Use audiotape or videotape; consider transcribing the most useful comments.

- **Collect administrators' and officials' stories and histories about writing programs and WAC.** As a WAC program proceeds, seek the perspectives that administrators and other officials (e.g., state legislators, district curricular specialists, state educational officials) have on how and why a WAC program came into being, what purpose(s) it accomplished/is accomplishing, who benefited/is benefiting, who was served/is served. Encourage administrators or officials to talk about the cost of such programs, the timing, the challenges involved, and the responsibility for evaluating the program and making sure that it succeeds. Use audiotape or videotape; consider transcribing the most useful comments.

- **Collect program artifacts.** As a WAC program proceeds, gather the documents that teachers and administrators generate as part of a WAC program: lists of program goals, institutional statements, curriculum descriptions, definitions of writing-intensive courses, tutoring/writing center reports, presentations to boards of control and parents.

- **Conduct classroom observations, observations of small groups, and observations of individuals working within WAC programs. Combine these observations with interviews.** As a WAC program proceeds, observe how WAC goals and assignments are being instantiated within different classes and why—and with what results. Observe the writing instruction that goes in large-group sessions, small group sessions, and among peers—note who talks about writing, what kinds of writing instruction is going on, and what criteria are being used to indicate success. Ask both teachers and students which writing assignments work, which are less successful, and why. Among other topics, talk to both faculty and students about how—or if—WAC has changed instruction in this classroom.

- **Collect performance artifacts from students in WAC programs.** Ask not only for completed written assignments, but drafts, papers that were not turned in for a grade, peer-group commentary, notes, audience analysis descriptions, reflections on an individual's writing progress, and complete portfolios of written work. Collect this information from various sizes of groups depending on the focus of the formative evaluation effort: For example, collect all the writing that several case-study students do in one year or in one course. Alternatively, collect all the student portfolios from a particular course or in response to a common assignment that extends across sections. If possible, collect teacher commentary on individual assignments and on portfolios as whole documents. In interviews, ask both teachers and students to comment on portfolios, assignments, peer responses, etc.

- **Conduct interviews with both students and faculty.** As a WAC program proceeds, ask students about their attitudes toward their writing skill, and their understanding of writing requirements in particular careers—before individuals begin working within a WAC program, after they have experienced the program, and when they are leaving the program. In faculty interviews, ask about what criteria individuals use to gauge success in students' writing efforts, what elements successful writing assignments must have, and how a teacher knows when writing assignments have succeeded. Also conduct interviews with alumni from various disciplines, asking them about writing practices within their career path, what they think of the WAC assignments that students are given, what kinds of writing instruction students will need.

CONCLUSION

As the participants at the 1994 CCCC session noted[2], contextual assessments of WAC programs (site-based evaluations efforts designed by teachers and

---

[2] The teacher–researchers at this session were attending a CCCC work group that focused on "formative" evaluation techniques, a term taken from Davis, Scriven, and Thomas (1981) that refers to

Evaluation aimed at the improvement of an ongoing enterprise... formative evaluation is done for the purpose of improving a program that is still in the process of development or implementation, and this kind of evaluation is given to the people who can still effect improvement... its intentions and process are clearly dedicated to improvement. (p.7)

Reflecting back on this session as I drafted and redrafted this article, I began to identify some important connections between the impetus of formative evaluation and the more robust theoretical model suggested by evaluation literature on contextual evaluation methodology: both approaches regard assessment as an ongoing, site-based process that involves the active participation of program participants, and both approaches suggest the importance of close ties between assessment efforts and curricular change. Through the writing of this article, then, I have come to understand formative evaluation better as an early, and more narrowly defined precursor of the contextual assessment model. Although participants in the CCCC workshop that I describe herein were talking about—and suggesting techniques and approaches for—formative evaluation, their insight and experience applies equally well to the efforts described by the broader project of contextual evaluation.

other program participants to gather information about programs in-progress and to yield understanding about how instruction and curricula can be improved on an ongoing basis) are useful projects for teachers, students, and administrators. Such projects, grounded intellectually in theories of reflective professional practice and social agency, can provide practitioners with the information they need to make productive changes in WAC classrooms, curricula, and programs. Contextual evaluations, when they are carefully designed and conducted by program participants with a penetrating understanding of the contexts within which they function, can provide richly textured data and artifacts that tell the story of a WAC program as it unfolds in time and as it is enacted by those humans who imbue it with purpose and meaning.

In practice, contextual evaluation locates the task of program assessment, the habit of reflective practice, and the responsibility for curricular improvement at the local level, with those practitioners closest to programs as they are enacted in classrooms and writing centers. The significance of locating the responsibility for ongoing program evaluation with those individuals who have a first-hand understanding of institutional constraints and possibilities; the concrete material conditions under which students, teachers, and administrators function; and the ways in which a particular program develops at the point of enactment cannot be underestimated.

REFERENCES

Berlak, H., Newmann, F., Adams, E., Archbald, D., Burgess, L., Raven, J., & Romberg, T. (1992). *Toward a new science of educational testing and assessment.* Albany, NY: SUNY Press.

Davis, B., Scriven, M., & Thomas, S. (1981). *The evaluation of composition instruction.* Inverness, CA: Edgepress.

Fulwiler, T. (1988). Evaluating writing across the curriculum programs. In S. McLeod (Ed.), *Strengthening programs for writing across the curriculum* (pp. 61–75). San Francisco: Jossey-Bass.

Giddens, A. (1979). *Central problems in social theory: Action, structure, and contradiction in social analysis.* Berkeley, CA: University of California Press.

Guba, E., & Lincoln, Y. (1989). *Fourth generation evaluation.* Newbury Park, CA: Sage.

Hartzog, C. (1986). *Composition and the academy: A study of writing program administration.* New York: MLA.

Herndl, C. G. (1993). Teaching discourse and reproducing culture: A critique of research and pedagogy in professional and non-academic writing. *College Composition and Communication, 44* (3), 349–363.

Huot, B. (1992). Finding out what they are writing: A method, rationale and sample for writing across the curriculum research. *WPA: Writing Program Administration, 15,* 31–40.

Huot, B., & Williamson, M. (1997). Rethinking portfolios for evaluating writing: Issues of assessment and power. In K. Yancey & I. Weiser (Eds.), *Situating portfolios: Four perspectives*. Logan, UT: Utah State University Press.

Moss, P. (1994). Validity in high stakes writing assessment: Problems and possibilities, *Assessing Writing, 1*(1), 109–128.

Phelps, L. (1991). Practical wisdom and the geography of knowledge in composition. *College English, 53*(8), 863–885.

Schön, D. (1987). *Educating the reflective practitioner: Toward a new design for teaching and learning in the professions*. San Francisco: Jossey-Bass.

White, E. (1985). *Teaching and assessing writing: recent advances in understanding, evaluating, and improving student performance*. San Francisco: Jossey-Bass.

Young, A., & Fulwiler, T. (Eds.) (1986). *Writing across the disciplines: Research into practice*. Upper Montclair, NJ: Boynton/Cook.

Chapter 5

•

Beyond Accountability:
Reading With Faculty as Partners
Across the Disciplines

Brian Huot

ACCOUNTABILITY: THE NEED TO EVALUATE

For those of us who administer, work in, or wish to establish writing-across-the-curriculum (WAC) programs, accountability and assessment are important and inevitable. The continued funding, support, and accreditation of WAC often depend on our ability to demonstrate that such programs contribute to students' ability to write and learn. Apart from outside pressures, WAC assessment can provide important feedback about the strengths and weaknesses of each program. This does not mean, however, that all assessment procedures will provide valuable information. Historically, educational assessment has demonstrated the potential to produce results that satisfy outside pressures for accountability without producing any information of value to the programs themselves (Berlak, 1992). Unless we who understand how our programs function become involved in their assessment, evaluation procedures are likely to produce results that are insensitive to the values which inform and drive successful WAC initiatives.

When considering options for evaluating a WAC program, it is important to note that conventional writing assessment procedures require that students write to a single prompt in a timed testing environment. Normally, each paper is scored by at least two individual raters trained with a scoring guideline used to ensure rater agreement (i.e., interrater reliability). Given the constraints of conventional writing assessment and the most common designs of WAC programs,[1] it is not difficult to figure out that assessing writ-

---

[1] For example, the three major designs for WAC consist of: (a) writing courses designed and taught by writing specialists for specific disciplines like the humanities, social sciences, business, etc; (b) linked writing courses of smaller enrollment taught by writing specialists in conjunction with larger courses taught by the faculty in the discipline; and (c) writing-intensive content area courses taught by faculty in the disciplines.

ing in the various disciplines in any meaningful way can be a difficult enterprise. This is especially true for programs like the one at the University of Louisville which utilize writing-intensive courses taught by faculty in the disciplines, thus reflecting the autonomy of individual instructors and the differences inherent in the disciplinarity of academic discourse.

Given the history of assessment procedures and the often tenuous nature of many WAC programs, WAC administrators and writing teachers often view assessment as a necessary evil. One purpose of this chapter is to construct assessment as a more positive force on WAC. Unlike most of the chapters in this volume, my chapter does not describe a comprehensive approach to WAC assessment nor does it provide interesting and encouraging data about how well our WAC program is functioning. Instead, I focus on a specific method used to read student writing with faculty across the disciplines that develops the partnerships necessary for assessment procedures to reach beyond accountability and establish relationships and provide direction to truly improve WAC. Because programs at other schools may utilize different organizational designs and exist within disparate political and educational missions and climates, one should not apply our particular scheme wholly or uncritically to another institution or program. Instead, I hope that my experiences give an idea of some of the options available for dealing with the need to evaluate. I believe that although evaluation is difficult and time consuming, it can yield benefits which stretch beyond the mere assessment of student writing or the certification of existing programs, if done well. Although I describe only a small portion of an ongoing assessment program, there are some promising signs that the institutional need to evaluate has helped particular units within the university understand and meet more local needs that deal with curriculum reform and instructional development. I also believe that our efforts have helped to strengthen ties with faculty who teach the writing-intensive courses that comprise our WAC program. Faculty have learned to recognize their expertise and to articulate it in ways that support the university-wide effort to teach and value student writing. These kinds of benefits extend beyond the initial impetus associated with assessment and accountability.

OUR WAC PROGRAM

At the University of Louisville we have a mandated WAC program that is part of our general education requirements. Along with two sections of first-year composition, all students must pass two writing-intensive courses at the 300 level or above to satisfy the written communication requirements for graduation. These courses are designated writing intensive by the individual school or college's curriculum committee which is responsible for other decisions about curriculum and instruction. A writing-intensive course includes 2,400 words of writing, has a research component, and gives students the opportunity to improve their writing within the context of the course. The courses are taught by the faculty within the various departments. Faculty across the disciplines are supported by a WAC staff appointed from the English Department and funded through the Provost's office. The WAC staff consists of an English faculty person with course release and two graduate assistant lines from our doctoral program in rhetoric and composition. We have, at times, split up the teaching assistant lines to have as many as four half-time graduate students. This staff consults with and supports faculty who teach writing-intensive courses. We have run workshops, brought in outside speakers, convened committees, conducted luncheon discussions and faculty seminars, and supported an electronic discussion list for those instructors teaching or interested in teaching WAC. A few years ago, the university began devising a plan to assess the general education program because it was nearing its fifth year, and we had to report on its effectiveness for the Kentucky Commission on Higher Education and for our impending self study. The scheme we created for evaluating the general education program consisted of a quantitative strand in which students take a standardized test before and after their general education courses. We also established a qualitative strand in which a small sample of students compile portfolios of the work they do in their general education classes, and this work is judged as being acceptable, unacceptable, or exceptional. The writing students produce in their writing-intensive courses is also included in the portfolios and is evaluated as part of the general education assessment.

PORTFOLIOS

We decided to include full portfolios of student work from individual classes to assess WAC because writing portfolios offer several assessment advantages. First, they allow the collection of many different kinds of writing and provide a comprehensive record of the writing a student does in a particular class. Portfolios also have a successful track record in assessing student performance in WAC programs (Haswell & McLeod, this volume; Larson, 1991; Mills-Courts & Amiran, 1991; Thais & Zawicki, this volume). The multiple writing samples provide evaluators with a range of rhetorical and linguistic tasks with which to assess writing ability and to eliminate the possibility that a single task might favor particular students. In addition, the multiple samples let evaluators consider the growth exhibited by students during a specified period. Portfolios can also include reflective and discursive material that give students the support to develop an identity within the discipline they are writing their way into. In this way, portfolios not only provide a sample of student writing but actually encourage student learning. Portfolio assessment furnishes the opportunity for diverse and multiple samples, while at the same time retaining the disciplinary nature of academic prose. Portfolios use writing that students have already produced for class, thus eliminating the need for writing sessions and, more importantly (especially for programmatic assessment), providing a better example of the kinds of writing students are actually doing. In other words, if we want to evaluate the efficacy of a WAC program, it is more sensible to use writing being written by students in that program, rather than using writing samples produced specifically for evaluation.

Although writing portfolios solve many problems connected with assessing WAC, they do create others. The crux of these new problems involves (a) who will read the portfolios and (b) what they will base their assessment on. The remainder of this chapter focuses on how instructors from the disciplines read and set up guidelines for evaluating student writing in particular disciplinary contexts. Before faculty can be assembled to read student writing, a set of guidelines or rubric needs to be established that is sensitive to the type of writing students do in various disciplines and to the values their teachers hold about this writing. Where will these guidelines come from? If we believe in the diversity of writing done across the disciplines, and we want our assessment procedures to reflect these differences, then individual guidelines need to be articulated for specific disciplines. It should be apparent that only those who teach, write, and work in specific areas are really competent to set guidelines and evaluate student writing.

OUR ASSESSMENT SCHEME

The use of faculty across the disciplines to create scoring rubrics and to assess student writing creates additional problems. Before faculty can be ready to judge how well their students' writing meets recognizable standards, these standards, themselves, need to be articulated. This creates new problems because only faculty within the disciplines are qualified to set such guidelines. Our colleagues in other disciplines often feel inadequate in their ability to describe student writing and respond to the various competencies this writing may exhibit. Faculty who don't normally consider the teaching of writing part of their jobs often lack the vocabulary and facility with language-specific phenomena to engage in meaningful dialogue about student writing. Without the skill to examine writing as an object, to recognize, describe, and name its rhetorical and linguistic features, frustrated faculty are often reduced to talking about student writing wholly in terms of its ability to approximate mechanical correctness. Faculty who are reading student writing to articulate guidelines must read beyond their normal roles as evaluators in a particular course. This can be a particularly difficult issue because the method employed will have to give faculty space to exercise their expertise while at the same time supplying them with the necessary support to engage student writing in ways that empower and utilize their knowledge, interests, and values.

To create guidelines, we solicited from faculty teaching writing-intensive courses collections of student writing at the three levels of evaluation being used in the qualitative assessment of the general education program: acceptable, unacceptable, or exceptional. We invited faculty who teach in the various areas to read student portfolios and describe the writing at three different levels. Teachers representing six different areas met and read a sample of student writing. Although we would have liked to conduct sessions for each school or college or even each department, our limited resources determined that we decide on the following areas: (a) Natural and Physical Sciences and Engineering, (b) Humanities and Liberal Arts, (c) Business, (d) Education and Social Sciences, (e) Nursing and Allied Health, and (f) Composition.

These six groups of teachers received a small stipend for their efforts. Three or four faculty met with two members of the WAC staff three separate times for a 2-hour session. During each session, the group read a paper that best represented one of the categories of achievement. These sessions were taped and transcribed, and from the transcriptions a tentative set of guidelines were developed for each of the three categories. Faculty readers received a copy of the guidelines and had a chance to modify or comment on them. These guidelines are then used to judge writing portfolios in the assessment of the university's WAC program.

The guidelines that are defined, articulated, and developed by the six faculty groups come from the writing being produced by University of Louisville undergraduates and the reading given by university faculty. These guidelines reflect student ability, curricular concerns, and faculty perceptions of student ability and performance. The purpose of the reading is to produce criteria that match the writing of the students and the reading of the faculty involved in the assessment program. By giving faculty the facility to work with student writing, we can help them create assessment schemes that are discipline specific and pedagogically relevant, because the guidelines themselves come from teachers reading student writing.

READING ACROSS THE CURRICULUM

To give faculty the ability to set guidelines and articulate goals for their students, we use an assessment technique developed by Patricia Carini, a pioneer in alternative education and assessment. This method, which has been called a reflective conversation, is based loosely[2] on theories of phenomenology. It has been used to gather groups of faculty to describe and articulate student writing ability for various purposes and at different levels. We at the University of Louisville are the first, however, to use it to read with faculty across a college campus. The Prospect School in Bennington, Vermont, a well-known alternative school, relied extensively on this method of assessment in which an archive of works was collected for each student. Assessment of student progress consisted of a reflective conversation on selected student works. Barrit, Stock and Clark (1986) used a similar method to comment on the University of Michigan's placement program. Himley (1989) employed this technique in a chapter in *Encountering Student Texts* to design composition curriculum. She also used the method in her book *Shared Territory* as a way to explore children's writing development (1991). This technique for reading has many applications and works well for the purposes to which we have adopted it. I must caution that this method is rather difficult to explain. Himley (1989, p. 6) provides a useful breakdown of the basic components of reflective reading which include reading a text aloud, attempting to describe it communally, and eventually moving on to a discussion of more inferential characteristics of student work.

Members of each of the individual groups receive the portfolios ahead of time and are instructed to read them before the first meeting. A warm-up exercise begins each reading. These warmups set the tone for the reading and help us visualize the writer and student within the text. For the first reading we ask the group to talk about themselves as writers. It's intriguing how many faculty tell us that they don't see themselves as writers, though they realize they do much writing and that producing written documents is a major part of their professional lives. This warm-up focuses on the phenomenon of writing and being a writer and lets faculty expand their ways of reading beyond the role of evaluator.

The second warmup usually consists of having faculty talk about who their students are and lets them think about their classrooms and teaching. This warmup can produce some especially clear insights of the relationship that faculty have with their students. One such insight came from an experienced part-time composition instructor who reminded us that "our students are not us," a phrase I have now used countless times in conversation and class with teachers and student teachers about their students and teaching.

Immediately after the warmup, the rest of the 2-hour session is spent reading and commenting on one paper, though we often refer to other papers

---

[2] For a good description of the method and rationale for using reflective conversation to read student writing see Carini's (1994) essay, "Dear Sister Bess: An Essay on Standards, Judgement & Writing."

from the student's portfolio. Initially, the student paper is read in its entirety, with different members of the group taking turns. One purpose of this is to get the student's words into as many different voices as possible. Once the entire paper has been read aloud, different members of the group take turns reading small sections, usually a half page or so, but the segments are often dictated by the paper itself. After reading a short piece of the paper, the reader paraphrases what she has read and then members of the group take turns commenting on what they see happening within this small section of text. The entire paper is read this way, with one member of the group summarizing the reading after two or three of the smaller segments. The tone is descriptive and nonevaluative. The readers attempt to find the student in the paper, what logic is at work in the various choices she makes, and where and with what she struggles. Readers not only comment on the writing but on each others' comments, building and expanding the reading of each section until the paper becomes more than the written word, reflecting the very complexity of trying to read and write. The effect is to slow down the reading process and to insert the voices of many readers within a single reading, creating a rich and diverse tapestry of readings that has the capability of capturing the labor of the student writer within the context of the assignment, the course, and the curriculum. It's humbling and enlightening to realize how much work can go into writing which is not very successful and how easy it is to miss the struggling writer within an imperfect text.

Although this way of reading has given us an important tool for supporting faculty interpretations of student writing and for constructing guidelines for the qualitative strand of the general education assessment, the best endorsement we can offer has been the reaction of the faculty who have read with us. For example, the composition instructors stated that they thought the readings were something that every incoming composition teacher should experience. One nursing reader stated in a presentation she gave at the Second Annual National Conference on WAC that she now reads her student writing differently because of her experience with reflective reading. On their request, I have returned to read with more of my nursing school colleagues and to conduct focus groups to help them as they struggle with the process of redesigning their curriculum. They believed they were able to see some of the strengths and weaknesses of their program within the readings of their students' work. We are presently working with nursing faculty to explore the possibility of using portfolios for program assessment as more and more instructors use them in their classrooms. Business faculty confided in us that they now realize that students at all three levels have similar discourse-level problems in their writing and that business faculty have been distinguishing writing quality primarily on the basis of surface correctness. The business school has also started a series of inquiries into not only their students' ability to write but also the curriculum and instruction the students receive in their business courses. They are currently exploring the possibility of having students compile portfolios of all the writing they do in their major in order to get a better sense of each student's strengths and weaknesses as writers and to assess the ability of their faculty to respond to that writing.

These kinds of reactions indicate the real potential of evaluation. Quality assessment enriches the programs it attempts to describe and evaluate by increasing our understanding of curricula, teaching, and learning. In this sense, we see these faculty reading groups as the beginning of a partnership with content area faculty that encourages them to look at the writing they are requiring, at how well their students are writing, and at what faculty response to this writing says about their individual goals as teachers and the overall goals and mission of their programs. This interaction empowers content area faculty as it recognizes their ability to teach and assess the kind of writing they hope to foster in their students.

BEYOND ACCOUNTABILITY: BECOMING PARTNERS

One of the most important and pervasive though less tangible effects of reading with faculty deals with the level of communication and trust that faculty across campus can bring to the various stakeholders in a university WAC program. To illustrate this point, I would like to tell a story about an experience I had with an engineering professor who was one of the readers. During the second warmup, when we talked about our students, I became aware that he had said some profoundly accurate, touching, and beautiful things about teaching. Because I was presenting a paper on how faculty read (Huot, 1994), I asked him if I could use the transcript of what he had said. He was flattered that I wanted to use his words and surprised that he had said anything remarkable enough for me to want to highlight it in my presentation:

> I can sing and dance and teach up a storm, but in the end, learning is an active activity which requires their part. I find my students to be a potpourri with different backgrounds both technical, societal, cultural and environmental. I find ones with a desire to learn, some who are there to succeed and learning is secondary. It's something that has to be done in the process. Some who want to make a good grade. I had one student raise his hand in class and tell me one day that I was assuming that he was there to learn and that he was really there to get through the course, to get a grade, and I admired him for his honesty. There are those who are there to make money or on some level to please a relative in majoring in whatever the major is. Some are smart. Some not so. Some quick. Some slow. Some lazy. Some industrious. They are human beings with their own hopes, fears, desires, needs, and I find the one single charac-

teristic necessary other than their being thrown in the common space and finding that they walk a common ground. I find them largely a people who carry more family and work responsibility than I feel can be managed effectively together with being a full time student. I want them to enjoy the material. I want them to think. Some times they've been trained not to. I want them to demonstrate an understanding of the material and of the concepts, to be able to know what, how and why. For some who are willing to take the chance, I'd like them to discover what they love, what they have a passion for and to follow it.

During our conversation, I shared with him my pleasure and surprise at what he had said. I'm afraid my surprise revealed my bias toward certain disciplines and their motives and insights into teaching. He fixed me in his eye and went on to say that we across the disciplines don't trust each other. I think he was right. Trust is a word that is usually absent in discussions about WAC and assessment. This is unfortunate.

I can't say that our experiences with reading across the curriculum have solved the lack of trust between English faculty who staff and administer WAC programs and the faculty who teach in them. My experience has, however, illustrated for me my own biases and lapses of trust. I am more aware that we college instructors, like our students, walk a common ground. Unfortunately, this common ground is often obscured by disciplinary boundaries and professional loyalty. Our experiences with WAC assessment, however, seem to indicate that involving faculty across the disciplines as partners in reading, discussing, and evaluating our common program has the potential to uncover and strengthen the bonds of all of us who strive to help students "discover what they love." I am also trusting that our efforts have not only provided viable and valid means for assessing WAC but have also promoted the information, cooperation, experience, and relationships necessary to ensure the success of the WAC program itself.

REFERENCES

Barrit, L., Stock, P., & Clark, F. (1986). Researching practice: Evaluating assessment essays. *College Composition and Communication, 37*, 315–327.

Berlak, H. (1992). Toward the development of a new science of educational testing and assessment. In H. Berlak, F. M. Newmann, E. Adams, D. A. Archbald T. Burgess, J. Raven, & T. A. Romberg (Eds.), *Toward a new science of educational testing and assessment.* Albany, NY: SUNY Press.

Carini P. (1994). Dear sister bess: An essay on standards, judgement and writing" *Assessing Writing, 1*, 29–66.

Himley, M. (1989). A reflective conversation: Tempos of meaning. In B. Lawson, S. Sterr Ryan, & W. R. Winterowd (Eds.), *Encountering student texts* (pp. 5–19). Urbana: NCTE.

Himley, M. (1991). *Shared territory: Understanding children's writing as works*. New York: Oxford.

Huot, B. (1994). *Reading across the curriculum: Understanding how content area faculty assess writing*. Annual Conference on College Composition and Communication, Nashville, TN.

Larson, R. L. (1991). Using portfolios in the assessment of writing in the academic disciplines. In P. Belanoff & M. Dickson (Eds.), *Portfolios: Process and product*. Portsmouth, NH: Boynton/Cook.

Mills-Courts, K., & Amiran, M. R. (1991). Metacognition and the use of portfolios. In P. Belanoff & M. Dickson (Eds.), *Portfolios: Process and product*. Portsmouth, NH: Boynton/Cook.

Chapter 6

·

How Portfolios for Proficiency Help Shape a WAC Program

Christopher Thaiss
Terry Myers Zawicki

This chapter describes how our 7 years of experience evaluating portfolios from students in many disciplines has provided *indirect* formative assessment of writing across the university. We also show how what we have learned from these portfolios has helped shape the focus of our faculty development program—by showing us what we need to accomplish and what we don't need to do. We call these uses of our portfolios indirect assessment because their primary purpose is, and always has been, individual student assessment to determine students' exemption from an upper-level required course. Nevertheless, we have discovered that this regular reading of cross-curricular student prose has been indispensable to our work with faculty and the curriculum.

We also illustrate in this chapter how writing-across-the-curriculum (WAC) assessment—in the absence of money and time for elaborate direct measures—can still occur by using tools already at a program director's disposal. In our case, those tools include the proficiency portfolios and the advanced composition course required of all students.

This chapter is presented in four parts. The first section describes the origins, purposes, and contents of our portfolio program. In the second section, Terry offers a close analysis of her process as a portfolio reader, showing us how she evaluates the submissions. This section will demonstrate that, although the portfolio gives us information about WAC, that information in turn helps us become more sophisticated portfolio readers. The third section outlines the types of data we glean from the portfolios about writing across the university and about faculty attitudes toward writing. We describe the ever-more-detailed picture of writing in our university that these hundreds of portfolios continue to draw for us. The final section shows how this data help to enhance our curriculum by telling us what to emphasize in our in-house WAC workshops and publications.

PART I: PORTFOLIOS FOR A DIFFERENT PURPOSE

The portfolios described here have never been used directly to assess either our WAC activities or the full spectrum of writing at George Mason University (GMU). Rather, we have been using the portfolio procedure for seven years to certify the writing proficiency of students who are attempting to gain three hours of credit for a course, Advanced Composition, which is required of all GMU juniors and seniors. This course, which is offered in different versions for humanities, social sciences, natural sciences/technology, and business majors, focuses on proficient writing for both disciplinary (specialized) and more general audiences. In each version, the course gives particular attention to research-based writing and the skills that requires. (See Figure 6.1 in the Appendix for a typical course description in an Advanced Composition syllabus—this one drawn from a social sciences section.)

We request that students include in the portfolio certain types of writing: a research-based paper (eight page minimum) from a course in the major, plus three or four other works, at least two of which should demonstrate the writer's ability to organize clearly information in support of a central idea. After a preliminary screening of these contents for completeness and for mechanical proficiency in English, we ask the writer to compose a reflective "process" essay on two of the pieces in the portfolio, and then we evaluate the total package (see Figure 6.2, the portfolio instruction sheet for students and Figure 6.3, the instructions for the reflective essay, in Appendix). If we can't come to judgment (pass or no pass) on the portfolio, we ask for a teacher in the student's major discipline to offer a third reading.[1]

As outlined in an earlier article (Brady & Thaiss, 1993), we had developed this proficiency option in pragmatic response to two factors: (a) the university's financial inability to offer enough sections of the course—at twenty-two per section—to meet the demand, and (b) our recognition, from our faculty's having taught the course during the previous three years, that there were several students for whom the requirement was superfluous: these students were already deft writers in their majors and/or experienced, competent writers on the job. Hence, it seemed appropriate to create a credit-bearing option to reward these writers and to free up space in sections.

Our seven years of experience with this proficiency option have made us confident that we are identifying a good number of students—about seventy per year, roughly 3% of those who take the course—whose prior writing demonstrates their ability to accomplish the kinds of tasks that are at the

---

[1] We have used this third-reader option no more than a half dozen times over the years; we anticipated occasions when the specificity of a format or the technical difficulty of the language might make judgment of organization, syntax, documentation, etc., difficult, but this has not proved to be the case.

center of the course. We continually modify the procedure in small ways, but we believe that it basically fulfills its designed purpose. But that purpose, as we say, was not WAC program assessment.

Nevertheless, as we have thought about possible, even if indirect, connections between the exemption procedure and our ongoing work with WAC, we have realized that the program-shaping role of the portfolios has been considerable. We have come to rely on information from our portfolio assessment, for instance, as we confer with colleagues about the goals for writing in the university, in the many venues in which it occurs at GMU:

1. in required first-year composition and third-year Advanced Composition courses;
2. in the "linked" introductory sections of disciplinary courses we have set up for new students in tandem with first-year composition sections;
3. in the writing-intensive (WI) courses that students are now required to take in their majors;
4. in two interdisciplinary programs that emphasize writing in all courses without requiring completion of separate composition courses (i.e., Plan for Alternative General Education and New Century College); and
5. from course to course, major to major, throughout GMU.

Because we have not formally and over a long period of time thought about the Advanced Composition portfolios as a WAC program assessment tool, we must stress that we have not done the analysis of data that would allow us to report numbers and precise categories of each type of prose that has been included in the folders—the kind of analysis that can be seen, for example, in the work by Richard Larson (1991). We do know, impressionistically, that portfolios have included an amazing variety of subjects in a wide array of genres, including personal essays, case reports, lab reports, technical specifications, manuals, book and performance critiques, advertising, business reports and recommendations, questionnaires, short fiction, plays and scripts, and so on, in addition to the documented research papers we specifically request. And, as Terry's reading will demonstrate, our long experience with the portfolios has led us to generalizations in which we have confidence; for example, (a) most faculty are not very concerned about documentation style, as long as the writer is consistent; and (b) some faculty, but far from most, allow many inconsistencies in punctuation, particularly in comma usage.

To indicate the factors we bring to bear on our reading and the kinds of questions we ask of the writing and of ourselves, Terry details in the next section the reading strategies she has developed over the past seven years, and which Chris, for the most part, shares. What these reading strategies demonstrate is that evaluating portfolios and developing a WAC program are mutually reinforcing activities. Just as reading portfolios teaches us more about writing in the university, so teaching the different versions of our Advanced Composition course on a regular basis helps us become careful, more knowledgeable portfolio readers, as do the frequent interactions we have with faculty in other disciplines about writing. This "course-taught expertise," as coined by William L. Smith (1993), is the best way to ensure reliability in holistic scoring situations. Indeed, Smith concludes from his study that the adequacy and reliability of the judgments of experienced teachers are so high it is "largely redundant" to solicit a second opinion from a rater who teaches the same course (pg. 198-199). In our discussions of our portfolio procedures, we have found, as Smith suggests, that we agree about how we read and the criteria we apply—criteria derived from our years of teaching the Advanced Composition course and reading writing across the disciplines. Terry's description, then, is meant as an illustration of our very similar decision-making processes. Our larger purpose in this section, however, is to highlight the kinds of meaningful information that we have gained through the portfolio reading.

PART II: HOW TERRY EVALUATES PORTFOLIOS

One of my duties as Associate Director of Composition is to read Advanced Composition (English 302) proficiency portfolios. I read the majority of the submissions—typically thirty-five to forty a semester—although Chris frequently provides a second reading of problematic portfolios and reads the twenty to twenty-five portfolios submitted during the summer. Over time, I have developed reading strategies that help me make knowledgeable judgments about awarding proficiency credit. My judgments are also informed by my experience teaching the Advanced Composition course; that is, I have certain criteria in place to judge the writing students produce in English 302, and I expect the writing in the portfolio to meet similar criteria. In both instances, I must negotiate criteria based on my understanding of what constitutes good writing in a range of disciplines, understanding which is derived from teaching English 302 as well as from reading portfolios.

When I teach English 302, I learn about my students. Over the semester, I glean this knowledge by reading their writing as well as by listening to them talk in class and in conference. I also see writing they are doing for other teachers. One important component of English 302 is a "dual-submission" research paper, which means that students are encouraged to work on a paper that has been assigned by a teacher in another course, preferably in their major. Because students are working with me and are also graded by me on assignments other teachers have given them, I am in a position to hear how they have interpreted those other teachers' assignments and expectations. To help the students understand *my* expectations, I give them a fairly elaborate syllabus including course goals and objectives. In addition, for every assignment I write out detailed instructions and explanations of what I'll be looking for as I read and evaluate their papers. Although I always keep in mind some general criteria for good writing in an advanced composition course, many other variables help determine my criteria and ultimately the grade a student receives on a paper. In other words, my perception of what constitutes a good paper is mediated by the experience of working with the writer in a classroom setting—often on papers assigned by teachers in other disciplines. In the same way, as students participate in the class and receive feedback on their writing, they learn to "read" me as a reader and to negotiate among different teachers' criteria for good writing. In contrast, students submitting portfolios for proficiency credit have not had the opportunity to "read" me as a reader, and, in many cases, are also not clear about what criteria were used by the teachers in their other courses to evaluate the papers they are now going to submit for writing course credit.

Thus, to help students select papers to submit, we give them a double-sided sheet of directions telling them what to include in the portfolio (Figure 6.2) and the description of the two-hour reflective examination they will be asked to take if their portfolio passes the initial screening (Figure 6.3). In order to qualify for an exemption, the papers the students submit "should demonstrate a proficiency equal to that of students in English 302 who have successfully completed intensive practice in writing from research and critically analyzing a variety of expository forms." Accordingly, in their portfolios, students must have samples that demonstrate proficiency in writing from sources, analytical reasoning, and logical coherence. From these general guidelines, students must ascertain what constitutes a passing mark according to the reader(s) who will be evaluating both the portfolio and the accompanying reflective examination.

By excluding more discipline-specific criteria, we are telling students that there are certain commonly held criteria for "good" writing which cross disciplines and also that teachers are in agreement about what those criteria are. Chris and I believe this to be an accurate perception. Even though disciplines, courses, teachers, and assignments vary in obvious ways, we see enough similarities among portfolios and in working with students in English 302 and with faculty across disciplines to justify this assertion. We have found from passing portfolios that most of the students at GMU who submit portfolios can

1. write fluently and correctly;
2. write from research and use sources to support arguments; and
3. cite and document sources correctly, using the style appropriate to a particular discipline.

While passing portfolios indicate that we have much in common with faculty across the disciplines when we evaluate the merits of a piece of writing, borderline or nonpassing portfolios give us some insight into how our criteria may differ from those of other teachers. When I come across a portfolio that seems to be less proficient than the others, I don't automatically assume that the difference is idiosyncratic to the student. Instead, I question the reasons for the differences. Could the differences be in teacher criteria, or could there be basic differences in criteria across disciplines? To help answer these questions, I look at the student's transcript, which is included in the portfolio packet. When we designed the process for submitting a portfolio for English 302 proficiency credit, we intended the transcript to show us only that the student had completed the prerequisite forty-five credits to qualify for admittance to the course and thus to qualify for the exemption. In addition to giving factual information such as that the student is eligible to submit a portfolio and that he or she did in fact take the courses for which he or she is submitting the papers, the transcript also tells us whether the student has generally been successful in upper-level courses, especially those from which the student is submitting papers.

The portfolio packet does not include such potentially helpful information as assignments, teacher grades, or comments on the individual papers. That students should submit "clean" copies of papers was a decision made early on when we designed the portfolio process, our thinking being that we wanted our evaluations—toward proficiency credit for advanced composition—to be free of extraneous influences (i.e., judgments made toward meeting criteria for professors in other courses).[2] We do not ask for copies of the assignments which generated the papers because, in our experience, students most likely will not have kept the assignment instructions or have not been given written instructions. Instead we ask students to indicate on each sample when the piece was written and for what course, if applicable.

When a portfolio is troublesome, then, I find myself consulting the transcript to see if it can provide partial answers to questions I have about deficiencies I perceive. I wonder, for example, how much weight a paper I consider problematic has carried in the final grade that the student earned in the course, especially if the grade is high. When I think a paper is marred by surface errors or is not appropriately documented, I speculate on what criteria the other teacher may have privileged A strong transcript, then, helps me read the papers more generously and can help make decisions about borderline portfolios somewhat easier, just as variables other than the papers (e.g., class participation, skill in peer review, strengths as a collaborator, etc.) might affect the grades I give when I'm teaching English 302.

---

[2] For further discussion of this point, see Ed White (1992), who recommends the submission of clean copies when a portfolio is being used to generate a grade in a different context.

In summary, if a student has done a significant amount of writing in upper-level courses as indicated by the quantity of papers in the portfolio and has achieved high grades in those courses, I am more inclined to give the student the benefit of the doubt. At the same time, in thinking about writing across the university, I question whether the other teachers and I have placed the same value on writerly criteria such as fluency and technical correctness. I consider again the kinds of surface errors which bother me yet may not have influenced the other teachers' grades. As so much of the research on error analysis shows, teachers' ideas about what constitutes serious and/or distracting errors vary widely, often according to how errors are constructed by and interpreted within discourse communities (see, e.g., Williams, 1981; Lunsford & Connors, 1988; Hull, 1985; Lees, 1987; White, 1985).

Besides the insights I might gain from looking at a student's transcript, my course-taught knowledge of other teachers' assignment and evaluation practices often mediates my judgments of borderline portfolios. If a student has made citation errors or used what I consider to be inappropriate or incorrect documentation in an upper-level research paper, I consider how the teacher may have designed the research assignment. I know by now, for example, that many teachers give students packets of materials to work with and that often these packets lack adequate information about the source of the materials. I know, too, that when students are analyzing a text as a class activity, they are often told they can disregard rules for citation. In addition, it is not uncommon for teachers to tell students that they may use any documentation style they choose as long as they are consistent. These kinds of differences, Chris and I believe, are specific to teachers and courses and do not pertain to entire disciplines. Besides our course-taught experience, our evidence for this statement is based on reading portfolios, most of which include well-documented and technically correct papers.

Whenever a portfolio is borderline, I consult with Chris as a second reader. If I am leaning strongly toward a no-pass grade in the initial screening and Chris confirms this opinion, the student is not asked to take the two-hour examination. If, however, after we have both read, Chris and I think the examination will give us additional useful information to help us make a decision, we call the student in. Talking through what troubles each of us helps us clarify not only our portfolio criteria and procedures but also the goals of the English 302 course. The conversation also helps us identify issues that we want to discuss with faculty across disciplines. For example, in part as a result of questions that emerge from the portfolio readings, we have created panels of teachers in the social sciences, business, natural sciences, and humanities to talk to English faculty about criteria in their courses.

When a student doesn't pass and is nearing graduation and needs credit for English 302 to finish on time, I know I'll be hearing protests. I can also almost guarantee that I'll be getting calls from students who have received high grades in the courses from which they submitted papers. Our conversation invariably starts like this: "I don't understand how I could have gotten A's on these papers in my other courses and not have a passing portfolio." In response, I first remind them that they are seeking three proficiency credits in English 302, a specific course which has its own goals and objectives. Next, I generally talk about how criteria for evaluating writing may differ from teacher to teacher depending on what a teacher is privileging in his or her grading. I describe some of the problems I've noted in their portfolio papers. Students usually point out that their other teachers didn't care about whatever it was I've said is a problem, and they wonder why I do. The subtext, of course, is that I am being too picky or that the standards of English teachers aren't realistic outside of English departments.

Every so often students will agree with my assessment of their papers, saying that they know, in retrospect, that there were problems in certain papers. Why, they wonder, didn't the teacher in the other course take off points, for example, when they failed to document and cite sources in a research paper, especially when they were using quoted material? Why were fragments, run-ons, subject–verb agreement errors, and garbled syntax not noted? Occasionally, if students seem to understand very clearly what they need to do to make the portfolio papers passing, I agree to let them revise and resubmit. Rereading revised portfolios (and sometimes acting as an ad hoc tutor) adds an unforeseen and time-consuming dimension to our portfolio process, but it is one we believe is worthwhile if students can revise successfully without taking the English 302 course.

Whether students agree or disagree with my negative reading of their portfolio, our dialogue is not completely one-sided; as we negotiate the criteria for passing portfolios, I learn from students as well. I discover, for example, that teachers rarely discuss with students the criteria they have used to evaluate a paper (or so the students tell me). In most cases, students seem to intuit what the teacher values from his or her lectures and from remarks made in class discussion. I learn that some teachers tend to be remarkably tolerant of inconsistent or unrecognizable documentation styles. Indeed, most students who have errors in documentation tell me that their teachers (a) never mentioned documentation to them or (b) told them to use whatever style they knew best. Students also tell me that teachers outside of writing classes "do not care about little things" like sentence structure, grammar, punctuation, and spelling. Usually, of course, the students have misread the teachers, who—as I frequently hear from the teachers themselves—do care a great deal about these "little things," but who consider it unfair, they sometimes tell me, to penalize students for writing mistakes in a content course.

I grant that these anecdotes about writing for teachers in other disciplines come from students who have not received English 302 proficiency credit; I seldom have the opportunity to talk with students who have sub-mitted passing portfolios. Yet I am also able to learn a great deal from the passing students' two-hour reflective essays (Figure 6.3), which they write after passing the initial screening. These essays, in which students describe the writing processes and the rhetorical scene of two of their portfolio papers, reveal that students seldom (about 10% of students) ask for feedback on a draft from the teacher who assigned the paper. Almost never does a stu-dent volunteer that the professor has asked to see an early draft. In addition, students rarely write about the assignment itself helping them develop their sense of the teacher's criteria, but instead say such things as "From writing these kinds of papers I know…" or "In class, the teacher kept repeating the idea that…" or "From our readings in class, I could tell…." All of these com-ments—from face-to-face conferences and from the reflective essays—give Chris and me additional insights about WAC at GMU.

PART III: WHAT THE PORTFOLIO PROCESS IS TELLING US ABOUT WAC

While Terry's discussion of her reading strategies in the foregoing section focused on some of the issues that come up for us when we read portfolios, this section describes generalizations that the portfolio process has helped us make about characteristics of student writing across the university at GMU and about faculty practices and attitudes.

We have discovered that we have much in common with teachers in other disciplines. Perhaps most important, we have found that other facul-ty and the students share our appreciation for certain characteristics of prose. The evidence for our community of shared beliefs about good writing is what we regard as the phenomenally high pass rate for the portfolios. Over the years, more than 75% of the submitted portfolios have passed without the need for revision and resubmission. Even though this is a rela-tively small, self-identified population from which to draw conclusions, we are confident in the generalization because of the remarkable consistency across all of the portfolios we have read over the years. We also believe in the significance of this figure because two key factors pertain to our procedure: (a) we *don't* feel under pressure to pass a high quota of students; and (b) it is reasonable to assume that students submit papers that their professors have graded highly. In regard to (a) our freedom to assess: Because we are evaluating for exemption from a specific course that we teach and supervise and which it is the *norm* for students at GMU to take, a no-pass can be given with relatively little stigma to the student or to the other teachers the stu-dent has had. This would not be the case, for example, in a mass writing-competency testing situation, in which a no-pass would obligate the student to take a remedial course and might cast aspersions on writing faculty who had previously passed the student—indeed, teachers don't know that students are submitting these portfolios. As a result, the pressure on us to pass students is minimal; rather, we feel more pressure to maintain high standards because taking the course is the norm and because we and the faculty at large believe strongly in its value. In regard to (b), the likelihood that students submit papers that have received high grades: to corroborate the psychological plausibility of such a move, students' transcripts show overwhelmingly that they submit papers from courses in which they've received high marks. As Terry has shown, anecdotal evidence from student conferences also supports this view.

What are the characteristics of "good" academic writing that we and faculty across fields seem mutually to perceive? Among these are

1. Respect for standard edited English grammar, punctuation, and spelling (many of our applicants for proficiency credit are nonnative speakers of English, and their portfolios show that faculty across the disciplines are willing to tolerate a small amount of divergence from standard idiom). We need to reiterate, though, that students do submit clean copies of their papers, so an inestimable proportion of what we see may have been copy edited just for us. Nevertheless, if, as we assume, students are submitting the work that their professors have already highly praised, we'd imagine relatively little overall change; the fact remains that most portfolios contain almost no mechanical errors.

2. Expectation of the more or less conventional American essay framework, with a thesis at or near the beginning of the piece, evidentiary details from primary and secondary texts, from empirical research, and/or from analyzed personal experience, and clear transitions between paragraphs.

3. A sense of an audience neither esoteric nor so general that only the simplest language must be used; rarely do we get a paper so dense with jargon that we cannot follow an argument or narrative, though, of course, we regularly receive papers with references to sources we've never heard of and to statistics the accuracy of which we have to assume.

4. "Voice" in the writing; perhaps surprisingly, given the stereotype of the academic prosewriter, portfolios tend overwhelmingly to show a blending of first and third person, and the prose rarely has that "written by committee" feel. Writers use active voice much more than passive, and most portfolios include at least one piece that details personal experience in some way.

These findings, which our accumulating experience continues to strengthen, initially surprised us. We expected to receive a great many portfolios that we would find difficult to comprehend because of the technical jargon or strange formats; we also partly believed—or were tempted to believe—that stereotype of the professor who won't tolerate use of the word "I." When we designed the procedure, we anticipated that many portfolios would receive the third reading we described earlier, by a faculty member in the student's major department—on the assumption that these faculty could tell us if we were applying criteria not pertinent to that discipline, and that, therefore, a portfolio that looked deficient to us was really adequate. To prepare for what we imagined would be a plethora of third readings, we secured the cooperation of the undergraduate coordinators in each department.

In fact, of the approximately 500 portfolios we have read over seven years, only 1% to 2% have required a third reading—about one or two folders a year in total. In these few cases, our quandary has arisen mainly over our unfamiliarity with what the student assures us is standard practice in his or her major, usually in regard to either the structure of a piece or documentation method. For example, even though we know that many teachers are tolerant of documentation styles which are not representative of the discipline, Chris was concerned about the style used in a research paper submitted by a senior political science major and asked the professor in the course to corroborate the student's contention that the particular style used need not be standard (APA, Turabian et al.) as long as it was clear and consistent. The professor agreed. As noted under characteristic 3 on the previous page, we rarely receive a piece that we find overly difficult to follow in terms of its structure or technical language. Those approximately 25% of portfolios we turn down fail most often for four reasons, none of which pertains to idiosyncrasies of a disciplinary discourse community:

1. Procedural problems—insufficient number of pieces, lack of pieces that show use and documentation of sources, pieces not in categories we've sanctioned (e.g., we don't allow pieces that have been used to satisfy the first-year composition requirement).
2. Significant number of errors in Standard Edited English grammar, punctuation, and usage.
3. Difficulty in paraphrasing and in otherwise integrating primary and secondary source material into a work—uncontextualized "block quotation" paragraphs, series of unanalyzed quotations from different authorities, etc.. The research-based essay is the one genre of writing specified in the portfolio instructions (see Figure 6.2) because it receives the most attention in the course; hence, our reading of the portfolios tends to be concentrated more on this piece than on others in the folder.
4. Inconsistent or unrecognizable documentation style—very slight use of citations in essays that clearly depend on secondary sources, lack of correlation between textual citations and source lists, mixture of styles in describing references, etc. Problems (3) and (4) occur frequently enough

in the portfolios for us to conclude that faculty across the curriculum are relatively less concerned about these features than about those features of academic prose we've listed under the characteristics we share. Nevertheless, we consider them grounds for not passing a portfolio because not only does English 302 devote a good deal of time to these skills, but also most of the portfolios display the writers' deftness in performing them.

PART IV: HOW PORTFOLIO READINGS HELP SHAPE
WAC ACTIVITIES AND PROGRAM STRUCTURE

The lessons we've learned from seven years of WAC portfolios have probably helped us see more clearly what we *don't* need to do in our WAC program than what we do need to attend to.

First, through surveys of students and regular conversations with faculty, we have always believed that GMU undergraduates are writing extensively in most majors, at least in some courses, and the portfolios support this view. The lack of portfolios from specific majors reinforces our sense of those areas of the curriculum in which we need to concentrate our efforts.

Second, our shared beliefs about the characteristics of good academic prose have given us confidence in the objectives of the Advanced Composition course, which was designed to reinforce the writing in the majors. Had we been flooded with portfolios that were incomprehensible to us because of discourse differences among disciplines, or had we seen large numbers of students submitting, as exemplary, papers with glaring deficiencies in standard grammar and usage, we would have been forced to reexamine the basic premises of the course, including the most basic premise: that it is feasible for an English Department to offer a course that purports to serve the needs of students majoring in such seemingly disparate fields as dance, computer science, marketing, and history.

Third, these shared beliefs, as demonstrated by the portfolios, have told us that we don't need to concentrate in our workshops and in our newsletter articles on trying to convince faculty about the importance of writing, about avoidance of esoteric jargon, or about upholding standards for effective essays.

Instead, our newsletter issues and our workshops tend to showcase the variety of techniques, assignments, and purposes that writing serves across the university, as well as to publicize new programs and new media. In some cases, the portfolios have introduced us to faculty whom because of their innovative assignments we want to invite to workshops and panels or ask to write pieces for the newsletter.

Moreover, we focus instruction in workshops and articles on practices that the portfolios have revealed as gaps in faculty method. The most frequently repeated topics are

- assignment writing and the importance of articulated criteria;
- the giving of feedback; and
- the usefulness of revision.

As Terry noted earlier, conferences with students who fail the initial reading consistently indicate that many faculty write vague assignments, with few specified criteria—if they write their assignments at all. (Feedback in workshops and tutors' experience with clients in our Writing Center reinforces this perception.) As Terry also noted, only about 10% of the reflective essays in the portfolios mention that a professor has given the student feedback on a draft, and almost always the student notes having taken the initiative to request it.

CONCLUSION: THE EFFECTIVENESS OF THE PORTFOLIO AS "INDIRECT" WAC ASSESSMENT

As valuable as the portfolios have been in shaping our assumptions about writing in the disciplines at GMU and thus, in part, shaping our WAC agenda, we don't recommend that such an indirect method be used in lieu of more direct measures. We stress again that evidence from the portfolios has *reinforced* evidence accumulated over the years from conversations and meetings with faculty and with students in our courses, as well as from faculty and student survey responses.

Nevertheless, the portfolios do provide a vital kind of data that would be difficult to obtain under other circumstances. Because students are attempting to gain credit and exemption for a course, they readily supply samples of their writing in diverse contexts and, at our request, write reflectively about it. Thus, although the data are not systematically even across the curriculum, the participants are highly motivated and the data plentiful.

Moreover, because the samples are provided by the students, they perhaps more accurately reflect the standards of their teachers than would samples we'd request from the faculty directly. We say this because, as we have mentioned, students are most often giving us papers that have been favorably received by their professors. Faculty, on the other hand, might be more likely to try to find samples that met what they perceived to be our standards rather than standards they indeed applied in the classroom. Because we are English teachers, they might be reluctant, for example, to share "exemplary" papers that were flawed in standard grammar or documentation style.

The great drawback of the Advanced Composition proficiency portfolios is that they by no means give a balanced picture of the writing that faculty across the curriculum see. Portfolios come from a self-identified "proficient" group of writers that comprise at present about 4% of all the students who take English 302 in a year. We in English get a much better sense of the full range of writing from the Advanced Composition course itself because all students must take it, and because the course includes the option for students to work on one project for a course that the student is also preparing for a teacher in the discipline. With money for assistants and more time for ourselves, we could use those multitudinous data to do a more systematic study of writing at the University than the proficiency portfolios would allow us to do.

However, lack of money and time kill most assessment dreams, so the upshot, at least for us, is to do as much direct assessment as we can afford to, and then to look imaginatively—yet realistically—at indirect evidence such as the WAC portfolios we solicit to meet a different purpose.

Indirect measure or not, the basic lesson we've learned from this long-term portfolio experience is that if one wants to operate a WAC program, it's a good idea to read regularly pieces that students are writing for their teachers in other fields. One can see what students are being asked to write about and in what formats, and one may even be able to see, as we have, what other faculty really think is good prose.

REFERENCES

Brady, L., & Thaiss C. (1993). What student portfolios are teaching us. In K. Gill (Ed.), *Process and portfolios in writing instruction*. Urbana, IL: NCTE.

Hull, G. (1985). Research on error and correction. In B. McClelland & T. Donovan (Eds.), *Perspectives on research and scholarship in composition*. New York: MLA.

Larson, R. (1991). Using portfolios in the assessment of writing in the academic disciplines. In P. Belanoff & M. Dickson (Eds.), *Portfolios: process and product*. Portsmouth, NH: Boynton/Cook.

Lees, E. (1987). Proofreading as reading, errors as embarrassments. In T. Enos (Ed.), *A sourcebook for basic writing teachers*. New York: Random.

Lunsford, A., & Connors, R. (1988). Frequency of formal errors in current college writing. *College Composition and Communication, 39*, 395.

Smith, W. L. (1993). Assessing the reliability and adequacy of using holistic scoring of essays as a college composition placement technique. In M. M. Williamson & B. Huot (Eds.), *Validating holistic scoring for writing assessment: Theoretical and empirical foundations*. Cresskill, NJ: Hampton Press.

White, E. (1985). *Teaching and assessing writing: Recent advances in understanding, evaluating, and improving student performance*. San Francisco: Jossey-Bass.

White, E. (1992). *Assigning, responding, evaluating: A writing teacher's guide* (2nd ed). New York: St. Martins.

Williams, J. (1981). The phenomenology of error. *College Composition and Communication, 32,* 152–168.

APPENDIX

Figure 6.1.   Advanced Composition: Social Sciences
English 302

Course Description

Advanced Composition: Social Sciences provides you with extensive and intensive practice in expository writing and research. Our focus will be on ways of knowing within the social sciences, that is, on how knowledge is constructed through the research methods and discourse styles the social science disciplines employ. As we progress, you will gain experience in observing closely and reporting what you see, separating "facts" from interpretation, defining concepts, abstracting, analyzing, and synthesizing the work of other writers, finding and evaluating research materials, and presenting your ideas and your research in several types of papers. Throughout the course, you will be demonstrating your ability to use the language of your discipline but also to "translate" that language for a lay audience. Ultimately, I hope that you will understand how your voice can be heard in the ongoing conversation of your discipline.

Figure 6.2.   Petition for Exemption from English 302,
Advanced Composition

To apply for exemption you must have completed at least 45 credit hours and fulfilled the English 100 or 101 and the 200 level literature requirements for your major. If you are currently enrolled in English 302, you must complete the whole exemption procedure before the end of the add-drop period, so that you may adjust your schedule. If the process will not affect your schedule, then you may submit your portfolio at any time. The portfolio requirements are outlined in the next paragraphs. If your portfolio receives a positive evaluation after an initial screening by the Department of English, we will make an appointment with you for a two-hour essay examination in which you will write about a topic assigned at the time. The portfolio and the exam are evaluated by a faculty member from English, and by a faculty member from the department of your major (if necessary).

In order for you to qualify for exemption, your writing should demonstrate a proficiency equal to that of students in English 302 who have successfully completed intensive practice in writing from research and critically analyzing a variety of expository forms. Therefore, we ask you to submit a portfolio of several writing samples that testify to your expertise. These pieces should be your best work, demonstrating your range of skills as an academic writer.

Requirements for portfolio of writing

1. Completion of at least 45 credit hours. You must provide a transcript reflecting these credit hours. Unofficial copies may be obtained from the Office of the Registrar in Krug Hall room 101.
2. One long writing sample (8–15 pages) that demonstrates knowledge of research techniques relevant to your major field of study, proficiency in the integration and citation of sources, analytic reasoning, and logical coherence. This paper should be from an upper-level course in your major, or from an upper-level course related to your major field of study.
3. At least three shorter pieces (3–5 pages each) that demonstrate the following aspects of writing:

   A. A range of audiences and purposes
   B. A mastery of analysis, argumentation, and persuasion
   C. Logical coherence and evidence in support of arguments

Note: Because you are seeking exemption from an advanced writing course which focuses on intensive research and writing in a discipline, you may not submit papers from 100-level English courses. In addition, you may not submit more than two papers from any one course. Further, unless you are an English major, you may not submit more than one paper from a 200-level English course that was used to fulfill the literature requirement at GMU.

Directions for arrangement of portfolio items

Please submit the portfolio in a manilla or simple pocket folder. Do not bind the items together with anything other than paper clips.

Include a top or cover sheet with your name, address, phone numbers for home and work, major, and social security number.

Following the cover sheet, include a descriptive table of contents. This table of contents should list the title of each piece in the portfolio, the class or context in which it was written, an explanation of why you feel this piece demonstrates the kind and quality of writing we would expect in English 302, and any other information you think is important to guide the evaluators in their reading.

The first piece(s) in your portfolio should be the long writing sample described in #2 of the Requirements for Portfolio of Writing. Use your judgment for the placement of the remainder of the pieces, recognizing that as the evaluator reads each piece he/she is forming an overall impression of the writer's knowledge of the materials, competencies, and skills.

Evaluation of the portfolio

Please make sure that all of your writing samples are typewritten. Indicate on each sample when the piece was written and the course for which it was written (if applicable). *Submit copies that are free of comments.* If any of your samples are collaborative job-related projects, please show evidence of your authorship and contribution to the project. Edit and proofread all material since you must also demonstrate stylistic and grammatical proficiency.

You must submit xerox copies, not your originals, as the portfolio will not be returned to you. Be sure to include the following information:

CURRENT TELEPHONE NUMBER
PERMANENT ADDRESS
MAJOR
SOCIAL SECURITY NUMBER

You will receive 3 credit hours of advanced placement credit if you pass both parts of the petition process. Do not expect the process to take less than 6 weeks. The turnaround time depends on the number of portfolios that need to be read. No matter when portfolios are submitted, they will only be read from September 1 to April 15.

**Figure 6.3. George Mason University Department of English:
English 302 Proficiency Exam**

Refer to two pieces included in your portfolio. Write about each. Explain your motivation to write the piece; describe your process of collecting information (sources used, problems encountered in the research); describe your process of drafting and revising, including, for example, your favorite tricks for getting started, for organizing your work, for understanding your audience, for getting feedback on your writing as it progresses.

Please read and sign the following **HONOR CODE** pledge before you turn in your completed essay and portfolio:

I HAVE NEITHER GIVEN NOR RECEIVED AID ON THIS EXAMINATION, NOR AM I AWARE OF ANY BREACH IN THE HONOR CODE, AND I PROMISE NOT TO REVEAL THE CONTENTS OF THIS EXAMINATION.

_____   _____

Sign Here   **Date**

Chapter 7

.

Listening as Assessment: How Students and Teachers Evaluate WAC

Larry Beason
Laurel Darrow

In many ways, the writing-across-the-curriculum (WAC) program at Eastern Washington University resembles WAC efforts across the United States. Teachers attend a workshop in which they explore ways to use writing as a resource for learning and communicating; afterwards, the teachers apply concepts and strategies from the workshop to their own courses (cf. Kelly, 1985; Fulwiler & Young, 1990).

Our WAC program, again like many others, was a response to a pressing concern from across the disciplines for improving student writing and learning. One aspect of the origin of WAC at our campus, though, is less common: The key factor in developing and sustaining the program is that it was tied directly to state-mandated assessment of students' writing skills. In fact, if it had not been for this connection, we might not have gained the administrative and financial support needed back in 1989 to establish a WAC program.

Washington state required our school, along with others in the state, to assess students' writing abilities, but the school was allowed great flexibility in determining what assessment means and how to carry it out. After several hearty discussions and committee meetings, faculty and administration decided not to use assessment to confirm the obvious (i.e., students don't write very well), but to explore and assess new approaches to improving student writing—approaches that were designed, promoted, and implemented by faculty for faculty and students. In all honesty, our WAC program was developed on one hand to provide a mechanism for securing and assessing samples of student writing, but on the other (and more important) hand, it was developed as a new approach on our campus for improving student writing and learning. A strong link between WAC and assessment was forged from the beginning.

Because of the pressure on colleges to assess students, teachers, and departments, the assessment dimension of our WAC program helped provide it with administrative support and approval, but assessment also proved beneficial in that it was tied to examining the strengths and weaknesses of the program. Recently, this program has been less reliant on assessment backing and funding, having gained more widespread support. We continue, however, to assess the program because we learned that even mandated assessment offers useful information.

The survey study we describe here grew out of this connection between WAC and assessment. Our assessment efforts have ranged from case studies to conventional pre/post testing of student writing, and one reason we used a survey approach was simply to vary our methods and capitalize on the strengths of surveys (such as the expedient way in which a questionnaire offers feedback from a large group of people, and the in-depth feedback that can be obtained by orally surveying a few individuals). But we had another reason: A survey approach reflects the "bottom up" attitude that was important in creating and sustaining our WAC program.

Although the link between WAC and assessment facilitated crucial administrative support, this established connection among WAC, assessment, and administration also led to the possibility that faculty and students would see WAC only as a tool of assessment implemented by the administration. In addition, it was well known that the state government had mandated the assessment, making it appear even more "top down" and threatening because bureaucrats and outsiders—rather than teachers—instigated assessment. Our initial WAC efforts depended solely on faculty volunteers, and it was essential to create a nonthreatening approach to assessing WAC. The campus has now institutionalized WAC, requiring some courses to be writing enriched, but our WAC program remains fundamentally dependent on the willing cooperation of teachers. To secure this support, we have stressed a nonthreatening, teaching-centered approach that has led to two major principles for our WAC assessment. First, assessment goals should focus on specific concerns raised by teachers and students (as opposed to researchers, WAC directors, or state officials); we believe that data useful and available to teachers are the only data worth gathering. Second, assessment methods should reflect a respect for teachers and students (by avoiding, for instance, methods that greatly intrude into the classroom). Assessment, then, means gathering information in a way that shows genuine respect for individuals in the classroom. To respect people, we must listen to them—pay attention to what they have to say about their situation. This value led us to considering an apt methodology—to listening as a means of assessment.[1]

Thus, the present study grew out of a vital historical link between assessment and WAC, with assessment being broadly aimed to go beyond, and avoid when possible, evaluating student or teacher performance. This study also grew out of a desire to provide assessment that values teachers' and students' perspectives on what is worth assessing and how to assess it.

In regard to assessment goals, this study examines the value of specific teaching strategies. Our WAC workshop offers teachers many approaches to using writing in their classrooms and focuses on two basic objectives of WAC: improving students' writing and learning the content of a given course.[2] A question that these teachers (as well as others) have posed is whether these various methods accomplish these two objectives; the teachers generally accepted the notion that writing assignments help students improve their learning and writing skills, but they were less enthusiastic about the effectiveness of certain activities, such as peer-response groups. Likewise, some teachers thought they could not incorporate all the workshop ideas into their teaching and wondered which strategies were most valuable in terms of improving writing or increasing the learning of course content. "I *must* get from A to Z in covering certain material," one computer-science teacher stated, "and don't have time to use everything we've talked about, so what works best?" To help us explore such issues, this study focuses on the following questions:

1. Do students and teachers perceive an improvement in students' writing abilities because of the writing activities done in a WAC classroom?
2. Do students and teachers perceive that these writing activities improved students' ability to understand course content?
3. How do various writing activities compare in terms of improving either students' writing or their understanding of course content?

This study, with its focus on listening, is limited to gauging respondents' *perceptions* of what students learned about writing or course content, and perceptions can be biased in numerous ways (Mishler, 1986; Sudman & Bradburn, 1982; Tomlinson, 1984). In reviewing dozens of studies that

---

[1] We wish make it clear that, throughout this chapter, our use of the term "listen" is a metaphor for conscientiously considering the expressed thoughts and feelings of others, whether the medium of expression is writing, oral speech, sign language, or some other form.

[2] Many teachers and WAC administrators forefront one of these goals of WAC, and some believe these two goals frequently clash. We share the perspective of Kirscht, Levine, and Reiff (1994), who argue that this conflict is based on a false dichotomy—that even if a student is asked to write strictly according to disciplinary norms, such writing offers the student a way of thinking about a subject.

investigate end-of-course evaluation forms completed by students, Cashin (1988) and Braskamp and Ory (1994) conclude that such surveys provide sufficiently reliable, valid, and trustworthy measures. For instance, surveys often correlate well with other measures, such as ratings by colleagues, instructor self-evaluations, and student-achievement tests. Empirical evidence therefore suggests that classroom surveys can be a useful resource in assessment.

In addition, we have described why our WAC is established on the principle of respecting individual teachers, which means valuing and listening to their perspectives. Although this attitude applies to many programs, it is especially important for our site given the close relationship between WAC and formal assessment. An extension of this respect for teachers is a respect for individuals in general; thus, in this study, we pay special attention to students, who traditionally have had little input in formal assessment efforts. The emphasis on student and teacher feedback is not a mere diplomacy ploy, or just an attempt to "sell" WAC and assessment to faculty and students. Because these individuals understand firsthand how a WAC classroom operates and because of the demands of WAC on their energy and academic lives, they have a right to be heard and have an insider's perspective on how WAC works.

In short, we invited teachers and students to speak because we felt their voices were worth hearing, and then we listened.

HOW WE LISTENED:
METHODOLOGY AND INSTRUMENTS

Our school refers to WAC courses as Writing Enriched Courses (WECs). A codirector of the program, Dana Elder, suggested this name because students found "WAC" obscure, and teachers and students alike found the "Writing Intensive" designation intimidating. WECs are not identified as such in course announcements, but the term is widely used around campus. Our WEC workshop is composed of four half-day sessions during the summer break, and most teacher participants implement a WEC in the subsequent fall quarter. The teachers, who voluntarily attend the workshop, are asked to require at least three writing tasks in their WECs and to offer various forms of writing assistance, such as prewriting and revision activities.

This study incorporates questionnaires and interviews to examine how students and teachers in WECs perceived selected writing activities. Student questionnaires (see Appendix) were administered in 12 WECs taught by 10 teachers who participated in a summer workshop. These courses represented a range of fields: accounting (two different sections of the same course); applied psychology (two different courses); biology; business administration; dental hygiene; education; management information systems; mathematics; speech communication; and urban and regional planning. A total of 262 students responded during the last week of the fall quarter (no teachers reported students who declined to complete the questionnaire). A student in each class collected the completed forms and mailed them to us, and respondents were informed that their teachers would not see individual students' answers. At the end of the quarter, all 10 teachers completed a similar questionnaire.

Our questionnaire differs in key ways from those used in other survey studies of WAC, which tend to fall into two categories: (a) studies gauging the frequency of writing activities and (b) studies evaluating either writing or approaches to teaching writing. The most common survey study, the first category, calculates the frequency of selected writing activities and practices, such as Bridgeman and Carlson's (1984) survey of types of writing assigned in 190 academic departments at 34 universities. The second major category examines teachers' or students' beliefs about effective writing and writing instruction. For example, Beadle (1989) asked teachers to indicate what they thought were the major problems in student writing.[3]

The questionnaire we used, with its focus on respondents' beliefs about effective writing activities, falls into this second category. Ours is the only one to our knowledge that focuses on asking both students and teachers to evaluate a range of specific writing activities in terms of two distinct outcomes: (a) the effects on writing skills and (b) the effects on the learning of course content. Most studies falling into this second category of WAC surveys concentrate on *either* writing skills *or* learning of the course content, or they examine a limited range of writing activities. For instance, Freeman and Murphy (1990) selected two writing tasks—keeping a journal and writing summaries—and asked students if these helped them understand mathematics and, in a separate question, if these tasks improved their writing style. Other studies attend to the two discrete functions of WAC but do not focus on how *specific* writing activities relate to each function (e.g., Duke, 1982; McGee & Starnes, 1988; Schurle, 1991). Hilgers, Bayer, Stitt-Bergh, and Taniguchi (1995) report, for example, that 83% of surveyed students said that

---

[3] The most common type of survey study of WAC gauges the frequency of specific writing activities and practices (see Beadle, 1989; Bernhardt, 1985; Bridgeman & Carlson, 1984; Donlan, 1974; Duke, 1982; Eblen, 1983; Goetz, 1990; Harris & Hult, 1985; Huot, 1992; Kalmbach & Gorman, 1986; Maimon & Nodine, 1978; Parker, 1985; Pomerenke, 1993; Selfe & McCulley, 1986; Swinson, 1992; Tighe & Koziol, 1982; Zemelman, 1977). The second type of WAC survey goes beyond frequency counts by examining what students or teachers believe to be important features of writing or writing instruction (see Beadle, 1989; Duke, 1982; Freeman & Murphy, 1990; Fulwiler, Gorman, & Gorman, 1986; Hilgers et al., 1995; Maimon & Nodine, 1978; McGee & Starnes, 1988; Schurle, 1991; Selfe, Petersen, & Nahrgang, 1986).

writing-intensive courses improved their learning of course content. Later, the researchers explain that students believed certain teaching strategies, such as feedback, made the courses work well, and the researchers understandably define "working well" as a composite of several features, such as improving writing, learning content, and developing problem-solving abilities. However, the extent to which feedback is linked specifically with the learning of course content among the 83% of students is not clear. Learning to write and learning course content are interrelated, but we wanted to see if some activities might work more effectively in one way or the other.

In sum, our questionnaire asks both students and teachers to consider not just writing in general but also specific writing activities. This study also investigates effects on learning of course content as well as writing abilities. Therefore, by focusing on measuring two vital aspects of WAC and how they are addressed in specific activities, this questionnaire offers an approach that builds on and extends the approach of existing WAC surveys.

Most of the questionnaire has a multiple-choice format, but the final item on the student version is an open-ended question that asks students to indicate what would most help them improve their writing. As the first step in analyzing student responses to this question, the authors of this chapter read the comments and formed—individually and then collaboratively—general categories based on this initial reading. Later, two graduate students in English categorized each response based on these categories (see Figure 7.6 for the categories as well as results).

To complement the questionnaire approach, one of the authors of this chapter (Laurel Darrow, a former journalist experienced in interviewing) conducted individual interviews with both students and teachers. These were audiotaped, with portions transcribed later. Some interviewees were randomly selected, whereas others were deliberately chosen because we wished to follow up on particular types of questionnaire responses. Because interviews provide more data than we can cover here, this report focuses on four students from two classes. We wanted to interview students who were generally satisfied with their WECs, as were most respondents, but whose questionnaire responses were occasionally quite critical. Focusing on students whose responses were not entirely favorable helped us explore some perceived shortcomings of WAC. This in itself is valuable because it can suggest improvements, but we also wanted to focus on listening to those who, too often, are ignored—students who say the system is not working. Although institutions develop elaborate or mysterious ways to channel student complaints through the bureaucracy so that it appears they were heard, such approaches are frequently confrontational or used as damage control, rather than actually leading to real change and growth. Thus, we listened to these particular students because we wanted to improve WECs and demonstrate a true respect of students' perspectives, even when they are critical of our own.

WHAT WE HEARD: QUESTIONNAIRE RESULTS

To gauge the frequency of the writing activities, we examined Questions 1 to 12 and noted how many students did not choose the C response (C = "This class did not use or have this activity"). The results are shown in Figure 7.1 (a few students did not answer each question, but we included their responses to other questions).

Figure 7.2 indicates the extent to which students believed the writing activities improved their writing abilities (the survey form notes that "writing ability" is not limited to grammar or punctuation skills). We were

Ranking and Type of Activities	Percentage of Students Who Reported Their WECs Used the Activity	
1. Doing writing assignments for the class	97%	(251 of 260)
2. Doing short writing tasks (1–3 typed pages)	91%	(236 of 260)
3. Receiving teacher feedback about students' writing	88%	(228 of 260)
4. Receiving teacher's criteria for writing	86%	(223 of 259)
5. Receiving written directions for writing assignments	84%	(219 of 261)
6. Revising at least one rough draft	83%	(215 of 259)
7. Receiving student feedback about a draft	68%	(178 of 261)
8. Giving feedback to other students about their drafts	64%	(167 of 261)
9. Taking essay exams	56%	(146 of 260)
10. Doing long writing assignments (more than 4 typed pages)	56%	(145 of 260)
11. Receiving a sample or model paper from the teacher	54%	(141 of 260)
12. Keeping a journal	35%	(91 of 259)

Figure 7.1. Frequency of Each Writing Activity

Ranking and Type of Activities	Percentage of Students Who Strongly Agreed or Agreed the Activity Improved Writing	
1. Revising at least one rough draft	84%	(180 of 215)
2. Receiving teacher feedback about students' writing	79%	(179 of 228)
3. Receiving written directions for writing assignments	77%	(169 of 219)
4. Doing short writing assignments (1–3 typed pages)	76%	(180 of 236)
5. Doing the writing assignments for the class	76%	(190 of 251)
6. Receiving teacher's criteria for writing	73%	(162 of 223)
7. Receiving a sample or model paper from the teacher	68%	(96 of 141)
8. Receiving student feedback about a draft	65%	(116 of 178)
9. Doing long writing assignments (more than 4 typed pages)	63%	(92 of 145)
10. Taking essay exams	57%	(83 of 146)
11. Giving feedback to other students about their drafts	56%	(93 of 167)
12. Keeping a journal	46%	(42 of 91)

Figure 7.2. Students' Perceptions of How Much Each Activity Improved Their Writing

interested in the use of these activities in specific WECs, so the following figures are based only on students who reported using a given activity in their WEC (on the questionnaire, students had a way to indicate that an activity was not used).

We did not expect that students would perceive revising a draft as the most helpful activity. As Fitzgerald (1987) shows in her review of the literature, theoretical as well as empirical research indicates that revision is an important part of learning to write effectively—especially when students revise global features of the text. Students, though, generally see revision as merely "cleaning up" a text and avoid global revisions (Crowhurst, 1986; Sommers, 1980), and we did not expect them to perceive revision as particularly helpful, because we assumed they were probably aware of the limited extent to which they and their peers revise. Our preconceived notions were not accurate, however. The respondents found revising to be helpful; perhaps they do more global revision than we thought, or perhaps even the non-global revisions are more useful than we thought they would be. The results also indicate general approval of a related aspect of writing: feedback (although, as noted later, the interviews reveal notable reservations about feedback they received). Not surprisingly, the WEC students considered peer feedback less effective than teacher feedback, but most students considered either form useful. Corroboration for this finding was found in a previous study of WEC students who, during revision, indeed addressed student as well as teacher feedback, although the teachers' feedback received far more attention during revision (Beason, 1993).

By averaging the responses for all 12 writing activities, we see that 68% of students believed their writing improved as a result of the activities. In fact, the only activity that failed to receive a favorable response from most

Ranking and Type of Activities	Percentage of Students Who Strongly Agreed or Agreed the Activity Improved Learning	
1. Doing the writing assignments for the class	84%	(207 of 247)
2. Doing short writing assignments (about 1–3 typed pages)	83%	(196 of 235)
3. Revising at least one rough draft	77%	(165 of 215)
4. Receiving teacher feedback about students' writing	76%	(177 of 234)
5. Receiving written directions for writing assignments	75%	(169 of 225)
6. Receiving teacher's criteria for writing	67%	(151 of 227)
7. Doing long writing assignments (4 or more typed pages)	66%	(94 of 143)
8. Taking essay exams	65%	(91 of 141)
9. Receiving student feedback about a draft	63%	(110 of 174)
10. Giving feedback to other students about their drafts	62%	(105 of 169)
11. Receiving a sample or model paper from the teacher	61%	(91 of 148)
12. Keeping a journal	55%	(46 of 84)

Figure 7.3. Students' Perceptions of How Much Each Activity Improved Learning of Course Content

students was keeping a journal. Freeman and Murphy's (1990) study of journals in math classes also found that students' reactions were not altogether positive.

Figure 7.3 presents the activities from another perspective: whether they helped students understand course content. Some students answered inconsistently in that the number claiming to have used a given activity tends to differ in Figures 7.2 and 7.3. Perhaps some respondents were confused or apathetic; these problems can be artifacts of survey research. The inconsistencies are so small they do not affect the findings; the largest inconsistencies are with sample papers and journals (for each, seven students reported both using and not using the activity).

The results again speak favorably of WAC. In fact, from the writing-to-learn perspective, all activities were deemed effective by most students; averaging the responses for the 12 activities shows that 70% of students believed their understanding of course content improved as a result of the activities. The activities are ranked somewhat differently in Figures 7.2 and 7.3. Although journals are again ranked as least effective, revision dropped to third. Still, the six activities listed at the top of Figure 7.2 are also in the top six of Figure 7.3. Interestingly enough, the six activities listed as the most frequently used (see Figure 7.1) are the same six at the top of Figures 7.2 and 7.3, suggesting that the most frequent activities are also the most effective. The nature of this relationship is not altogether clear and requires additional research. Perhaps these activities are deemed most effective because students are exposed to them so often that they have gained experience and competence with them, and it seems likely that teachers frequently use these activities because they too perceive them as being the most effective (Figures 7.4 and 7.5 offer some support for this possibility).

Type of Activities	Percentage of Teachers Who Strongly Agreed or Agreed the Activity Improved Writing	
Giving written directions for writing assignments	100%	(10 of 10)
Requiring the writing assignments for the class	100%	(10 of 10)
Students' receiving feedback from teachers	100%	(9 of 9)
Requiring short writing assignments	100%	(8 of 8)
Students' receiving feedback from students about a draft	100%	(7 of 7)
Students' giving feedback to students about drafts	100%	(7 of 7)
Requiring long writing assignments	100%	(7 of 7)
Giving a sample or model paper	100%	(6 of 6)
Revising at least one rough draft	88%	(7 of 8)
Supplying teacher's criteria for writing	88%	(7 of 8)
Requiring a journal	75%	(3 of 4)
Requiring essay exams	50%	(2 of 4)

Figure 7.4. Teachers' Perceptions of How Much Each Activity Improved Students' Writing

Essay exams came in as the eighth most appreciated in terms of writing to learn. In some ways, this finding is counterintuitive because essay exams require students to demonstrate mastery of course material. The respondents' evaluations might have been tainted by their dislike of high-pressure tests; the students might have been unable to be objective, perhaps hoping that somehow essay exams would go away if the survey showed them ineffectual. Or, perhaps indeed, essay exams are not as pedagogically effective as their widespread use in education might suggest. Students often cram for such exams and probably are aware of the short-lived learning that results. In addition, students frequently must rush through essay exams and see them primarily as means for teachers to evaluate them. As a result, there is little opportunity and motivation for students to make meaning or develop new understandings through essay exams—only the displaying of memorized facts and hastily recalled information.

As noted, our study pays special attention to the perspectives that students brought to the WAC experience, but we wanted to compare, at least to some extent, these perspectives with those of the teachers. The teachers' responses are even more favorable than the students' but are difficult to rank because they indicate little difference in the efficacy of the activities, hence no rankings in Figures 7.4 and 7.5. Eight of twelve activities received unanimous approval. As with the students, teachers were not as enthusiastic about journals, and teachers were even less inspired than students about essay exams.

In the student version of the survey, the final question was open ended, asking students to tell us what could most improve their writing. Approximately 50% (132 of 262) gave 169 legible recommendations (some students offered more than one). After a training session, two graduate students individually categorized these responses and agreed on 93% (157 out

Type of Activities	Percentage of Teachers Who Strongly Agreed or Agreed the Activity Improved Learning	
Giving written directions for writing assignments	100%	(10 of 10)
Requiring the writing assignments for the class	100%	(10 of 10)
Students' receiving feedback from teachers	100%	(9 of 9)
Requiring short writing assignments	100%	(8 of 8)
Students' receiving feedback from students	100%	(7 of 7)
Students' giving feedback to students	100%	(7 of 7)
Requiring long writing assignments	100%	(7 of 7)
Giving a sample or model paper	100%	(6 of 6)
Revising at least one rough draft	88%	(7 of 8)
Supplying teacher's criteria for writing	88%	(7 of 8)
Requiring a journal	75%	(3 of 4)
Requiring essay exams	50%	(2 of 4)

Figure 7.5. Teachers' Perceptions of How Much Each Activity Improved Learning of Course Content

of 169) of the codings. As seen in Figure 7.6, the single largest response (26%) indicates a need for more writing in general (i.e., students did not specify the context for doing this writing). Although it makes perfect sense that people need practice in writing to improve, in one regard we were sur-

Type of Recommendation	Percentage of Responses Making the Recommendation	
A. More writing in general: Indicates more writing practice is needed but doesn't specify where it should be done (contrast w/ Item M focusing on courses).	26%	(41 of 157)
B. Feedback in general: Calls for useful feedback but doesn't specify source.	10%	(16 of 157)
C. Clear Expectations: Indicates a need to understand what students are supposed to do or what the teacher is looking for when grading writing.	9%	(14 of 157)
D. Teacher feedback: Calls for useful feedback from teachers.	8%	(13 of 157)
E. More writing courses: Indicates a need to take more courses devoted to writing.	6%	(9 of 157)
F. Better skills: Indicates a need to improve a specific skill(s) associated with writing (e.g., grammar or mechanics).	6%	(9 of 157)
G. Student–Teacher feedback: Calls for useful feedback from both (or either).	5%	(8 of 157)
H. Better topics: Calls for more interesting, suitable, or appropriate subjects to write about.	5%	(8 of 157)
I. Revision: Indicates a need for more revision of drafts.	4%	(6 of 157)
J. Sample writing: Indicates teachers should supply model papers or examples.	4%	(6 of 157)
K. Better composition courses: Indicates problems with English composition courses.	4%	(6 of 157)
L. Student feedback: Calls for useful feedback from students.	3%	(5 of 157)
M. More writing across the curriculum: Indicates a need for courses to include more writing.	2%	(3 of 157)
N. Less restrictive prompt: Calls for assignments with fewer "do's and dont's."	1%	(2 of 157)
O. Other: Makes a recommendation that does not fit above categories.	7%	(11 of 157)

Figure 7.6. Student Recommendations for Improving Writing

prised that the call for more practice was the most frequent response on the survey; our experience suggests that many—if not most—students try to avoid classes and situations requiring them to write. As seen in Daly's (1985) review of research on writing apprehension, many students indeed prefer to avoid such situations. However, this apprehension does not necessarily result in denial; even those students who avoid writing may well realize they need to write more to improve as writers.

Items B, D, G, and L in Figure 7.6 all deal with useful feedback. As shown below, together these account for 26% of the responses (also note that the second most frequent recommendation overall is Item B):

B. Feedback in general: 10%
D. Teacher feedback: 8%
G. Student–Teacher feedback: 5%
L. Student feedback: 3%

Hilgers et al. (1995) found that students perceived feedback as the most important teaching strategy that made writing-intensive classes work well for students, and feedback was commonly mentioned by our students as well. What was deemed "useful" feedback varied from student to student in our study, but many students indicated on the questionnaire that feedback should not merely point out errors, but should also suggest improvements or indicate where the writing succeeds.

One conspicuous result of the open-ended question is the sheer range of responses. Despite some agreement about practice and feedback, the findings illustrate one difficulty in improving writing skills: No single "fix" is available. The survey as a whole suggests that many activities improve writing skills, but students still perceive notable differences in terms of what would most help them. This disagreement might reflect different learning styles, the varied experiences they have had with writing in school, and the range of problems they think they have in regard to writing. For instance, students who call for teachers to provide clearer expectations may believe their writing skills are sufficient; the biggest problem these students face may well be not knowing what their readers want from them. Although we cannot fully account for why there is such variation in the recommendations, this range reinforces the pedagogical stance that teachers need to use diverse approaches to assisting student writers.

WHAT WE HEARD: INTERVIEW RESPONSES

We designed the interviews to address three issues related to the overall goals of the study: (a) determining specifically what writing was going on in these courses; (b) understanding how this writing was contributing to student learning and writing; and (c) obtaining insights that might help us improve the WEC program. We spoke to teachers and students from various disciplines: urban and regional planning; dental hygiene; accounting; speech communication; and business administration. In addition, we sought people who were generally pleased with the writing-enriched courses but whose responses to particular questions suggested that they might have some criticisms to offer, some suggestions for improvement.

Because past assessment efforts on our campus focused mainly on teachers' attitudes and concerns, the interviews described here focus on students, specifically on four who saw problems in their WECs. As noted earlier, we believed this approach was appropriate to reflect the overall principle of listening, especially listening to those whose voices are not often heard in institutionalized learning. Listening closely to their concerns followed up on the questionnaire responses (particularly the student recommendations depicted in Figure 7.6), but listening to students who have concerns is also useful in improving WECs. To promote frank responses, we conducted the interviews after students had completed the WECs. Further, students were granted anonymity and assured we were not evaluating their classroom performance; they were advised that we wanted to gather information that would help us improve the courses. Although every interview covered the same basic questions, students were encouraged to express any opinion of their WEC, writing, and learning.

The interview respondents included the following, identified by pseudonyms:

Lisa: A math-education major in an elementary-education math class;
Connie: An English-education major in an elementary-education math class;
Kevin: A business major in a business administration class; and
Helen: A business major in a business administration class.

We selected these four because they were in two classes that, like the other WECs, attained favorable responses on the questionnaire as a whole, but students in these two classes in particular indicated a need for improvement in specific areas, most notably with regard to feedback. Possibly, these students' concerns are course specific, but the questionnaire results indicate that feedback is a more widespread concern (see Figure 7.6). We began the interviews by talking about writing assignments in the WECs. Then we discussed how that work affected their writing and understanding of course content.

What they wrote

In both classes, students wrote short papers based on course-related readings. In the math class, students wrote eight papers on articles they had found in math-education journals; the goal of each paper was to summarize and evaluate an article in about a page and a half. In the business class, students wrote a weekly one-page paper answering questions from the textbook; their answers were to incorporate information from magazines, newspapers, and journals as well as from the textbook.

In both classes, the students also wrote a longer paper in collaboration with other students. In the math class, this project involved working in pairs to develop a detailed series of lesson plans for teaching math. In the business class, the project involved working in groups of four or five to write a research paper on a group-chosen business issue.

Writing to learn

All of these students indicated that their understanding of course content improved as a result of these assignments. Indeed, as discussed below, the assignments seem to have promoted not only learning during the course, but also continued learning afterwards by giving students the opportunity to consider their future roles as professionals.

The two math students valued the assignment involving the journal articles because it introduced them to important professional resources. Lisa said that this assignment made her aware of the useful information available in various education journals. She was certain she would continue to refer to those journals for teaching ideas. Connie liked the assignment because she said it made her more aware of current research in math education. In fact, this work seemed so valuable that she had saved the papers in a special notebook she hoped to use as a guide for her first teaching job. The assignment was valued because it encouraged professional reading. These students also valued the drafting aspect of the assignment. Lisa said that simply drafting the papers helped her understand the concepts better than if she had just read the articles, and Connie said that by explaining the concepts in writing, she began to develop strategies for explaining them to her own students.

In the business class, the students also appreciated how the short writing assignments introduced them to professional publications. Kevin and Helen said that doing the reading helped them draw connections between course concepts and "real world" problems, and both indicated that writing about these subjects enhanced the benefits of the reading. Kevin said the assignment helped him "tie things together"—to take the concepts in the textbook and apply them to the real-world scenarios he collected from newspaper and journal articles. Helen said this added a practical component to the course: "I learned to apply things instead of just reading from the book. You know how you just memorize things—you don't really apply them to the outside world, the real world.... It's just the book, the textbook." For both students, writing about the topics made the issues more tangible.

As for the longer papers, the students said these assignments also enhanced their understanding of course concepts. The two business students said the longer paper was helpful because it forced them to delve more deeply into issues that would affect them in their professions. Helen, for instance, said she became better informed about the topic her team researched: pay inequalities between men and women. Kevin said he learned more as a result of investigating his team's topic, communication strategies in business. In the math class, both students said the lesson-plan assignment was worthwhile because it introduced them to the sorts of planning they would do in their future careers. For example, Connie said the assignment was good because it was "real...doing real activities, real math, real things we would do in a class-room." "Real" is a word that we heard again and again in these conversations. In interviewing 82 WAC students, Hilgers et al. (1995) found similar results: A recurring theme of writing being valued as a practical job skill. Students in our study likewise said that the writing assignments offered a unique engage-ment with the material, an engagement that caused them to see connections between abstract concepts and specific applications in the work world. At least for these students in career-focused majors, writing seemed to form a bridge between the college classroom and their professional workplaces.

In addition, the students thought that writing about these topics increased their retention of the information. "For me," Helen said, "when I write things down like that, it helps me remember things. If I study for a test and just look at things and try to remember them, when I go and take the test, I'll do fine but the next day I won't remember things as well. But when I write things down and read back over them or rewrite them, it sticks in my mind longer."

The experiences of these students reinforce the questionnaire respons-es; students said that writing about a topic enhances their learning—both their exploration of course material and their recall of it. For these students, assignments creating connections between academic concepts and real-world issues were most valued. Although the students did other types of writing, such as essay exams, the out-of-class papers were best remembered, most valued.

Writing to write

A problem that arose during the interview was trying to define what stu-dents meant by effective writing or improvement in writing. Their conversation often faltered when approached on this subject ("Good writing is. . . .well, something that works with readers?"). They are certainly not alone; teachers in general have a history of struggling with these definitions. Despite these problems, we see no reason not to consider students' feedback on writing improvement; in fact, the interviews have pointed to a need for our future assessment to examine how students and their teachers define writing improvement. Although their criteria are not altogether clear, the students were able to explain reasonably why some aspects of WECs provided useful stepping stones for writers and why others proved to be stumbling blocks. The four students did perceive some growth in their writing development. Both on the questionnaire and in the interviews, they indicated that doing more writing helped make them better writers. At the same time, however, the four students said that they had not improved as much as they would have liked. All but one (Connie) pointed out several times that they still had a notable lack of confidence in their writing ability.

One reason they thought they did not greatly improve was their familiarity with the types of writing assigned in these courses. With both the short papers in each class and the research paper in the business class, the students indicated that they used what they had already learned about writing in their composition courses. In their own words, each of the students expressed the sentiment that any sort of writing was helpful in improving their writing; simply practicing their skills was worthwhile. Yet beyond that practice aspect, they did not seem to think these assignments imparted the new skills they needed. A comment by Lisa was echoed by the others: "I knew how to do those assignments already."

Assignments involving new types of writing for the students thus seem more meaningful than familiar academic assignments because the students seemed to define writing competency in terms of the skills needed for the genres of writing they would use as professionals. For example, the two math education students viewed the lesson plan assignment as very helpful because it was a new task and one they would use on the job. Kevin, a business major, said he wished there was less academic-type writing and more workplace-type writing (memos was a form he mentioned specifically). In contrast, the shorter papers (dealing with article reviews and textbook questions) and the longer research paper in the business class focused on traditional academic assignments; from the students' perspectives, these tasks helped in learning course content, but were less effective in helping students improve their writing.

The overriding factor contributing to the sense that they had improved but not enough was that they thought they were not getting sufficient feedback from instructors. Although the students said they benefited from the quantity of writing required in these courses, they frequently said that further improvement was possible only by receiving specific feedback about the quality of their writing. They said that the instructors were more concerned about giving feedback dealing strictly with the subject of a paper (e.g., math education) rather than feedback that indicated how students might better express their own ideas. But often there was simply not enough feedback to guide students. On the longer papers, students did not receive any comments before the end of the quarter. On the short papers, the students received little feedback aside from a grade. They said they doubted that the quality of their writing had been evaluated at all; they believed these assignments were judged simply for completion. Both Connie and Lisa, for example, suspected they could have put less effort into the article summaries and still have received the same grade. "I'm not sure if there really was an evaluation done of content or format or how well we had written," Connie said. Although she valued doing the work, Connie wondered at times why she had bothered to hand it in. These students wanted more than a grade; they wanted a response as to how they had approached the subject and assignment.

Although these interviews (like the questionnaire) reveal that students thought the writing tasks improved their writing skills to at least some degree, the interviews also emphasized several mixed feelings; the improvement was not all it could have been or not all that the students would have liked. The interviews also revealed that perceptions of WAC effectiveness are influenced by factors such as the "newness" of writing assignments and instructor feedback—or the lack thereof. Thus, interviews have proved to be a valuable component of our assessment. By encouraging participants to talk—and then demonstrating that we were eager to listen—we gained insights that we could not have gleaned from numbers alone.

CONTINUING THE CONVERSATION

This study has some implications for using surveys to investigate or assess WAC, and our belief is that other sites might benefit from the approach and instruments described here.

Certainly, surveys dealing with WAC are not new. Various studies have used them to examine the growth of WAC (Griffin, 1985; McLeod & Shirley, 1988; Stout & Magnotto, 1991) and the extent to which writing activities are actually used in WAC classrooms (Fulwiler, Gorman, & Gorman, 1986; Goetz, 1990; Kalmbach & Gordon, 1986; Selfe & McCulley, 1986). But even though WAC programs are growing in number and students are doing more writing, can frequency alone assess the value of WAC? Fulwiler (1988) suggests that WAC programs can be evaluated by a growing list of teacher participants: "These are significant data. Period" (p. 66). Griffin (1985) states, "My survey [on the growth of WAC programs] demonstrates that the WAC movement is a success" (p. 403). Growth and quantity of writing are indicators of success, but frequency is not enough to show that WAC programs improve writing and learning—especially when assessment results are presented to administrators and teachers who might not readily accept the assumption that more writing necessarily leads to better writing, better learning.

Because the goals of WAC typically focus on improving writing and the learning of course content, assessment must eventually return to these two desired outcomes. Some people might argue that surveys, being so clearly based around people's perceptions, cannot make this determination, but there has not yet been a single methodology that alone is satisfactory. The literature on WAC assessment is laden with concerns about effectively measuring improvement in writing and learning, particularly when the researcher uses an experimental design or tries to directly measure outputs of "good" writing or "good" learning. These concerns range from dealing with the logistical impositions placed on students and teachers by the assessment design to finding a valid way to measure the specific thinking and writing skills improved by WAC.[4] Although these difficulties are insufficient reasons to avoid experimental research or direct measurements of writing, neither should anyone assume there is only one way to assess WAC. Each approach has its own strengths and its own shortcomings. While recognizing the pitfalls of surveys, we chose them for our site because they offer an insider's perspective and because they are based on the assumption that our colleagues' and students' input is valuable for both assessment and WAC.

As discussed in the methodology portion of our chapter, this study differs from existing studies that use surveys to evaluate writing activities in WAC classes. Specifically, our approach differs in that it combines the following elements:

- responses from students as well as their WAC teachers;
- a population representing a range of disciplines;
- the use of both written questionnaires and follow-up interviews;
- evaluations of WAC in two distinct ways (improving writing and helping students learn course content); and
- evaluations of writing improvement and learning not just in terms of overall writing done for a course, but in terms of specific writing practices and activities used in WAC classrooms.

---

[4] Such concerns about effectively assessing WAC programs have been raised by Fulwiler (1988, pp. 69–70), Goetz (1990, pp. 6–7), Schumacher and Nash (1991, pp. 73–74, 83), and Selfe, Petersen, and Nahrgang (1986, pp. 202–203).

Even though our site has its own unique history and needs, our hope is that other schools can make use of the slant we have put on using surveys to assess WAC. Ours, of course, is not the only school that values input from students and teachers, nor is it the only one where teachers and students have asked if specific writing activities really make a difference on student writing and learning. Indeed, being listened to is a fundamental human need, a fact that assessment efforts should consider.

Listening, though, means more than just hearing. It also means we value what people have to say, and such valuing has taken many forms. The results have changed our WEC workshops. For example, greater emphasis is given to helping teachers offer clear, "contentful" feedback, and we work more with teachers in helping them design assignments which students will see as relevant to their professions. Our workshop approaches to journal writing have changed as well, moving toward journals that allow students to respond to one another's writing (a method described by Yaciw, 1994). The results not only help refine our program but also prove useful when our colleagues need more than theoretical arguments on the value of WAC. At workshops, we have shared the results—both the positive and negative—with teachers, who have often noted that the findings give them confidence in trying out what, for many, is a new way of teaching. In the results, these teachers find support for their WAC methods, but they also see that there are teachers who, like themselves, do not attain 100% success. The results have also been helpful when working with administrators who fund and support the WEC program. Some administrators are less than enthusiastic about qualitative assessment, but most believe survey results can be at least one part of credible assessment.

Our results do not conclusively prove that WAC works. This hope is impossible until everybody involved in WAC discussions (students, teachers, administrators, taxpayers, etc.) agrees on what it means to say "WAC works"—what it means to claim that effective writing and learning are occurring and that the gains overshadow costs. Nonetheless, we believe this study reveals considerable support from people who may be in the best position to perceive if WAC is worthwhile. The results indicate overall satisfaction with WAC experiences in terms of improving writing and learning skills. This study also shows there are specific approaches that teachers and students consider effectual in promoting learning and writing improvement.

In addition to helping validate existing practice, the results also point to areas that need enhancement and additional study. The interviewed students expressed a desire for more teacher feedback—especially feedback which indicates that the teachers have carefully read students' papers. But to give students better feedback, it may be necessary to find ways to help them recognize and articulate the types of responses they need. Another area in need of study is the link between WAC and what students consider "real" writing and response. The interviewed students suggested that assignments making connections between course concepts and "real-world" situations are particularly valuable. Similarly, they wanted "real" feedback—responses that let the writer know the reader not only entered a mark in a gradebook, but also took time to appreciate the content and the effort put into a paper.

These notions of classroom evaluation and writing done for more than just academic purposes return us to the issue of WAC assessment in general. In this project, as in most other studies of education, classrooms are assessed based on changes and learning during a given semester, quarter, week, etc. But certainly formal education is meant to produce long-term results. The interviews indicate that some benefits of WAC—such as familiarizing students with resources for the future or helping them make connections between course content and their future jobs—occur not so much in the WAC classroom as beyond it. Such effects suggest, then, that WAC has long-term values that cannot be assessed simply in terms of how well students perform in terms of an end-of-quarter exam or writing sample.

ACKNOWLEDGMENT

Funding for this study was provided by the Office of Academic Assessment at Eastern Washington University. We thank the students and teachers involved in this study for their participation. We also thank Dana C. Elder and Gary Beason for offering feedback on drafts of this report.

REFERENCES

Beadle, M. E. (1989, March). *Evaluating writing across the curriculum: Struggles and insights.* Paper presented at meeting of the American Educational Research Association, San Francisco. (ERIC Document Reproduction Service No. ED 316 562)

Beason, L. (1993). Feedback and revision in writing across the curriculum classrooms. *Research in the Teaching of English, 27,* 395–422.

Bernhardt, S. A. (1985). Writing across the curriculum at one university: A survey of faculty members and students. *ADE Bulletin, 82,* 55–59.

Braskamp, L. A., & Ory, J. C. (1994). *Assessing faculty work: Enhancing individual and institutional performance.* San Francisco: Jossey-Bass.

Bridgeman, B., & Carlson, S. B. (1984). Survey of academic writing tasks. *Written Communication, 1,* 247–280.

Cashin, W. E. (1988). *Student ratings of teaching: A summary of the research.* (IDEA Paper No. 20). Manhattan, KS: Kansas State University, Center for Faculty Evaluation and Development.

Crowhurst, M. (1986). Revision strategies of students at three grade levels. *English Quarterly, 19,* 216–226.

Daly, J. A. (1985). Writing apprehension. In M. Rose (Ed.), *When a writer can't write* (pp. 43–82). New York: Guilford.

Donlan, D. (1974). Teaching writing in the content areas: Eleven hypotheses from a teacher survey. *Research in the Teaching of English, 8,* 250–262.

Duke, C. R. (1982). *Survey of writing in various disciplines.* (ERIC Document Reproduction Service No. ED 232 167).

Eblen, C. (1983). Writing across-the-curriculum: A survey of a university faculty's views and classroom practices. *Research in the Teaching of English, 17,* 343–348.

Fitzgerald, J. (1987). Research on revision in writing. *Review of Educational Research, 57,* 481–506.

Freeman, M., & Murphy, M. (1990). The "write" thing in the mathematical sciences. *Mathematics and Computer Education, 24*(2), 116–121.

Fulwiler, T. (1988). Evaluating writing across the curriculum programs. In S. H. McLeod (Ed.), *Strengthening programs for writing across the curriculum* (pp. 61–75). San Francisco: Jossey-Bass.

Fulwiler, T., Gorman, M. E., & Gorman, M. E. (1986). Changing faculty attitudes toward writing. In A. Young & T. Fulwiler (Eds.), *Writing across the disciplines: Research into practice* (pp. 53–67). Upper Montclair, NJ: Boynton/Cook.

Fulwiler, T., & Young, A. (Eds.) (1990). *Programs that work: Models and methods for writing across the curriculum.* Portsmouth, NH: Boynton/Cook.

Goetz, D. (1990, August). *Evaluation of writing-across-the-curriculum programs.* Paper presented at meeting of the American Psychological Association, Boston (ERIC Document Reproduction Service No. ED 328 917).

Griffin, C. W. (1985). Programs for writing across the curriculum: A report. *College Composition and Communication, 36,* 398–403.

Harris, J., & Hult. C. (1985). Using a survey of writing assignments to make informed curricular decisions. *WPA: Writing Program Administration, 8*(3), 7–14.

Hilgers, T. L., Bayer, A. S., Stitt-Bergh, M., & Taniguchi, M. (1995). Doing more than "thinning out the herd": How eighty-two college seniors perceived writing-intensive classes. *Research in the Teaching of English, 29,* 59–87.

Huot, B. (1992). Finding out what they are writing: A method, rationale and sample for writing-across-the-curriculum research. *WPA: Writing Program Administration, 15*(3), 31–40.

Kalmbach, J. R., & Gorman, M. E. (1986). Surveying classroom practices: How teachers teach writing. In A. Young & T. Fulwiler (Eds.), *Writing across the disciplines: Research into practice* (pp. 68–85). Upper Montclair, NJ: Boynton/Cook.

Kelley, K. A. (1985). *Writing across the curriculum: What the literature tells us.* (ERIC Document Reproduction Service No. ED 274 975).

Kirscht, J., Levine, R., & Reiff, J. (1994). Evolving paradigms: WAC and the rhetoric of inquiry. *College Composition and Communication, 45,* 369–380.

Maimon, E. P., & Nodine, B. P. (1978, December). *Measuring behavior and attitude in the teaching of writing among faculties in various disciplines.* Paper presented at meeting of the Modern Language Association of America, New York City. (ERIC Document Reproduction Service No. ED 167 999).

McGee, D., & Starnes, C. (1988). *Evaluation as empowerment: Holistic evaluation across the curriculum.* (ERIC Document Reproduction Service No. ED 319 425).

McLeod, S. H., & Shirley, S. (1988). National survey of writing across the curriculum programs. In S. H. McLeod (Ed.), *Strengthening programs for writing across the curriculum* (pp. 103–130) San Francisco: Jossey-Bass.

Mishler, E. G. (1986). *Research interviewing: Context and narrative.* Cambridge, MA: Harvard University Press.

Parker, R. P. (1985). Surveying writing practices across the curriculum: Models and findings. *NASSP Bulletin, 69*(478), 34–40.

Pomerenke, P. J. (1993). Surveying the writing assigned in functional areas. *The Bulletin of the Association for Business Communication, 56*(4), 28–31.

Schumacher, G. M., & Nash, J. G. (1991). Conceptualizing and measuring knowledge change due to writing. *Research in the Teaching of English, 25,* 67–96.

Schurle, A. W. (1991). Does writing help students learn about differential equations? *Primus, 1,* 129–136.

Selfe, C. L., & McCulley, G. A. (1986). Student exposure to writing across the curriculum. In A. Young & T. Fulwiler (Eds.), *Writing across the disciplines: Research into practice* (pp. 86–96). Upper Montclair, NJ: Boynton/Cook.

Selfe, C. L., Petersen, B., & Nahrgang, C. L. (1986). Journal writing in mathematics. In A. Young & T. Fulwiler (Eds.), *Writing across the disciplines: Research into practice* (pp. 192–207). Upper Montclair, NJ: Boynton/Cook.

Sommers, N. (1980). Revision strategies of student writers and experienced adult writers. *College Composition and Communication, 31,* 378–388.

Stout, B. R., & Magnotto, J. N. (1991). Building on realities: WAC programs at community colleges. In L. C. Stanley & J. Ambron (Eds.), *New directions for community colleges* (pp. 9–13). San Francisco: Jossey-Bass.

Sudman, S., & Bradburn, N. M. (1982). *Asking questions: A practical guide to questionnaire design.* San Francisco: Jossey-Bass.

Swinson, K. (1992). An investigation of the extent to which writing activities are used in mathematics classes. *Mathematics Education Research Journal, 4,* 38–49.

Tighe, M. A., & Koziol, S. M., Jr. (1982). Practices in the teaching of writing by teachers of English, social studies, and science. *English Education, 14*(2), 76–85.

Tomlinson, B. (1984). Talking about the composing process: The limitations of retrospective accounts. *Written Communication, 1,* 429–445.

Yaciw, B. (1994). Students responding to student folders. *Teaching English in the Two-Year College, 21,* 10–11.

Zemelman, S. (1977). How college teachers encourage students' writing. *Research in the Teaching of English, 11,* 227–234.

APPENDIX
STUDENT VERSION OF THE WEC QUESTIONNAIRE

This class was not primarily designed to improve your writing ability, but it may have done so anyway. Using the following scale (A–E), identify how helpful you found each of the following in terms of improving your writing ability. Consider only this class. "Writing ability" refers to the general skill of producing effective writing; it does not refer just to grammar or punctuation.

(A) strongly agree   (B) agree   (C) this class did not use or have this activity
(D) disagree   (E) strongly disagree

1. My writing ability was improved by *keeping a journal* for this class.

2. My writing ability was improved by *receiving feedback (either oral or written) from fellow students* about writing I did for this class.

3. My writing ability was improved by *receiving feedback (either oral or written) from the teacher* about writing I did for this class.

4. My writing ability was improved by *giving feedback to other students about writing they did* for this class.

5. My writing ability was improved by *revising at least one rough draft of a writing assignment* for this class.

6. My writing ability was improved by *taking essay exams* for this class.

7. My writing ability was improved by *doing short writing assignments* (about 1–3 typed pages).

8. My writing ability was improved by *doing long writing assignments* (4 or more typed pages).

9. My writing ability was improved by *being told by the teacher how he/she would grade writing assignments* (the teacher explained his/her criteria for evaluating writing).

10. My writing ability was improved by *being supplied with a written explanation of what I was supposed to do for a particular writing assignment* (a written set of directions).

11. My writing ability was improved by *being given a sample (or model) of how some student responded to a writing assignment.*

12. Overall, my writing ability was improved by d*oing the writing assignments* for this class. (Writing assignments might include journals, essay exams, lab reports, short or long papers, etc.)

Using the following scale (A–E), identify how helpful you found each of the following in terms of improving your understanding of the subject matter of this class. Consider only this class. For instance, if you are in an accounting class, did keeping a journal in this class help you better understand the principles or practice of accounting?

(A) strongly agree   (B) agree   (C) this class did not use or have this activity
(D) disagree   (E) strongly disagree

13. My understanding of the subject matter was improved by *keeping a journal* for this class.

14. My understanding of the subject matter was improved by *receiving feedback (either oral or written) from fellow students* about writing I did for this class.

15. My understanding of the subject matter was improved by *receiving feedback (either oral or written) from the teacher* about writing I did for this class.

16. My understanding of the subject matter was improved by *giving feedback to other students about writing they did* for this class.

17. My understanding of the subject matter was improved by *revising at least one rough draft of a writing assignment* for this class.

18. My understanding of the subject matter was improved by *taking essay exams* for this class.

19. My understanding of the subject matter was improved by *doing short writing assignments* (about 1–3 typed pages).

20. My understanding of the subject matter was improved by *doing long writing assignments* (4 or more typed pages).

21. My understanding of the subject matter was improved by *being told by the teacher how he/she would grade writing assignments* (the teacher explained his/her criteria for evaluating writing).

22. My understanding of the subject matter was improved by *being supplied with a written explanation of what I was supposed to do for a particular writing assignment* (a written set of directions).

23. My understanding of the subject matter was improved by *being given a sample (or model) of how some student responded to a writing assignment*.

24. Overall, my understanding of the subject matter was improved by *doing the writing* assignments for this class. (Writing assignments might include journals, essay exams, lab reports, short or long papers, etc.)

What do you believe would most help you improve your writing skills? Even if they are already good, in the space below please take a sentence or two to explain what could help you write even better.

Chapter 8

.

Program Review, Program Renewal

Charles Moran

Anne Herrington

BACKGROUND:
HISTORY AND STRUCTURE OF PROGRAM

At the University of Massachusetts, the writing-across-the-curriculum (WAC) program is part of the University Writing Requirement, which includes both a required one-semester first-year writing course, given by the Writing Program, and a required one-semester junior-year writing course, given by each academic department to its own majors. Our WAC Program, what we refer to here as our Junior-Year Writing Program (JYWP), is therefore a distributed system, with responsibility for program quality and integrity located principally in the academic departments which design and offer the courses to their majors. This distributed system is overseen by a university-wide committee of the Faculty Senate—the University Writing Committee (UWC). On what has proved to be a 3-year cycle, this committee conducts a review and evaluation of each departmental JYWP.

The structure of our WAC program—distributed, rather than centralized, with responsibility for program quality located in individual departments—is based on two assumptions about the way writing is learned and taught in an institution of postsecondary learning.

First, we believe that responsibility for students' writing is a pan-university responsibility, not one located solely with a department of English. If all faculty, not just English faculty, are involved in the teaching of writing, the institution says by what it does that writing is important. If only English faculty, and, in the worst case, just English teaching assistant (TAs) and part-time instructors, are engaged in the teaching of writing—as is true of our first-year writing course—the institution says by what it does that writing is the province of the overworked and underpaid, the least prestigious members of the academic community. In the 1982 faculty senate document that created our JYWP, we argued that "Students write better when they are expected to write better; they are likely to develop the habit of careful writing when this expectation is satisfied in various intellectual contexts over a number of years" (see Forman, Harding, Herrington, Moran, & Mullin, 1990, for background). In the university's academic culture as things stood in 1982, writing was viewed as the responsibility of the rhetoric program, a unit that existed on the margins of the academy—dependent for its funding on the whim of a dean, a unit whose courses were taught almost entirely by graduate students. One of the JYWP goals was to build an institutional expectation, create an atmosphere—nothing short, finally, of an attempt to change a culture.

Second, we believe that faculty in the disciplines are a resource: They are the most knowledgeable about the kinds of writing they want their majors to do. Many of them are already accomplished writing instructors, potentially a resource for the rest of the campus. Our JYWP requirement is, therefore, closely connected to the major and to its faculty. The second semester of the writing requirement occurs in the student's junior year, once the student has chosen a major. The junior year was chosen in preference to the senior year so that after the JYWP course students would have further occasions to be writing in situations where expectations would be high and where they would be receiving instructive feedback. An instructive program was chosen instead of an "exit test" because we assumed that a program of summative evaluation—or competency testing—would not improve students' writing. In short, given limited resources, we put those resources into writing and teaching instead of testing.

What would it take to make such a program successful? Certainly the improvement of students' writing ability, the at-least-implied goal of all WAC programs, would be a direct measure of success—if this improvement occurred and if we could measure it. The document that established our JYWP made this promise explicitly, outlining the conditions that were required if one wanted to improve students' writing: "Students write better when...." Yet as Witte and Faigley (1983) have made clear, such a summative evaluation would be tremendously expensive and perhaps finally impossible. As we have indicated, we chose to spend our limited resources on teaching.

Still, the question of assessment could not, and should not, be side-stepped. We chose not to make students the object of the program-wide assessment for several reasons: Our student population was changing, so a longitudinal measure of students' writing ability would be compromised at the outset. A longitudinal measure would have to assume that the JYWP was introduced into an educational structure that was itself stable over time: Students taking the same distribution of kinds of courses, enrolling in majors in steady numbers, staying at the university for the same number of years. Further, this kind of evaluation would be radically out-of-scale with the university's general evaluation of its academic programs: The under-graduate programs in chemistry, for example, or forestry, are not given a summative, university-wide evaluation. Not surprisingly, we get the occasional call for summative evaluation, often the suggestion of an exit test for all students. But, at least for now, the arguments against such an evaluation have prevailed. Evaluations of students' satisfactory completion of the university's writing requirements are trusted to the teachers of the First- and Junior-Year courses; evaluations of the JYWP are made on the basis of other indicators directed related to the WAC program's goals.

PROGRAM GOALS

Our JYWP, like other WAC programs, hoped to improve student writing through nothing less than changing the university's culture: bringing about increased faculty involvement in, and responsibility for, students' writing. We hoped to move writing from its position outside the academic mainstream to a position in the center of that stream. Our chosen means of moving toward this goal was to find good writing teachers already on our faculty and to bring their work to light, asking them to lead training workshops for faculty, workshops in which they described ways in which they used writing to teach their subject. By discovering and disseminating what we thought to be good teaching practices, we hoped to change the ways in which writing was taught and learned at our university.

JYWP REVIEW AND ITS RELATION TO PROGRAM HISTORY, STRUCTURE, AND GOALS

The means of review that we decided on follow from our program's history, structure, and goals. The review is conducted by the UWC which is charged by the faculty senate to "approve and monitor the Junior-Year Writing Component in the university's academic units" and to "evaluate the program and, on the basis of this evaluation, to suggest changes in procedures or policies"(Bylaws, p. 19). Consistent with the pan-university conception of the prgram, this committee is composed of faculty from across the University. The review is periodic and by department program: "A regular review of all courses...provid[ing] periodic evaluations to the Faculty Senate" (Special Report, p. 4). Regularizing review as a recurring fixture of the Program underscores its formative function. The review would not be conducted by an outside agency but by colleagues: fellow-teachers. In practice this has meant that once every 3 years, each of the approximately 55 individual programs is visited by one of the 10 members (including three ex officio members) of the UWC. After the visit, this UWC member writes a short report to the committee as a whole for review, discussion, and committee action. This discussion provides an important occasion for problem solving if a program seems to be in difficulty. It also helps all committee members develop a sense of the status of the JYWP overall.

Part of the committee-member's report is the placement of the individual JYWP program in one of three categories: (a) exemplary programs, (b) programs that are functioning well, and (c) programs that are experiencing difficulty. This aspect of the evaluation process serves two important Program goals. First, it identifies outstanding programs, teachers, and teaching materials that we draw on for our teacher-training workshops and resource library. Second, it identifies programs that are struggling, and programs that need the help of the committee and of the writing program staff.

The evaluation process also serves a related program goal: It helps build and sustain a living system—the JYWP community. The JYWP had been collegial from its beginnings, built on talk about teaching among faculty who shared a concern for their students' learning. When the UWP was voted in April 1982, the first-year writing program (FYWP) was implemented almost immediately, in the following fall semester, but the JYWP was not implemented until 1984, when the first-year students who had come under the new dispensation became juniors. During this 2-year break, the UWC engaged in extensive dialogue, most of it face-to-face in small groups, with all academic units, helping them plan for the implementation of the JYWP requirement in their majors. In January 1983, during the University's semester break, members of UWC met with representatives from every academic unit on campus to help these units plan their JYWP courses and programs. These plans were submitted to the UWC as draft proposals in April 1983. The UWC returned the proposals with comments in May 1983, and revised proposals were submitted to UWC in August 1983 for the committee's approval. Once a department's JYWP proposal was accepted by UWC, any proposed changes in that program had to be approved by UWC before they could be enacted. This procedure was dialectical and collegial: Faculty talking to one another about the best ways of facilitating their students' learning.

The UWC's review of JYWP, based as it is on visits from UWC members to departmental JYWP personnel, continues and reinforces the already established connection between the Committee and the department. The UWC and the writing program staff are paying attention to the department's JYWP. They are, yes, asking for information, and yes, they are "evaluating" the program, but they come also as learners, looking for good programs and strategies to celebrate and disseminate, and they present themselves as a resource, ready to bring suggestions and alternative models from other departmental JYWP programs (for detail, see *Program Review: 1992–1993*).

The evaluation serves yet another JYWP goal: It helps UWC and WP staff present the JYWP Programs to the university community as a coherent whole. Part of the evaluation procedure is the gathering of information about the individual JYWP Programs. This information is compiled and summarized in a "Report" to the Faculty Senate—both a brief report and a longer document, a small book, really, containing a description of each of the departmental JYWP and a set of statistical summary sheets. Such a representation of the program as a coherent whole is particularly necessary for an interdisciplinary program that does not have a departmental structure, or a departmental faculty, to give it support and identity. Further, because our JYWP is located in approximately 52 (originally 58) departments, it can easily seem a fragmented and chaotic nonprogram. Because it is a relatively new structure, it competes for resources with departments that have long-established histories, budget lines, and tenured faculty to argue for those budget lines. The information-gathering and report-writing component of our evaluation was designed, then, to keep the JYWP viable in an institution where academic units are competing for a shrinking pool of resources.

PROGRAM REVIEW: 1992 TO 1993

But enough background. We turn now to our 1992 to 1993 JYWP evaluation. We give you actual documents from this evaluation procedure; the first is a memorandum from Paula Mark, chair of UWC, announcing the evaluation to the university community.

UNIVERSITY OF MASSACHUSETTS

Writing Program

Date: October 4, 1992
From: Paula Mark, Chair, University Writing Committee
To: Department Heads and Junior Year Writing Program (JYWP)
Representatives
Subject: Program Review, Fall 1992

As you may know, the University Writing Committee is charged by the Faculty Senate with the review and evaluation of the Writing Program at both the freshmen and junior year levels This year, the Committee will be undertaking an assessment of the JYWP. I am writing to you now to let you know what we expect to accomplish and invite your cooperation with the Committee as we review your department's JYWP.

Our aim this year is twofold:

1) to assess departmental programs with respect to JYWP goals, both to obtain a campus-wide view and to identify where specific strengths and problems lie; and

2) to develop further our collection of descriptions of each program (proposal, syllabi, sample assignments, etc.), a resource base that we expect will continue to be an important library for those teaching writing on the campus.

To complete the review, we need both printed information from your department and an interview with the principal JYWP parties in your department. The Writing Committee will arrange a one hour meeting that will bring together a member of the Writing Committee and as many as possible of the persons in your department most directly involved with your department's junior year program: the JYWP representative; other faculty teaching JYWP courses; as appropriate, teaching assistants, in your junior year program; and, if feasible, the Director of Undergraduate Studies. The meeting will take place in your building. The enclosed "Interview Worksheet" indicates the kinds of questions we would like to ask. Please share it with all who will participate in the interview. We would also appreciate it if teachers of your JYWP course would bring along to the inter- view examples of assignments, students' writings, and any other teaching materials that would be helpful in illustrating the nature of your JYWP course. These materials provide a valuable resource for other faculty.

Before the interview, we would like you to complete and return the enclosed brief "Preliminary Request for Information." Please send it and a syllabus for your JYWP course to the Writing Program Office, Bartlett 305 by November 2.

Someone from the Writing Committee will contact you soon to set up a convenient date and time for the interview We look forward to talking with you.

We draw your attention to the second paragraph which describes the aims of the review: "to assess departmental programs with respect to JYWP goals," "to obtain a campus-wide view," "to identify where specific strengths and problems lie," and "to develop further our collection of descriptions...a resource-base that we expect will continue to be an important library for those teaching writing on this campus." We note, too, Paragraph 3, that "The meeting will take place in your building." The UWC deliberately goes to the "home" of the JYWP being reviewed to keep the program in its context, insofar as we can.

Finally, we note that the chair's letter introduces two documents that accompany it: a "Preliminary Request for Information" sheet (which gathers information that will be useful in furthering several Program goals listed above), and an "Interview Worksheet" (a document that prompts the visited department to reflection and self-evaluation and that serves as a guide for the UWC member conducting the interview). We include the first of these, the "Interview Worksheet," below; we include the "Preliminary Request for Information" sheet as an appendix.

As the interview worksheet makes clear, the UWC is concerned with

---

INTERVIEW WORKSHEET
JUNIOR YEAR WRITING PROGRAM REVIEW

Date of Interview: Interviewer:

Department Interviewed: Place:

Members Present:

Copies of course syllabus and other materials used by the department are attached: Yes No

I. Organization and Structure of the Current Course [If the current course is different from the one approved by the Writing Committee, discuss changes and the reasons for those changes.]

To ask of the instructor(s):
    What sort of writing do students do? (e.g., number, type, and length of major assignments? any other sorts of writing?)
    Have you made use of the techniques of peer review, draft revision, and completion of several short papers instead of a single one? How has each worked?
    How do you respond to student writing? (e.g., peer review, written comments on drafts? on final version? conferences?)
    How is the student's grade determined?

Is the present instructor going to teach the course next time? If not, who will?

If the JYWP in your department is multi-sectioned, how, if at all, are the sections coordinated?

Describe the involvement of full-time faculty in curriculum
design, training and supervision of TAs (if they are involved),
and evaluating student writing (if TAs are involved). If TAs are
involved, what is their role?

II. Your Evaluation of Your Current Course
What are satisfactions and difficulties with the course?

What's the nature of the feedback that you have received
from students about the course?

What suggestions do you have for refinements or developments
in future semesters?

III Resource Issues
Did the instructor or TAs attend a JYWP faculty workshop in
the past year? Was it useful/informative? Would a follow-up
workshop be useful? What sort of workshop?

Has the instructor used any other Writing Program resources,
e.g , library? videotapes? consultation? Are there other ways in
which the Writing Program staff could assist?

IV. Relation of Course to Major
How does the JYWP course advance or detract from the goals
you have for the major?

What is the relation of the JYWP to other courses in the
curriculum? Are there other courses that complement the JYWP?

Describe the impact that your junior year writing program
has had on students and faculty. If you wish, you may include
historical data, student evaluations, or other kinds of commentary.

program continuity and stability (Section I), self-evaluation (Section II), the departmental JYWP's connection to the larger program of which it is a part (Section III), and the relation of the departmental JYWP to the unit's undergraduate major (IV). Implicit in the Worksheet are the criteria that guided the design and review of the original program proposals in 1983 and have guided subsequent reviews. They include the following, as culled from various documents and summarized here in our words:

Each departmental JYWP will be embedded within the major: "The function of writing in the course will be to enhance and reinforce the subject being studied, not to teach grammar and spelling at the expense of that subject. . . . The quantity of writing required is less important than how writing is incorporated into the course" (Special Report, 1982).

Faculty from the major will be directly involved—preferably by teaching the course; if not teaching, then keeping in close contact with and/or supervising the person who does teach it.

The curriculum and teaching approaches will reflect sound principles of writing pedagogy, e.g., a series of shorter, rather than one long writing assignment; attention to matters of style, line of reasoning, disciplinary conventions; writing to various audiences and in various genres; opportunity to draft and revise; opportunity for feedback from peers and/or the teacher on work in progress.

THE REVIEW PROCESS:
WHAT WE LEARN AND WHAT WE GAIN

Using the documents generated by the JYWP reviews from 1986–1987, 1989–1990, and 1992–1993, and drawing on our own memories of conversations we have had over the years with faculty from specific departments, we here report on what the UWC learned and how it used what it learned. We begin with summary information about the campus-wide JYWP and move to two case studies of the JYWP in individual departments: One a JYWP that grew and changed substantially over time and whose development can certainly be connected to the JYWP review process; and one a JYWP that has been exemplary from the start and whose excellence can be seen to have been sustained and rewarded by the review process. We have selected these to illustrate the two primary ways in which the committee's program review information is used.

SUMMARY ASSESSMENT OF THE OVERALL PROGRAM

The UWC assesses the overall health of the JYWP on the basis of what it learns from the reviews of the individual programs in relation to the review criteria. Obviously, special concern is given to the number of programs that are identified as having difficulty and the reasons for those difficulties. The low number of such programs is taken as one indicator of the health of the overall program. For instance, the committee's report on the 1992 review indicated that "Of the fifty-two courses reported on (some departments have created joint programs) only one seems to be ineffective; another is being redesigned; and a third is in need of revision. In each case, corrective action is underway; these units will be revisited in Fall 1993 and reviewed again at that time." This statement should not suggest that the committee has an idealized picture of, or complacent attitude about, the JYWP. Clearly, as the case studies that follow indicate, "corrective action" is not always easy, and, as we know from experience with any large, multisectioned program, the quality of individual sections varies even for those that are generally "functioning well."

A second indicator of overall program health is the number of exemplary programs. Programs are judged "exemplary" on the basis of the curriculum and pedagogy of the JYWP course, evidence of integration of the JYWP with the major, and evidence of direct faculty involvement in teaching the JYWP. On this basis, 15 of the 58 programs reviewed from 1986–1987 were judged exemplary; in 1992 11 of the 52 programs in 1992 were judged exemplary.

As we have indicated, direct faculty involvement is valued, although not mandated. Because faculty ownership of their department's JYWP and commitment to it are founding principles of the program, we tally the degree of faculty involvement in instruction in each review. Looking back over the past three reviews, we find that from 1986–1987, 65% of the courses were taught by faculty alone or with a TA; 11% by a part-time lecturer alone or with a TA; and 21% by a TA alone. The 1989–1990 review indicated an increase in faculty involvement, as 79% of the JYWP courses were taught by faculty alone or with a TA; 10% were taught by a part-time lecturer alone or with a TA; and 10% (instead of 21% in 1986) were taught by a TA alone. This increase in faculty involvement was noted favorably in the committee's report for 1989–1990:

> Though the aims and the theoretical and pedagogical foundations of the university's JYWP have remained relatively stable, practical applications of these principles show some interesting developments. For example, the percentage of courses taught by department faculty has risen since the 1986-87 program review....

We note that the lead clause, above, also indicates a committee judgment about the overall quality of the JYWP, a judgment formed as they reviewed specific programs.

Unfortunately, the 1992–1993 review indicated that this relatively high degree of direct faculty involvement had decreased. Indeed, it dropped to 61%, with corresponding increases in both the percentage of courses taught by a part-time lecturer alone or with a TA (19%) and courses taught by a TA alone (19%). While this decrease in direct faculty involvement is of concern to us, it is also not surprising when viewed in our institutional context: Between 1989 and 1993, the University suffered a severe budget crisis, losing 27% of its state funding during this period. As a result of the cut, more university courses generally are being taught by part-time faculty and TAs. So what is true of the JYWP is true of our university's academic programs generally. Indeed, the fiscal crisis was so great that funding for the JYWP was almost eliminated. That such a move was considered is evidence of the continuing marginalization of writing instruction. The JYWP survived, and even prospered, because the director and the UWC were able to mobilize faculty support and lobby the senior administration. Faculty support for the program was there to be mobilized, we believe, at least in part because of the formative and participatory nature of the JYWP review and the heavy faculty involvement in this process.

Still, beyond the one "crisis" year, budgets still remain tight. In most departments, many faculty have declined while teaching demands have not. Regardless of all we say about recognizing a university-wide responsibility for the development of our undergraduates' writing, when choices have to be made about whether a professor will teach a graduate course, an undergraduate course for majors, or a JYWP writing course, the choice is not likely to be the JYWP writing course. Particularly in programs where the JYWP is "free-standing"—for example, a distinct "Writing in Exercise Science" course—faculty are likely to choose to teach in their home department's graduate course or undergraduate major. In departments where JYWP are integrated into existing courses required of majors—e.g., "Problems in Anthropology I and II"— the faculty do not have to make this choice.

In some instances, the committee has thought that the decline in direct faculty involvement reflects a lack of commitment to the JWYP. For example, in the 1992 review this loss of direct faculty involvement was a reason we identified one program as having difficulties. In this particular instance, a TA had been given sole responsibility for the course, and the JYWP contact professor had had very little contact with the TA. One sign of that was that only the TA and not the faculty contact attended the review interview with the writing committee member. In other instances, however, the shift from full-time faculty to a lecturer or TA has not meant a lack of contact with departmental faculty. For example, in Slavic Studies, an adjunct professor, who is highly respected by the faculty, teaches the course and, not surprisingly, the faculty perceive it as important to the major. These differences indicate that although we believe in our review that we need to look at overall trends, we know that we also need to look at the specific situation in each department. In general, direct faculty involvement in the JYWP course is good; in a particular case, however, the lack of such involvement may be compensated for by other factors in the JYWP's departmental context.

We turn now to two case studies of departmental JY reviews.

JYWP REVIEW: MATHEMATICS

Between 1984 and 1989, instead of having their own faculty teach a JYWP course, the Department of Mathematics contracted with the Department of English to provide their JYWP course. This meant that a TA from English taught a specially designated expository writing course that focused on general skills of exposition and argument.[1] The curriculum and pedagogy of the course seemed sound, but there was no attempt to connect the writing with the work of mathematics. These limitations were noted in the 1986–1987 review report by a writing committee member to the full committee: "...both the design of the course and the staffing deviate a good deal from the aims of the JYWP." The overall evaluation was as follows: "The course seems sound, but given the lack of involvement by the Mathematics Department, the program is not exemplary."

On the basis of its review, the writing committee chair wrote a memo to the Mathematics Department *encouraging* that it become more involved in the course: "We fear that the full-time faculty are not directly involved in the design and in the teaching of the course.... We are offering our assistance to solve the problems described in the evaluation report. We hope we can assist your department in finding a solution to the problems you are encountering."

Unfortunately, the Mathematics Department at that time did not think it had a problem. Indeed, the Mathematics professor who was the JYWP contact person expressed general satisfaction with the course on behalf of the Department. Further, while direct faculty involvement in the JYWP is desired, it is not mandated. The UWC was not in the position to "force" direct involvement. Indeed, as the tone of this letter implies, the UWC's authority is exercised through collegial consultation and persuasion—more through interpersonal contacts than through formal letters or memos. In the case of Mathematics, that persuasion was exercised over time as members of the committee—principally, Associate Director for the Junior Year Program, William Mullin, Professor of Physics; his successor, Annaliese Bischoff, Professor of Landscape Architecture; Chair of the UWC, Paula Mark, Reference Librarian; and then Director of the Writing Program, Charles Moran, Professor of English—sought out faculty within mathematics who valued writing and supported the underlying principles of the JYWP.

That pressure was exerted more intensively after the 1989–1990 review

---

[1] While "contracting" out to another department was not a favored option, the Faculty Senate document creating the JYWP allowed for it. The primary instance is the School of Engineering which contracts with English for Technical Writing courses, taught by Teaching Associates from English who have been trained by an English professor with technical writing experience.

that indicated that no change had been made in the program since 1986. In a letter of January 1990, following up on a telephone conversation, Paula Mark wrote to the Undergraduate Program Director of the Mathematics department urging them to "to think again about the way your majors meet the requirements of the JYWP and to consider a departmental alternative to English 350M: Expository Writing." Her tone was clearly cordial ("We appreciate your offer to bring this up in the Spring semester . . .)," and she ended by offering any assistance she or the Director or Associate Director of the Writing Program might be able to offer.

Finally, in the fall of 1992, the Mathematics Department proposed to the writing committee its own Writing in Mathematics course taught by its own faculty. In developing the proposal, Mathematics faculty consulted with both Professors Mullin and Bischoff and reviewed the course designs of other JYWP, including the JYWP Program in Physics, on which they modeled their own course. Their rationale for the new course-echoes concerns that were expressed in their 1986–1987 UWC evaluation:

> It [the Junior Year writing course offered by the English Department] is a source of great discontent because the students find no material relevant to their major field. We intend to offer a more mathematically oriented course.

The proposal was approved by the UWC, and for the past 2 years Writing in Mathematics has been offered and taught by faculty from the Mathematics Department. That Mathematics came forward with this proposal is testimony, we believe, to both their commitment to their undergraduate program and the persistent efforts of writing committee members and writing program directors.

The 1992–1993 evaluation of the new Mathematics JYWP was positive. The reviewer noted in his report to the committee that, "The faculty is supportive of the writing course, and glad to see it taught within the department. Other faculty members will likely be involved in the course in the future."

JYWP REVIEW: ANTHROPOLOGY

In contrast to the review of the Mathematics JYWP, which focused on the need for change, the review of the Anthropology JYWP focused on the program's excellence, identifying it as a resource for other university JYWP teachers and programs. With its initial program proposal of 1983, Anthropology showed early signs of being an exemplary program: It had direct and substantial faculty involvement in the course, a sound curriculum, and creative teaching. In its original form, the Anthropology JYWP program was a free-standing, three-credit "Writing in Anthropology" course with a topical focus that varied according to the interests of the professor.

The 1983 review by the UWC served no formative function for Anthropology beyond formally approving its course; it did, however, serve a formative function for the JYWP as a whole by identifying a key professor, Sylvia Forman, and exemplary teaching approaches and materials that could serve as resources for other programs. From that time on, materials from the Anthropology JYWP course have been used in JYWP workshops and shared with JYWP faculty on an individual basis. Forman was recruited to join other colleagues in conducting faculty workshops. With colleagues from the Physics, Management, and English Departments, she conducted JYWP workshops at other institutions and coauthored an article on the JYWP (Forman et al., 1990). The initial review and the subsequent recruitment of Forman as a teacher of teachers also led one of us (Charlie, who was then Director of the Writing Program) to introduce Sylvia to the Anne, as an interested researcher of writing–learning relations. This meeting led to a classroom-based, qualitative study of the course and subsequent publications that shared with an even wider audience Forman's way of conceptualizing her course and working with her students (Herrington & Cadman, 1991; Herrington, 1992). The review process thus had a formative effect within and beyond the university's JYWP, as the exemplary work of one teacher was shared with an ever-enlarging circle. This process has repeated itself, as many faculty identified through the JYWP reviews have published their work in academic journals in their own disciplines (e.g., Ahearn 1991; Marston [Bischoff] 1990, Mullin, 1989). Others have copublished in WAC literature with members of Program staff (e.g., Mullin & Moran, 1991; Forman et al., 1990; Schneider et al., In press).

In the 1986–1987 review, the Anthropology JYWP was again identified as exemplary. In his report to the UWC, the reviewer noted, however, that the Department was considering revising its JYWP program from a one-semester stand-alone course to a new two-semester sequence of courses that would combine two existing courses: the one-semester JY writing course and a one-semester theory course. The Department's rationale was based on curricular and financial concerns. The Department thought that each existing course was too full, and that students did not have sufficient time to develop as writers and theorists. According to the proposal, in the new two-course sequence the focus would be on both "writing for thinking" and "writing for communication." Further, the number of Anthropology majors was growing, and the Department thought this plan would better use faculty resources than the perceived alternative: both a new two-semester theory course in addition to the one-semester JYWP writing course. The course proposal was coauthored by Forman and a colleague she had recruited, Professor Ralph Faulkingham. An outstanding teacher himself, Faulkingham has also contributed materials and his teaching talents to workshops and is now Chair of the UWC. And, so, the cycle of teachers-teaching-teachers continues, stimulated and sustained by the process of JY program review.

The Anthropology Department's 1988 proposal was approved by the Writing Committee, and the subsequent 1989–90 review concluded, "This course is an example of how well a junior-year program can work if the people in charge are not only competent but also believe in the concept." The same conclusion was reached by the 1992 review. And, extending beyond the review, in faculty workshops and our resource library, we continue to use teaching materials from Forman's early course and the course syllabi from the new two-course sequence. A similar story could be told for other programs. The initial review of proposals served to identify and recruit the first Associate Director for Junior Year, William Mullin from Physics; subsequent reviews served to identify and recruit the current Associate Director, Annaliese Bischoff, of the Department of Landscape Architecture. More generally, reviews of all exemplary Programs have identified course designs and teaching materials that are used in workshops and available in the resource library for interested faculty.

The history of the Anthropology JYWP and its relationship to the review process illustrates another way in which the JYWP review is formative: If a Department wishes to change its JYWP, it must bring a proposal to the UWC for review and approval. In developing a proposal for program change, Departments are encouraged to seek out the Associate Director or Director for advice and are encouraged to consult sample course designs and teaching materials in the writing program's resource library. As the case of Mathematics illustrates, many Departments find this consultation and these resources useful. When a proposal comes before the committee, it is referred to two members for review and recommendation to the full committee. Their review may occasion consultation with the Department and some revisions if the committee thinks the proposal is not in line with JYWP aims and guidelines.

OTHER INDICATORS OF PROGRAM QUALITY

During the course of the JYWP review, committee members and program staff stay alert for unconventional and unexpected indicators of JYWP health. The 1989–1990 Program Review notes the following:

> Other noteworthy outcomes are visible as well. Students themselves have attained recognition through their writing activities. For instance, one Landscape Architecture student designed a mural competition that has been subsidized by the UMASS Council of Arts. And for faculty, involvement in the

Junior Year Program constitutes not only an important contribution to their departments, but to their own professional development as well. Members of the Physics, Anthropology, and School of Management faculties have published their material on their programs in the 1990 *Programs that Work*, a compendium of writing-across-the-curriculum programs nationwide (Forman et al., 1990); a Landscape Architecture professor has published a major article on her department's program in a professional journal (Marston [Bischoff], 1990) and other faculty offer workshops and consulting services at other schools and colleges.

The most recent JYWP-generated publication was coauthored by faculty from Education, Landscape Architecture, and English, and an instructional services librarian (Schneider et al., forthcoming).

Although these other outcomes are not formally considered by the UWC in its review of JYWP, they are nevertheless signs of a lively program. By collecting and publishing these items, the UWC is saying to the University community, "Here's what your colleagues have done. And here's what you could do, too."

CONCLUSION

The present University Writing Program was designed by a faculty senate committee composed of members of various disciplines. That it is a university-wide, faculty-initiated program accounts in large part for its success and, in turn, the success of the JYWP review process. The review process is actually an extension of the initial program-design process as UWC faculty work collegially with faculty teaching JYWP courses to assess and revise these courses and thus the program itself.

If the university's periodic JYWP review had functioned solely as an exercise in collecting information and making evaluative judgments about each program, it would not have nourished and strengthened the program in the ways we believe it has. In this review process, what happens as a result of each review is more important than the review itself: problem-solving work with departments having difficulty; renewing a network of personal, collegial contacts around writing and teaching; identifying teachers and teaching resources; and disseminating exemplary practice through workshops, articles, and a resource library.

As we write this, the university's JYWP reviews continue to be an integral way to maintain a self-regulating organism: renewing contacts, providing feedback, and working to revise and regenerate from within. Not incidentally, the JYWP review is, in our minds, itself a model of good teaching.

APPENDIX

PRELIMINARY REQUEST FOR INFORMATION
DESCRIPTION OF THE JUNIOR YEAR WRITING PROGRAM
IN

Major: Anthropology   Date: October 30, 1992

Please complete this page and return to the Writing Program, Bartlett 305 by Monday, November 2, 1992. Attach a copy of the most recent syllabus for your department's JYWP course(s).

Course number(s) and title(s):
Anthropology 364: "Problems in Anthropology I" (Fall, 3 credits)
Anthropology 365: "Problems in Anthropology II" (Spring, 3 credits)
    (note: both courses are required)
Credits offered: 3 each

Average class size: 50   Majors served per year: 50

Semester(s) offering JYWP course(s) this year:
Fall _X_   Spring _X_

Names and ranks of persons involved in your junior year writing program.
For '91-'92   For '92-'93
JYWP Rep.:   JYWP Rep. and Phone Number:
    Ralph Faulkingham, Professor, 5-2065 (both years)

Teacher(s):
Ralph Faulkingham, Professor, Anth. 364: Fall '91 & '92
Helán Page, Assistant Professor, Anth. 365: Spring '92 & '93
Elizabeth Chilton, TA, Anth. 364: Fall '92
Diana Fox, TA, Anth. 365: Spring '92 & '93, Anth. 364: Fall '92

For 1992–93, amount/nature of departmental support beyond the JYWP allotment.
    (none)

If to your knowledge the syllabus you attach represents any change from your department's JYWP as approved by the University Writing Committee, please note the nature of the change(s) and the reason.

No, what we have been doing last year and this is what we proposed to do and what the University Writing Committee approved (and applauded!).

Describe features of the program which deserve special mention.

Our JYWP reflects our belief that integrating writing into the curriculum beyond a single "writing" course enhances the education our majors receive. Anthropology 364 requires seven short papers, where peer critiques are employed.

The primary objective is to let writing be a means for critical thinking, rather than writing to communicate. What we find is that as students write for thinking in Anthropology 364, they come to write well in Anthropology 365, where 4 essays employing multiple drafts and peer critiques are required. The emphasis in Anthropology 365 is writing for effective communication. We find that students not only write better out of this sequence, but they think critically and well on theoretical issues usually reserved for graduate students in many programs.

REFERENCES

Ahearn, J. (1991). Writing to learn in Landscape Architecture. *CELA Conference Proceedings.*

Bylaws, University of Massachusetts Faculty Senate.

Forman, S., Harding, J., Herrington, A., Moran, C., & Mullin, W. (1990). The University of Massachusetts Junior Year Writing Program. In T. Fulwiler & A. Young (Eds.), *Programs that work* (pp. 199-219). Portsmouth, NH: Boynton/Cook.

Herrington, A. (1992). Composing one's self in a discipline: Students' and teachers' negotiations. In M. Secor & D. Charney (Eds.), *Constructing rhetorical education* (pp. 91-115). Carbondale: SIU Press.

Herrington, A., & Cadman, D. (1991). Peer review and revising in an anthropology course. *College Composition and Communication 42*, 184-99.

Marston, A. [Bischoff, A.](1990). *Teaching as if writing mattered.* Proceedings of the Second International Design Communication Conference. Tucson, AZ: University of Arizona College of Architecture, 51-53.

Mullin, W. (1989). Writing in physics. *The Physics Teacher*, 442-447.

Mullin, W., & Moran, C. (1991). Dialogue across the two cultures. In M. Schwartz (Ed.), *Writer's craft, teacher's art* (pp. 69-78). Portsmouth NH: Boynton/Cook.

Schneider, H., Bischoff, A., Herrington, A., & Mark, P. (forthcoming). The University of Massachusetts Writing Program and library connections. In J. Sheridan (Ed.), *Writing across the curriculum and the academic library*. Westport, CT: Greenwood.

Special Report of the Academic Matters Council Concerning a University Writing Program, April 29, 1982. University of Massachusetts Faculty Senate Document 82-057.

Witte, S. P., & Faigley, L. (1983). *Evaluating college writing programs*. Carbondale: SIU Press.

Chapter 9

•

The Crazy Quilt of Writing-Across-the-Curriculum: Achieving WAC Program Assessment

Meg Morgan

A friend of mine makes quilts. She takes big pieces of fabric and cuts them into little pieces. She sews them all together to create a coherent design, then attaches the batting for warmth and substance and sews a plain, often contrasting, backing to the multipieced front. Then she gives the quilts away to friends, to friends' babies, and to relatives. She makes quilts to be distributed at the local battered women's shelter. In the past, during hard times in graduate school, she sold them at craft fairs. Finally, she does something that I think is very unusual: She takes pictures of her quilts to show them to people who, for any number of reasons, may be interested in seeing the results of her efforts once the quilt itself is gone.

Such quilting provides a very nice metaphor for creating, developing, and assessing programs in writing-across-the-curriculum (WAC). We create programs by piecing together student, faculty, and administrative needs and wants; we develop programs (attach the batting) through writing intensive courses, faculty development workshops, and a multitude of other efforts; we back this with a philosophy of learning and writing and of goals or ways to implement that philosophy. We give our programs away to anyone in the university who wants to receive them. However, unlike my friend, we seldom take pictures so that others can see that program once it is gone. In other words, we are not very good at program assessment.

My original idea for this article was to evaluate all the efforts at assessing WAC programs in the last 15 or so years. But, I found few pictures I could examine. What we do know is that many institutions do offer WAC programs. In 1987, Susan McLeod surveyed 2,735 U.S. universities to find out information about WAC (McLeod, 1988, p. 103). She received 1,112 returns; of that number, 427 indicated that they had WAC programs in place (McLeod, 1988). For the past months, I have been trying to find information in print that describes the systematic (empirical) evaluation of these WAC programs. I have found nothing like 427. Instead, I found tiny photographs of minute cuts of fabric. I have read much about how faculty or students feel about writing (Behrens, 1978; Bernhardt, 1985; Gere, 1977; Zemelman, 1977); about the learning that occurs or does not occur as a result of putting writing into courses or a curriculum (Connolly & Vilardi, 1989; Day, 1989; Herrington, 1985; Hirsch & King, 1983; Parker & Goodkin, 1987; Penrose, 1992; Pittendrigh & Jobes, 1984; Walvoord & McCarthy, 1990); about the effects of WAC programs on student performance in writing (Hillocks, Kahn, & Johannessen, 1983); and about the development of WAC programs (Fulwiler & Young, 1990). The above citations do not constitute a complete—or even nearly complete—list. In one sense, of course, all these studies are efforts at program evaluation. However, in another sense, none are because they are too isolated, within a course or sometimes between courses, and although some try to look beyond the immediate (such as Bernhardt's faculty survey that included faculty within an entire university), many are not located within the context of a program.

It could be that I have a too prescribed, reductive, and narrow definition of program assessment. Let's look at what I mean by an academic program. For me, an academic program is a unit composed of multiple parts leading to one or more ends. The parts in an academic world are usually courses, although they could be credit or noncredit, for undergraduates, graduates, faculty, or staff, or courses offered for the community at large. A WAC program, then, is a conglomerate of courses, for just about anyone in or outside the university, that are geared to a certain end: In this case, writing as a way of knowing and learning. I cannot imagine that one course offered to meet a requirement constitutes a program, unless I want to change my definition. At present, in the department where I teach, we have one course in composition-like writing (that is, nonliterary, nonprofessional writing) at the upper division. Even though we offer multiple sections of that course taught by several members of the department, we do not have a departmental program in this type of writing. At the same time, we have several courses in technical writing that lead to a minor. Although the faculty is smaller, the students are fewer, and the total sections offered fewer, it is a program. The assessment of these two programs differs because one can be called program assessment whereas the other cannot.

However, WAC program assessment is different still. The assessment of a program within a department, like the technical writing program, is relatively easy compared to the assessment of a WAC program, perhaps like comparing a quilt of a simple design to a complex one. WAC programs are incredibly complex because they are typically woven throughout the entire university—not located in a single department with a coherent set of goals. WAC goals are often multiple, unstated, and even conflicting on the surface.

For example, Fulwiler (1988) uses the terms "student-centered" and "faculty-centered" to describe different activities, but also to suggest different goals within a WAC program. They are also difficult to assess for other reasons. WAC program directors are often caught up in the day-to-day operations that make any program tick; yet, to successfully assess a program, the director must be involved in that assessment and be able to look both broadly and longitudinally—both of which require discipline and, more than anything, time and patience. Fulwiler (1988) also points out that WAC programs "grow, evolve and mutate at alarming rates" (p. 62) and that what directors are trying to evaluate is often difficult to quantify and even more difficult to attribute to a WAC program. So as Fulwiler writes, "[w]hat you end up with will depend more on what can be measured than on what is happening" (p. 64). I would further add that almost anything can be measured, and that "what you end up with" is what you choose to measure.

Finally, I believe that some university and WAC program administrators see program evaluation in ways that further complicate any evaluation. Recently, when I mentioned program assessment to a very knowledgeable friend who coordinates a technical writing program, she immediately thought of money and intrusion. She imagined an outside agency coming on campus to evaluate a program, the anxiety and uncertainty this assessment would evoke, and the high cost of such an effort. Although this kind of program evaluation is common, it's not what I'm writing about in this chapter. At its most effective, program assessment is that which is done by people in the program. Although any assessment can be intrusive, that which is conducted by and for program participants is less so.

SOME EFFORTS AT PROGRAM ASSESSMENT

Because of my definition of program assessment, I had to abandon my original design for this piece which was to review and evaluate efforts at WAC program assessment: There is very little in the WAC literature that is directly *program* assessment. In 1988 Fulwiler said what I am going to say in this chapter, 11 years later: Nothing much is happening or, at least, nothing much has happened in print that provides direction for WAC directors in their efforts to assess their programs. Few researchers frame the assessment within the context of a program and measure the assessment against larger goals or problems. The following paragraphs describe some individuals who have framed assessment this way.

In 1989, Mary E. Beadle tried to evaluate the WAC program at Walsh College in Canton, Ohio and reported her findings at the 1989 meeting of the American Education Research Association (AERA). The program at Walsh was divided into stages, and at the end of Stage 1, Beadle wanted to know if student writing had improved, if student learning had improved, and if the forms teachers used to evaluate writing helped improve their assessment of student writing. Beadle concluded that both writing and learning improved and based her conclusions on how well students performed on essay exams when they were allowed to rewrite answers. She concluded that students learned more and wrote better because the answers on the rewrites showed improvement "in accuracy and understanding of concepts." Her assessment is also based on faculty anecdotes about improvement in test grades. Although the ways that Beadle chose to measure improvement are questionable, she did try to measure it within the context of program assessment.

An earlier attempt at program assessment occurred at the University of Northern Iowa (1983). One of the questions the researcher (Eblen) asked was: "[T]o what extent do overall faculty standards for student writing fit with the criteria established for a university-wide competency requirement?" (p. 343). Unfortunately, Eblen did not articulate the "criteria" and stated that "faculty as a whole concur with the criteria established by the English Department for writing competency," without elaboration (p. 348). Because the article focused more on local- or classroom-based assessment, even this article which looks at a writing competency requirement in the context of university level standards does not adequately assess that *program*.

From the late 1970s to the mid-1980s, Art Young and Toby Fulwiler led a group of faculty in the implementation of the now-famous WAC program at Michigan Tech. Although the focus of the program was faculty development through workshops, the authors also tried to measure the impact of those workshops on student attitudes and student writing in addition to measuring the impact of the workshops on the target audience: the faculty. So, in 1981, they began assessing their program, mainly through a series of surveys of both faculty and students. The faculty surveys intended to measure how the workshops changed the attitudes and behaviors of faculty, and were conducted at two points in the program. The first effort measured change in faculty attitude; a survey was administered to faculty before they took faculty development workshops and immediately after completion.

The second faculty questionnaire that Young and Fulwiler administered surveyed faculty in late 1982 after all the workshops had been completed, and after faculty had had time and opportunities to implement what they learned in the workshops in their teaching. After extensive analysis of the data from the questionnaire, they concluded that although the WAC program "had a strong impact on faculty" (p. 81), the impact was not uniform across all disciplines. In general, the "composition faculty [was] the most strongly affected and the engineering faculty the least affected" (p. 82).

Young and Fulwiler also tried to assess the impact of the program on students—an effect they admitted was several steps removed from the thrust of their program: faculty development. However, team members Selfe and McCulle embarked on an attempt to measure student "exposure" to the kinds of writing experiences promoted in the workshops. In another study, Selfe, Gorman, and Gorman tried to measure changes over time in student attitudes toward writing by looking at how students responded to the Daly/Miller Writing Apprehension Test, taken by students when they entered the university, and by comparing those results with results from the same test that these same students took as seniors. The final measure conducted by the Young-Fulwiler team looked at changes in writing abilities in a sample of students in engineering. What the researchers discovered was that writing quality of students across several years (as determined using a primary trait scoring guide) "first went up, then fell back down," a trend that the researchers found "difficult to explain" (p. 127).

The most recent attempt to assess the quality of a WAC program is occurring at the University of Hawaii at Manoa, where a team of researchers is looking at the ways the writing program has improved the quality of the writing experience for its students. The writing program began in 1987 with the mandate that all students must take at least three writing-intensive courses. Assessment of the program is ongoing and includes data collected from "end-of semester" surveys, "[c]ommentaries and intention-statements from the professors and students who constituted the observed classes," and "a few 'case-studies'" (p. 61). Hilgers, Bayer, Stitt-Bergh, and Taniguchi (1995) also interviewed 82 seniors who had taken at least three writing-intensive courses in order to identify possible "cumulative effects" of taking those writing-intensive courses (p. 63). The program assessment efforts cited here show both the problems with WAC program assessment but also some of its possibilities.

In this chapter, I argue that WAC program assessment is achievable. Although it might not be as easy as taking a snapshot of your product, assessment within a WAC program can be accomplished by looking at the pieces that lead to the whole, like examining the pieces that lead to the creation of a quilt. A thorough examination of each piece will take time, and some pieces will take more time, expertise, effort, and expense than others. All will be examined against the backdrop of goals. But it will be possible to achieve a good picture of the quality of a program after a few rounds of assessment.

QUALITY IN PROGRAM ASSESSMENT

Program assessment is an effort at improving quality: It's really that simple. Whether we discuss "summative" assessment (the measure of quality at the end of a program) or "formative" assessment (the measure of quality during the program), the results of our inquiry can give us a good picture of the quality of our program. Quality has become an increasingly important issue in U.S. corporate cultures, and corporate United States has hopped on the quality bandwagon through quality enhancement programs (the Malcolm Baldridge award) and sloganeering ("Quality is job one."). The cynic in me realizes that the downward spiral of consumer faith in U.S. manufacturing and the resultant efforts to improve quality have little to do with intrinsic rewards and more to do with economic disaster. Nonetheless, these efforts have resulted in increasing attention in both the corporate and the academic world to principles of a program of evaluation called total quality management (TQM). Those involved in academic program evaluation can learn from principles of TQM—especially as academic arenas are increasingly under the scrutiny of legislators, trustees, alumni, or parents concerned with accountability and evidence of worth.[1]

Although the term TQM may have already passed into buzzword heaven, the philosophy has left behind certain ways to look at quality and issues of evaluation that can change the way we think of program assessment. There are four principles of TQM that are particularly relevant for academic program evaluation.

First, leaders must be able to demonstrate a vision of the program. The most crucial part of this principle is the role that leaders play. Instead of the major impetus toward program assessment resting in university administrators or in outside agencies, efforts toward program assessment begin with the program administrator. Without the leadership of this administrator, assessment can be seen as threatening and intrusive. How does the program administrator lead? Leaders should begin the evaluation process by eliciting "claims, concerns, and issues" (Guba & Lincoln, 1989, p. 42) from all stakeholders and by considering the mission and goals of the program, program standards, values, and tacit belief systems. Adopting this principle of TQM means that subsequent assessment decisions are made within these constraints. For example, if a program's mission is to enhance the writing abilities of students and to develop faculty awareness of student writing issues, then measuring only student written products will assess only half of a program. After this initial discussion, administrators can then discuss the purpose of the evaluation and how the evaluation is related to concerns and issues.

---

[1] According to Brocka and Brocka, TQM "is a way to continuously improve performance at every level of operation, in every functional area of an organization, using all available human and capital resources" (p. 3). There are several names associated with TQM in its various transformations, most of whom began their work in the 1950s, 1960s, and 1970s. They include such recognizable names as Philip B. Crosby, W. Edwards Deming, Joseph M. Juran, and Tom Peters. They all seem to have "steps" or "principles" in common that, if followed, will lead to improvement in quality. Some of these are: strong, visionary leadership; working in teams; faculty development through education; and systems of open communication, often non-hierarchical. TQM, thus, is "both a philosophy and a set of guiding principles..." (p.3).

The second principle of TQM that can help with program assessment is the idea that "continuous analysis" improves quality. In TQM, this ongoing analysis invokes the principle called *kaizen:* "day-to-day, week-by-week discovery of small slips that make the process [of work] increasingly more efficient, more economical, and more dependable" (Schmidt & Finnigan, 1992, p. 40). One aspect of this principle is the issue of "continuous" or ongoing. Another is the idea of "small slips." Program assessment does not have to be large scale and performed at prescribed times, although this is also possible. Instead, a WAC administrator can identify one small area for assessment each year based on these discovered "slips." The converse is also true: While slips can lead to assessment, assessment can lead to the discovery of slips and become occasions for improvement. Slips enable program administrators to see exactly where improvement needs to occur. Perhaps the best outcome of such an approach to program assessment is that it makes the assessment manageable. In the overwhelmingly complex patchwork of WAC programming, singling out a piece to evaluate within articulated program goals is one sane approach.

The third principle of TQM that seems valuable to import into WAC program assessment is the idea that all members of a program must be empowered to act within that program. One of the best ways to empower all constituents or stakeholders of a program is to involve them in the evaluation, in what then becomes a *collaborative* evaluation process (Guba & Lincoln, 1989). A WAC program has a particularly complex network of stakeholders: faculty from many disciplines, administrators across a campus, students in general education courses as well as in a variety of majors, and often members of communities outside the university, such as parents, taxpayers, and secondary school teachers. Each group of stakeholders may hold different—even conflicting—notions about writing and what a writing program can and should do, notions that the leader of the program must negotiate. Involving stakeholders in evaluation may lessen the uncertainty that is often provoked when processes of evaluation are imposed from outside the program by university administrators, funding agencies, boards of trustees, accrediting agencies, testing companies, or state legislators. Such outside efforts can require little or no investment from the participants in the program and often do little more than produce anxiety and uncertainty evoked by the possibility of change (Sell, 1989, p. 29; see also Williamson, this volume). Making the evaluation process collaborative can also ensure that both the process and the results of the evaluation will be "owned" by those involved. (Davis, 1989, pp. 14, 16–17; Guba & Lincoln, 1989, p. 42). The successful outcome of this process depends on the involvement of the stakeholders and the articulation of concerns that *they* have identified. The stakeholders become the agents of inquiry, not the subjects of it, in ways that they could never be if the evaluation process were "top-down." Having some control over the questions, methods, and outcomes may not only alleviate uncertainty, but also may create a climate in which change is welcomed.

The fourth (and final for our purposes) principle of WAC assessment that comes from TQM is the idea that companies and employees must pay attention to the needs of the customers, defined as "anyone to whom you give your work" (Brocka & Brocka, 1992, p. 36). In the university, we generally do not call our students "customers." However, in that they are the primary receivers of our work, they are our primary customers. But because WAC work is so varied, WAC customers are varied. In a faculty-centered WAC program, the main customer would be faculty, and the work that is performed for them would be such activities as workshops, off-campus retreats, lunches, classroom observations, video teleconferences, etc. Customers of a WAC program might also be university administrators, members of the community outside the university, or even members of the profession.

A PROCESS FOR EVALUATING ACHIEVEMENT OF QUALITY

The principles of TQM place the responsibility for quality within the program itself. To document the achievement of quality, a program administrator must be able to lead stakeholders to articulate a mission statement—basically a statement of the purpose for which the program exists. Together, they must begin to set goals, the first step in documenting the achievement of quality. Altogether, there are three steps:

1. Create goals. What does the program want to achieve? The goal statement points to the future and should contain a "quality" word: better, highly motivated, effective, etc. The vision for quality first appears in the goal statement.
2. Establish goal-achievement activities. What activities will allow the program and its stakeholders to know if the goals have been achieved? Goal achievement activities, if done well, move the program toward achieving the goal.
3. Create measures. What measures will show the success of the activities? The program administrator creates measures to determine "done well." Measures will vary in complexity, depending on the complexity of the activity and the goal.

Creating goals, establishing goal-achievement activities, and creating measures should be done with the consultation of other members of the program. This goal, activities, and measure need some illustration.

Consider: A new WAC program director wants to make sure that writing

activities in the writing-intensive classes in the university effectively challenge the students to think at higher levels. So, her goal will be that all writing-intensive classes in the university include activities that effectively
challenge students to think at higher levels. She (and her faculty or another
stakeholder group) now must decide what evidence will demonstrate that the
goal has been reached. They have several choices: They may choose to examine student writing; they may discuss the writing assignments with the students or the teachers, asking questions that get at the challenging nature of
the assignments; they may examine the syllabus of each teacher and also the
writing assignments detailed in those syllabi. In fact, they might do all three.
They choose to examine the syllabi of all teachers and request syllabi and
descriptions of the writing assignments.

Finally, they have to decide on a way to measure "thinking at higher levels." They decide to use Bloom's taxonomy as a way to gauge the intellectual difficulty of the writing assignments. Bloom maintains that there is a
hierarchy of cognitive behaviors that ranges from simple to complex. Recall
is the simplest; evaluation the most complex.[2] Our new WAC administrator
believes that if the assignments in the writing-intensive courses fall at the
simple end of Bloom's scale, she would consider them unchallenging. She
gathers a group of teachers to act as raters, trains them to recognize the taxonomy, to apply it to the descriptions of the assignments, and to make judgments about the degree of complexity of the assignments.

At the end of this process, she has some assurance that the writing
assignments either are or are not challenging; she knows which teachers
seem to be (or not to be) challenging their students; she knows where to
place her training efforts and where not. She might even know that no training is needed. She does not, of course, know how well the students perform
on those challenging assignments, how they are evaluated by the teacher,
etc. That information could only be learned by designing a different set of
activities that would lead to different measures.

You might think that such an approach is obvious: We all offer programs
and evaluate them. We all want to know how well things are going and are
concerned that our students are learning. This may be true, but we all do not
think of this approach in terms of *program* evaluation, of documenting that
a *program* goal has been reached. You also may think that such an approach
is random; and, indeed, it can be. Yet, early in this chapter I used a metaphor

---

[2] Bloom's intent was to create a classification system that traced "changes produced in
individuals as a result of educational experiences" (p. 12). For this reason, our fictional WAC
director has chosen an established taxonomy based on educational behaviors in what Bloom
calls the cognitive domain as opposed to the affective domain. The taxonomy contains these levels arranged from most simple to most complex: knowledge, comprehension, application, analysis, synthesis, and evaluation. Bloom makes the point that the higher orders include the
objectives of the lower orders (pp. 15–18).

of a quilt to describe how I see WAC programs and their evaluation. Just as the quilter uses separate pieces of materials and chooses to create a specific design out of those pieces for her quilt, the process of program evaluation that I describe in this chapter and especially the matrix I describe next allows the program administrator to set up a *design* for evaluation.

And a qualifying note: Every metaphor falls apart at some point. This one does, also. After many hours of work, a quilt is eventually finished. An evaluation of a program is never finished until the last—summative—one, usually at the demise of the program. Any goal, any activity and its measures contribute only one square to the total patchwork design of WAC program assessment.

A MODEL FOR PROGRAM ASSESSMENT

To construct a model for program assessment, I created a triple matrix that schematizes certain critical relationships in program assessment. The matrix cannot incorporate everything; yet the force behind it includes the principles of TQM I already discussed as well as the idea of program goals, activities directed toward accomplishing the goals, and measures of the quality of the activities. The matrix calls for multiple goals across several dimensions, goals which should be articulated by the program administrator and also by the other participants in the program. The matrix is so complex that it forces the program administrator into a continuous, ongoing mode of evaluation. This complexity also encourages participation from many stakeholders in the program and, by naming some of them "agents," empowers them. Finally, the basis of the matrix is the effect of the program on each "customer." Because in academics, customers are beneficiaries or users, I will use the term "user" rather than customer. Any program assessment must be user-driven; it must ask "Assessment for whom?" and must consider the effects of any program on its users. In Figure 9.1 below is an example of an empty-celled matrix; completed matrices appear on subsequent pages.

This matrix, which looks strangely like a quilt, answers a need for a systematic, comprehensive way of viewing the activities of a program within the context of assessment. The matrix is built on the intersection of pertinent agents and pertinent users of a program, and assessment goals can be generated by asking the question: "How does Agent 'X' create a quality program for User 'Y'?" The cells are created by creating goals that answer this question. There are three variations to the matrix: one that articulates goals; a second, activities; and a third, measures. Each matrix is composed of cells that contain goals through a goal statement, activities, and ways to measure achievement of the goal.

Agents:	Faculty	Students	Administrators	Curriculum
Users: Students				
Faculty				
Administrators				

Figure 9.1. General Matrix

To illustrate this program assessment model, I created three matrices for a hypothetical WAC program. The phrase in each cell is a shorthand for the goals, activities, and measures in an assessment of this program. In all cases, the question that generates the goal, activity, and measure is centered on the user: For this particular program, I identify four pertinent agents (although some might argue that there are more and others that "curriculum" is not an agent, technically): students, faculty, administrators, and curriculum. I identify three users: students in the program; the faculty, who act in several roles within WAC programs; administrators, who include not only the primary administrator of the program, but also deans and administrators at the college/university level. Again, there could be more users, such as members of the community, trustees, professional assessment organizations, and state assessment agencies. This program assessment model also is driven by the question: How do the agents of the program (faculty, students, administrators, and curriculum) create a quality program for the users (students, faculty, and administrators)? See Figure 9.2.

Goals

Some of the goals can be achieved rather quickly, whereas others may take more than 1 year to achieve or may be ongoing. For example, a project that assesses university-wide "quality learning" may take several years to design and implement. Achieving valid student evaluations might take a year. And creating clear program guidelines for students might take a semester. A realistic timeframe should be part of the planning. Given that the matrix out-

Agents:	Faculty	Students	Administrators	Curriculum
Users:				
Students	Quality learning	Students helping other students write	Increasing services in the writing center	Clear program guidelines
Faculty	Creating learning environments among faculty	Valid student evaluations	Encouraging an atmosphere for innovation	Clear guidelines related to expertise
Administrators	Clear articulation of needs for future planning	Helpful feedback of program effectiveness after graduation	Allocation of adequate resources for development	Guidelines closely attuned to university mission statement

Figure 9.2. Assessment Matrix: Goals

Agents:	Faculty	Students	Administrators	Curriculum
Users:				
Students	Using end of semester writing to assess learning	Creating writing groups in dorms	Initiating semester-long tutorials for serious writing deficiencies	Rewriting writing-intensive guidelines
Faculty	Creating faculty writing groups	Revising student evaluations	Initiating an award for the most innovative writing assignment	Writing a WAC teacher manual that discusses ways writing can be used in various disciplines
Administrators	Writing a report that outlines WAC needs for 5 years	Contacting alumni to determine how well writing served them	Writing a report (from WAC program director) that outlines financial needs for the next 5 years	WAC program guidelines to match university mission statement

Figure 9.3. Assessment Matrix: Goal-achievement Activities

lined above has 12 cells (it actually could have more if you add more agents or users), a program administrator might construct 12 goals for any one year.

Goal-achievement activities

Each goal has an activity that helps the program administrator determine if the goal has been met. It is important to remember that any one goal may have several activities that demonstrate achievement. The next matrix, in Figure 9.3, shows one activity that might be used to show that a goal has been reached. The cells in this matrix are placed relative to the goals in the previous matrix.

Some of these activities will seem very familiar to anyone administering a writing program. For example, any program administrator wants to be assured that student learning improves through writing, or that working in groups helps students' writing. In fact, much of the assessment that has been done in WAC has been within the category of "students as users." However, as I have mentioned before, a program involves several users (even more than those listed in this matrix), and designing activities that will lead to goal achievement, though more comprehensive, is also more unfamiliar.

Because it is unfamiliar, a few cells may need some explaining. In the cell where the goal is "Valid Student Evaluation" (the intersection of "Agents: Students" and "Users: Faculty"), students can help faculty improve their teaching if they provide sound feedback to their teachers. To do that, students can help create valid instruments for measuring effective teaching. Creating a student task force to help revise the presently used evaluation instrument for writing-intensive courses might be one activity that the WAC administrator initiates. However, it is only one of several options. Another option could be studying the use of written evaluation instruments and deciding if, how, and when to administer them. Or studying the feasibility of an oral evaluation of teaching, or of alternative methods, such as videotaping. The cell demands only that students become the agent of the inquiry and that the faculty become the users of the outcome.

Measures

Program administrators must create ways to measure whether or not the activities have achieved the goals. There are many ways to measure outcomes. Some are quite simple: Has the report been written? Yes or No. If so, what has been the effect of the report? For example, in the "Activity" matrix, the intersection of "Agents: Faculty" with "Users: Administrators" calls for a report to be written that articulates future needs. A measurement of that activity could be the completion of the report. A further measure of the activity could be the completion of the report along with a response from the users. Ultimately, the success of the report might be measured by whether or not the needs articulated were funded by the administrators.

The matrix is open to many different research designs to measure goal achievement. Some cells call for the design and administration of questionnaires—a quantitative measure. Others require that faculty examine student writing, which could be a qualitative measure. With activities written differently, the measures might emerge as studies of groups of students over time (following student writers through 4 years to measure their growth in learning, for example), or as comparisons of written products between control and experimental groups, generally a quantitative measure in a true experiment. Some measures are easy to establish: A group of faculty meets in groups to receive feedback on articles they want to publish. Within a year, all articles have been accepted for publication; therefore, the goal has been achieved.

However, most things worth measuring are difficult to measure. Measuring the quality of students' learning through writing (the goal for the first cell) may require elaborately designed activities and more elaborately designed measurement techniques. For example, the decision to use end of semester writing to assess learning assumes that students will know what they need to at the *end* of the semester, not before and not after. Why not measure the learning 3 months after the end of the semester, or 2 weeks before? What kind of writing is the best to measure learning? Who will define quality? Yet, a well-designed measurement will result in the assessment of an activity that will have far-reaching implications for the WAC program.

The fourth matrix, Figure 9.4, in this set suggests ways to measure the success of the activities in achieving the goals. Because goals can be achieved through several activities and activities can be measured in several ways, this matrix, like the others, is only one possible design among any number of choices.

Designing levels of matrices that include goals, activities, and measures across agents and users creates a plan that has several advantages. First, it is flexible: If the goal seems worthwhile and if a particular way of achieving it does not seem to be working, it might be better to keep the goal and change the activity and measure than to give up the goal. If goal achievement cannot be confidently measured or if the quality cannot be built into the goal, it may and should be dropped. Second, the matrices also demand that the program assessment be viewed from multiple perspectives: They allow for multiple ways to achieve goals through activities, multiple ways measure achievement (qualitatively and quantitatively), and multiple ways to collect data (observation, surveys, interviews, experiments, etc.). The matrices also emphasize growth and process. Finally, the matrices allow opportunity for analysis, synthesis, and reflection through review of the plan by all stakeholders. Unfortunately, the matrices also magnify the complexi-

Agents:	Faculty	Students	Administrators	Curriculum
Users:				
Students	Students take an essay exam	Students complete questionnaire	Students complete questionnaire; before and after writing samples are rated by faculty	Students complete questionnaire
Faculty	Articles are accepted for publication	Faculty complete questionnaire	Award is granted	Faculty complete questionnaire
Administrators	Administrator is interviewed about the value of the report	Alumni complete questionnaire	Administrator includes WAC financial needs in university budget	Guidelines are delivered to university-level administrator

Figure 9.4. Assessment Matrix: Measures

ty of assessing any program; WAC programs are especially daunting. However, given the lack of program assessment in WAC, this matrix provides a clear, focused, and systematic way to begin the process.

CONCLUSION

Many WAC administrators may not have the patience to work with these matrices; many people do not have the patience to design and execute a quilt. Many may not have the ability to succeed in an environment where much of the work is accomplished through the vision of a leader working collaboratively with all stakeholders, and where the users of the program are one of the cornerstones of the assessment process. Some may be unsatisfied with the prospect of an evaluation process that really never ends. Yet, at a time when many programs are being cut back or eliminated, WAC administrators may not be able to afford not to create a plan for program assessment that does not take into consideration at least some of these characteristics. And even if cutbacks were not an issue, quality must be.

Handmade quilts at craft fairs and auctions are valuable not only because of the materials used to make them, but also because of the skill and the hours of patient attention that put those materials together to create a thing of beauty. But quilts are not ineffable; programs are. And we need assessment snapshots to demonstrate that we are, indeed, quality makers.

REFERENCES

Beadle, M. E. (1989). Evaluating writing across the curriculum: Struggles and insights. Paper presented at the Annual Meeting of the American Educational Research Association, San Francisco, CA. (ERIC Document Reproduction Service No. 316 562).

Behrens, L. (1978). Writing, reading and the rest of the faculty: A survey. *English Journal, 67*(6), 54–66.

Bernhardt, S. A. (1985). WAC at one university. *ADE Bulletin, 82,* 55–59.

Bloom, B. S. (Ed.) (1956). *Taxonomy of educational objectives: Book 1 the cognitive domain.* New York: Longman.

Brocka, B., & Brocka, M. S. (1992). *Quality management: Implementing the best ideas of the masters.* Homewood, IL: Business One Irvin.

Connolly, P., & Vilardi, T. (Eds.). (1989). *Writing to learn mathematics and science.* New York: Teachers College.

Davis, B. G. (1989). Demystifying assessment: Learning from the field of evaluation. In P. J. Gray (Ed.), *Achieving assessment goals using evaluation techniques* (pp. 5–20). San Francisco: Jossey-Bass.

Day, S. (1989). Producing better writers in sociology classes: A test of the writing-across-the curriculum approach. *Teaching Sociology, 17,* 458–464.

Eblen, C. (1983). Writing across-the-curriculum: A survey of a university faculty's views and classroom practices. *Research in the Teaching of English, 17,* 343–348.

Fulwiler, T. (1988). Evaluating writing across the curriculum programs. In S. H. McLeod (Ed.), *Strengthening programs for writing across the curriculum* (pp. 61–75). San Francisco, Jossey-Bass.

Fulwiler, T., & Young, A. (1990). *Programs that work: Models and methods for writing across the curriculum.* Portsmouth, NH: Boynton/Cook.

Gere, A. R. (1977). Writing and WRITING. *English Journal, 66*(8), 60–64.

Guba, E. G.,& Lincoln, Y. S. (1989) *Fourth generation evaluation.* Newbury Park, CA: Sage.

Herrington, A. J. (1985). Writing in academic settings: A study of the contexts for writing in two college chemical engineering courses. *Research in the Teaching of English, 19,* 331–359.

Hilgers, T. L., Bayer, A. S., Stitt-Bergh, M., & Taniguchi, M. (1995). Doing more than "thinning out the herd": How eighty-two college seniors perceived writing intensive classes. *Research in the Teaching of English, 29,* 59–87.

Hillocks, G., Jr., Kahn, E. A., & Johannessen, L. R. (1983). Teaching defining strategies as a mode of inquiry: Some effects on student writing. *Research in the Teaching of English, 17,* 275–284.

Hirsch, L. R., & King, B. (1983). *The relative effectiveness of writing assignments in an elementary algebra course for college students.* Paper presented at the Annual Meeting of the American Educational Research Association, Montreal, Quebec, Canada. (ERIC Document Reproduction Services No. 232 872).

McLeod, S. H. (1988). Appendix. In S. H. McLeod (Ed.), *Strengthening programs for writing across the curriculum* (pp. 103–130). San Francisco: Jossey-Bass.

Parker, R. P., & Goodkin, V. (1987). *The consequences of writing: Enhancing learning in the disciplines.* Upper Montclair, NJ: Boynton/Cook.

Penrose, A.M. (1992). To write or not to write: Effects of task and task interpretation on learning through writing. *Written Communication, 9,* 465–500.

Pittendrigh, A., & Jobes, P. C. (1984). Teaching across the curriculum: Critical communications in the sociology classroom. *Teaching Sociology, 11,* 281–296.

Schmidt, W. H., & Finnigan, J. P. (1992). *The race without a finish line.* San Francisco: Jossey-Bass.

Selfe, C. A., Gorman, M. E., & Gorman, M. E. (1986). Watching our garden grow: Longitudinal changes in student writing apprehension. In A. Young & T. Fulwiler (Eds.), *Writing across the disciplines: Research into practice* (pp. 97–108). Upper Montclair, NJ: Boynton/Cook.

Selfe, C. A., & McCulley, G.A. (1986). Student exposure to writing across the curriculum. In A. Young & T. Fulwiler (Eds.), *Writing across the disciplines: Research into practice* (pp. 86–96). Upper Montclair, NJ: Boynton/Cook.

Sell, G. R. (1989). An organizational perspective for the effective practice of assessment. In P. J. Gray (Ed.), *Achieving assessment goals using evaluation techniques* (pp. 21–41). San Francisco: Jossey-Bass.

Walvoord, B. E., & McCarthy, L. P. (1990). *Thinking and writing in college.* Urbana, IL: National Council of Teachers of English,

Young, A., & Fulwiler, T. (1986). *Writing across the disciplines: Research into practice.* Upper Montclair, NJ: Boynton/Cook.

Zemelman, S. (1977). How college teachers encourage student writing. *Research in the Teaching of English, 11,* 227–234.

Chapter 10

▪

Integrating WAC Into General Education: An Assessment Case Study

Martha A. Townsend

General education reform has been a catalyst for new writing initiatives at many colleges and universities. However, at the University of Missouri–Columbia (MU), somewhat the opposite occurred. By the time our first campus-wide general education proposal was put to a faculty vote in 1989, MU's writing-across-the-curriculum (WAC) program—the Campus Writing Program (CWP)—was already 5 years old, and its organizational structure provided the model for the new general education program. Those of us involved with WAC, though, were unsure how to best fit the established writing program into the new general education initiative. This case study describes the year-long assessment project—a self-study and external review—which helped the CWP make that transition. This chapter argues for social constructivist theory to undergird such an assessment and includes the array of activities MU undertook, the methods we used to collect data, the rationale for our choices, the multiple audiences and stakeholders involved, and the outcomes of the project for the institution.

There are several reasons for including such a case study in this volume. First, few WAC programs have undertaken lengthy self-examinations or requested external reviews. When they have, reports of them generally go unpublished. Second, surprisingly little exists in the literature on how WAC programs might conduct assessment; WAC needs examples and models to work from. Third, national, state, regional, and institutional mandates for assessment abound. Both educators and policymakers need more access to specific examples of assessment alternatives. Finally, assessment of any kind is usually threatening. Institutions and faculty are reluctant to open themselves to the kind of probing and introspection that an honest evaluation demands. As one new faculty member, interested in lobbying her department to support an external review, posted to the writing program administrators' (WPA) listserv recently, "Are there ways to convince my colleagues who have expressed hesitancy and doubt regarding the efficacy of such reviews?" This chapter demonstrates that WAC programs can not only survive the scrutiny, but that assessment can be a way of learning that leads to their improvement.

THE CONTEXT FOR MU'S ASSESSMENT PROJECT

A Carnegie I research university, MU is also the state's major land-grant institution with 25,000 students enrolled in doctoral, professional, and undergraduate programs, plus an extensive outreach mission. The 20,000 undergraduates are dispersed among nine colleges. MU's initial 1984 WAC requirement called for all undergraduates to complete a semester of first-year composition taught in the English Department and one writing-intensive (WI) course taught in the disciplines. Each of the nine colleges, however, maintained its own general education requirements. CWP was created to oversee the development of WI courses, faculty, and teaching assistants (TAs) across the disciplines in which the courses were to be taught. Situated on a permanent budget line, CWP had full-time staff of four individuals (a director, a learning resource specialist, an administrative assistant, and a secretary), sufficient graduate TAs to assist faculty so that classes would not exceed a student-to-instructor ratio of 20:1, and additional graduate TAs to staff a writing center for students enrolled in WI classes.

Three main factors influenced MU's decision to launch the year-long assessment project. First, whereas the fairly flexible 1984 requirement allowed students to take the WI course anywhere in the curriculum at any level as long as the first-year composition prerequisite was completed, the 1989 requirement required a second WI course for all students, with the new course to be taken at the upper-division level in the major. Second, the program had never been systematically evaluated; assessing the progress of the original WI requirement prior to implementing the new one seemed only appropriate. Third, I had just been hired as CWP's director, and my biggest challenge would be to oversee the implementation of the new requirement. So, even though university officials urged caution ("Assessment is a highly charged issue around here—the 'A' word on this campus. Don't even bring it up," was the warning I was given during my interview), I lobbied for a formally commissioned self-study and external review. By the time I was hired, undertaking the assessment project was a foregone conclusion.

SOME WORDS ABOUT THEORY AND PRACTICE

If this account has an autobiographical edge, it's because a significant part of the project grew out of how I believe writing programs ought to be assessed. This is not, however, to suggest that the many others involved shared those views or even knew them. Few people were interested in devoting committee time to philosophical discussion of assessment theory. Most simply wanted to identify tasks at hand and plan timetables by which various committees had to meet. Even so, the theoretical principles that guide my work allowed me to influence how the project was managed. As any literary or critical theorist knows, a theoretical position undergirds the analysis of any text, even if the author does not foreground it.

The same is true of writing program evaluation. A theory, or some combination of theories, undergirds the evaluation process whether or not those positions are made explicit. In MU's case, the process was informed by quantitative, empirical measures, but more importantly, these were combined with—or folded into—an adaptation of the social constructivist methodology espoused by Guba and Lincoln (1989). My recently completed doctoral work (1991)—an assessment of 19 writing-based general education projects funded by The Ford Foundation—had been influenced by Guba and Lincoln's approach which offers a means of addressing the politically charged, often threatening aspects of assessment. These authors believe that treating educational evaluation as a technical or scientific process misses "completely its fundamentally social, political, and value-oriented character" (p. 7). The alternative they offer to positivistic approaches is a "social constructivist" approach. This view holds that reality—especially social and behavioral reality (like writing and writing programs)—is not an absolute that is scientifically and objectively observable, but rather is a construction made by individual observers and participants, each of whom has something different at stake in the program and how it is evaluated. A constructivist evaluation tries to indicate through discussion the claims made, the uncertainties expressed, and the issues identified with regard to a program's effectiveness. Constructivist methodology seeks areas of both agreement and disagreement and then seeks to resolve, through "hermeneutic dialogue," the discrepancies in stakeholders' views, in order to arrive at a plan for action. The goals of this type of evaluation, Guba and Lincoln say, are to empower, to educate, and to open discourse. The product of evaluation is not so much a set of conclusions or recommendations as it is an agenda for negotiating the concerns and issues that are discovered. This approach seems particularly appropriate for WAC programs because so many different groups are affected by WAC and because the approach can consider features of programs that traditional approaches neglect.

Guba and Lincoln's model is admittedly time consuming and financially costly. I did not employ the full range of their "fourth generation" methodology which, in keeping with their goal of resolving disagreements through discussion, is lengthy, recursive and, in fact, ends only when time and money run out or agreement is reached. "Evaluation," they say, "is indeed a continuous process" (p. 222). But, by adapting the ideas behind the model, I found the Ford Foundation participants remarkably open to answering questions that might otherwise have been potentially threatening. Ford Foundation officials and I had assured them verbally and in writing at several stages throughout my study that any information they shared with me would not affect future funding. In scheduling my trips to the institutions, I collaborated with participants to "construct" a site visit that addressed the needs of their projects at that time; in other words, I talked to the campus representatives they chose, at locations they chose, and at times convenient to them. Several, for example, used my campus visit to "remind" their deans and provosts that The Ford Foundation was eager to know whether the WAC projects would be continued with campus funding. My protocol of questions was generative rather than closed. I asked permission to take close notes, but did not use a tape recorder. I assured participants that my reporting of data would not embarrass the institution in any way. I also agreed to circulate a draft of any material for their feedback if it were to be published. I was convinced that a similar adaptation should provide the philosophical framework for MU's project.

The practical framework for MU's project was provided by the Council of Writing Program Administrators' *Guidelines for Self-Study to Precede a Writing Program Evaluation* (pp. 304–313). These guidelines pose 80 or more questions under 5 headings (general background, curriculum, faculty, program administration, related writing programs and instructional units) intended not as an outline to be followed but as a heuristic to help programs shape their own review—an idea that coincides well with Guba and Lincoln's social constructivist approach. MU's final written report thus included all the information sought in WPA's document, but in finished form looked very different from the guidelines. Likewise, every institution's self-study will be different from the one described in this chapter. Just as WAC programs must be institutionally specific in order to function successfully, so must the assessments they undertake be particularized to their needs. It's the uniqueness—one might say the social construction—of each WAC program that makes standardized program assessment impractical. The combination of social constructivist methodology with the flexibility of WPA's guidelines makes these approaches appropriate for WAC program evaluation.

MU'S WAC INTO GENERAL EDUCATION DILEMMA

WAC and general education are natural companions. Few would question the wisdom of campus planners who integrate them, yet many campuses experience considerable problems in making the relationship work. The

Ford Foundation projects I had studied exemplified many of these problems, and MU was no exception. Our list of issues that we hoped the assessment project would help us resolve was substantial:

1. Many of the faculty who elect to offer WI courses are the same under-graduate teaching faculty who were also inclined to offer the other, new general education courses (in addition to the second WI class, a sopho-more seminar, a senior capstone, cluster courses, a science lab, and pro-ficiencies in computing, information literacy, and math). CWP needed to ensure that MU's pool of WI instructors wouldn't dwindle, nor that fac-ulty would spread themselves too thin.
2. Early on in CWP's history we realized that the optimum time to hold faculty workshops is the week immediately prior to the start of each semester. Faculty, recovered from the pressures of intense semesters, are ready to focus again on teaching and, not least, are available then to attend. But the general education planners realized this also, and our concurrent workshops were competing with each other.
3. The newly required sophomore seminar differed from the WI require-ment mainly in its emphasis on oral rather than written skills. We need-ed to articulate how these courses could complement rather than compete with each other, especially in times of limited resources.
4. Because WI courses had a 5-year history when the general education plan was adopted, CWP was cited as "the successful component" of gen-eral education. While this was pleasing for CWP, it also gave the impres-sion that our work was finished, and it negated the tremendous effort the campus would have to put forward to create the new tier of WI courses in the major.
5. The new general education plan was ambitious in part because it was MU's first curricular initiative to unite all nine colleges. Much uncer-tainty existed over whether the logistics of implementing all the compo-nents (clusters, capstones, labs, etc.) could be coordinated. Reform of this magnitude is difficult on any campus but especially so at a comprehen-sive, Research I institution. Moreover, MU was undergoing changes in high-level administration; faculty were unclear whether the needed philosophical and financial support would be forthcoming. CWP needed to ensure that in our becoming part of such an ambitious plan the effec-tiveness of the WAC effort to date wouldn't be jeopardized, that is, that we would lose scarce resources or, worse, collapse along with a plan so weighty that it simply couldn't be implemented on our campus.
6. Finally, to prepare for the future we needed to know more about the impact of the WAC effort to date. Sample questions under this heading included concerns such as: Had faculty changed their teaching practices as a result of workshops? Were students doing more writing in their

classes? Were enough WI classes being offered to allow for timely graduation? Did faculty feel sufficiently rewarded for their WI teaching to offer even more courses?

HOW MU'S SELF-STUDY PROCEEDED

The project contained two separate but interwoven strands: (a) a full-scale review of CWP by an "Internal Review Committee" commissioned by the provost and the Dean of Arts and Science and (b) concurrent, complementary data gathering conducted by CWP.

The structure of the Internal Review Committee (IRC) was unusual in that the ten members were selected specifically for their non-WAC, and therefore presumably more objective, orientation. In the spirit of a constructivist evaluation their being selected to serve was appropriate in that all ten represented constituencies on campus ("stakeholders," in Guba and Lincoln's terms) that are affected by the WAC requirement. Comprised of nine tenured faculty and one graduate TA from various disciplines—only half of whom had attended a CWP faculty workshop and only two of whom had taught WI courses—the IRC embodied both respect for CWP's prior work and skepticism born of their own or their colleagues' experiences with WI courses. I met with this group for their first four or five meetings to provide background and answer questions. Once grounded in CWP's basic history and current activities, they met independently to continue their review. Periodically, IRC would call on me or CWP staff to provide additional information or verify data they had collected. Meanwhile, CWP staff and I carried out concurrent research to supplement IRC findings. Although the split arrangement seemed awkward at first, and although it took us awhile to figure out what each group's responsibilities were to be, the separate strands ultimately benefited the project. Throughout the year, the IRC chair and I kept in close touch about what each group was doing, asked frequent questions of one another, and shared data as it was collected.

STRAND ONE: WHAT THE INTERNAL REVIEW COMMITTEE DID

IRC's activities were varied. They began by meeting with the English Department's composition director to learn about the WI prerequisite course, English 20, taught mainly by graduate TAs in English. IRC next surveyed English 20 TAs to determine their knowledge of WI courses and their perception of students' readiness for WI instruction. IRC surveyed deans of undergraduate divisions to ascertain colleges' goals for WI courses and perceptions about whether CWP was providing adequate support for WI faculty. IRC also surveyed faculty to find out why some faculty who, after attending CWP workshops, had not subsequently offered WI courses. IRC reviewed students' WI course evaluations, and they read summaries of CWP's end-of-semester WI faculty interviews. IRC members divided responsibility for interviewing selected WI faculty, TAs, and students, as well as the chair of the 1984 Task Force that established WAC at MU, Emerita Professor Winifred Horner. Finally, IRC members attended Campus Writing Board subcommittee and general meetings to observe this group's deliberative processes and to ask questions about WI policies and procedures.

CWP cooperated with IRC's review by (a) compiling a "blue book" of background material to familiarize them with the program; (b) drafting and revising survey instruments for IRC to send to the groups named above; (c) offering the services of our administrative assistant to keep minutes of their meetings; (d) and, most important, highlighting unresolved problems associated with WI teaching such as insufficient faculty incentives, difficult workloads, and an inadequate faculty reward system.

IRC's five-page, single-spaced narrative to the dean and provost found that, overall, the WAC program was "of high quality and should be continued as an integral component of the undergraduate curriculum." The committee presented its findings under five categories based on the MU audiences involved (WI faculty, TAs, students, administrators, and CWP staff) and offered 13 recommendations—both general and specific. Specific recommendations included requiring that TAs attend faculty workshops (and paying them for it); explaining the connections between English 20 and WI courses better; and reassessing the criteria for certifying WI courses to accommodate differing disciplines' discourse practices. General recommendations, due to their more open-ended and therefore less easily accomplished nature, included developing guidelines for increasing the value of teaching WI courses in raise, tenure, and promotion evaluations; exploring ways to reduce the workload of faculty teaching WI courses; and finding ways to improve the consistency of writing abilities of students completing different sections of first-year composition.

Consistent with the open and reciprocal operating procedures that I had worked to foster throughout the project, IRC asked us to review their report before they sent it to the provost and dean. It was this openness, and the sense that IRC was committed to enabling CWP, as opposed to disabling it, that contributed to the absence of threat in our project. And, despite the report's "recommendations" (which are not the intended product of fourth generation evaluation), the spirit in which IRC conveyed them was very much within Guba and Lincoln's call for "an agenda for negotiating claims, concerns, and issues that have been uncovered and not resolved."

For example, the context of IRC's entire report makes clear that their final recommendation—to develop guidelines for increasing the value of teaching WI courses in raise, tenure, and promotion evaluation—does not suggest that CWP had failed in its mission because this had not been accomplished; nor does IRC suggest that such guidelines be implemented by some specified deadline. Rather, the report reflects on larger institutional forces that inhibit such guidelines. By making the recommendation public, CWP now has a meaningful document to cite which validates our efforts toward making this change. Thus, IRC fulfilled Guba and Lincoln's goal to empower (a) the CWP to take an activist role on campus, (b) the faculty who may be uncertain about rewards for WI teaching, (c) departments to make specific commitments for rewarding WI teachers, and (d) administrators to acknowledge these commitments when departments forward raise, tenure, and promotion recommendations to campus-wide committees.

Another of Guba and Lincoln's principles—to educate, to open discourse based on added knowledge—was fulfilled when the journalism professor serving on IRC realized that in helping to conduct the review he had himself become educated about WAC. True to his journalistic instincts, he wrote about what he'd learned and his essay, "Overcoming Skepticism About Writing Across the Curriculum," appeared in *The Chronicle of Higher Education* (Weinberg).

STRAND TWO: WHAT THE CAMPUS WRITING PROGRAM STAFF DID

CWP's activities were as varied as IRC's. Thinking that a "thick description" would be a good place to start assessing the program, we began by systematically documenting and updating information on every possible aspect of CWP—information that hadn't always been organized or represented meaningfully. We sought to answer such administrative questions as: What WI courses were taught, when, and by whom? How many students enrolled in each one? Who attended faculty workshops, and why? Who had attended workshops, but not offered WI courses? How many students had been tutored? Who had served on the Campus Writing Board, and what had they gained from it? We also wanted answers to more complex and substantive questions such as: What kinds of writing are students doing in WI courses? How have faculty's teaching practices changed? What do students think of the WI requirement? and What difference has the program made on this campus? We tried to assemble, analyze, and then present data in ways that were meaningful to multiple audiences—ourselves, IRC, the campus writing board, the provost, the dean, and the WPA consultant–evaluators who would be conducting our external review. The process confirmed beliefs we had held but for which we lacked specific evidence. One such discovery was that faculty who had taught WI courses without having attended a workshop were those least likely to teach a repeat WI course. Another was that students were able to meet the WI requirement and still graduate on schedule. Another was that many faculty did not teach WI classes after having attended the three-day workshop because they taught only graduate classes (only undergraduates are subject to the WI requirement), yet they had chosen to attend anyway, believing the information beneficial to their graduate teaching. (Interestingly, one survey showed that the stipend faculty received for attending was positive factor for less than one third of the participants.)

CWP staff also adopted a more structured approach to our regular end-of-semester WI faculty interviews, as a means of better synthesizing responses than had been done in the past. These hour-long visits give faculty an opportunity to reflect on what worked well (and what didn't) in their WI courses. We notified faculty that the assessment project was in progress and foregrounded the interviews as a central feature. At the interview, in the faculty's office, we took special care to assure faculty that their responses would be accounted for in the self-study, that any information they shared would be confidential, and that only aggregate information would be presented in any reports. Our ten-question protocol was intended to be generative rather than closed; although we did not tape record the sessions, we took close notes. Question 1 was: "What do you think the overall goal of WI courses should be?" Of the 54 interviewees that semester, some form of "improving critical thinking" was given as the primary pedagogical goal for their use of writing in the course. The distant secondary goal was "teaching students to write in the discipline." Of the few who mentioned "improving student writing ability" as one of several course goals, all noted this as tangential to other, more far-reaching goals.

Toward the end of the project, CWP hosted a day-long "Retrospective" to which all faculty who had ever taught a WI course were invited. They participated in a structured exercise in which they reflected on their experiences and then offered recommendations about the program's future. Funded with an assessment grant from the Provost's office and facilitated by Pat Hutchings, director of the American Association of Higher Education's Teaching Initiative, this event paid stipends to attendees and produced a position paper in which faculty affirmed the value of WAC in their teaching. The position paper also demonstrated that, overwhelmingly, what faculty most wanted was university recognition for their WI teaching—in the form of reduced workloads, reduced class size, consideration for tenure and promotion, and salary increases. Other recommendations included: (a) increasing administrators' awareness of WI teaching, (b) ensuring overlap between the various new general education components (i.e., that cluster or capstone courses can also be WI), and (c) offering incentives to "repeat" WI teachers.

In addition to the thick description, the end-of-semester interviews, and the Retrospective, CWP staff also (a) collected papers and articles that faculty had delivered or published based on their WI teaching, (b) surveyed TAs who had worked with faculty in WI courses, and (c) transcribed students' responses to the open-ended questions on evaluation forms from 18 WI classes (one third of the WI classes taught that semester). All of this material was shared and reviewed with the IRC throughout the project.

Significantly, neither CWP staff nor IRC considered quantitatively measuring student writing improvement over the 5-year history of WI courses; nor did the provost, dean, or WPAs consultant–evaluators request such a measurement. For one thing, no baseline data had been kept. But more importantly, years of faculty workshops on writing, teaching, and learning had reinforced the notion that growth in writing is not demonstrated through standardized tests of writing or simple pre- and postwriting assessments. Moreover, MU's program transcends learning to write by including such goals as writing to learn, changing student and faculty attitudes toward writing, and enhancing the professional preparation of graduate students in the disciplines through their work with WI professors. We agreed that the multiple measures and methods our project was employing would be the best way to establish WAC's benefits to students and the university.

CWP's final task (or rather mine) at the end of the year was to actually "write" the self-study—in other words, to give sensible form to some 125 items comprising over 200 pages. The report consisted of (a) a three-page *abbreviated* table of contents, which categorized the items in 20 sections, (b) an eight-page *annotated* table of contents, which explained the various sections, summarized the analysis of each section, and posed questions we wanted the reviewers to focus on, and (c) 20 sections containing the collected data and extended analyses. The result was a genuinely collaborative document. IRC's report was the lead entry in this last part; remaining entries represented the combined work of both strands.

THE WPA CONSULTANT–EVALUATOR'S VISIT

The arrangements for the WPA portion of our project were made as collaboratively as had been the project to this point. The dean requested a list of potential reviewers from CWP and made the final selection in conjunction with us, IRC, and the director of WPA's consultant–evaluator service. Because of MU's mission and size, coupled with the scope of our general education reform, we all agreed that the external reviewers needed to be senior scholars from comprehensive universities if their report was to carry its weight with appropriately critical faculty on our campus. We were fortunate in securing Edward White, California State University–San Bernardino, then director of WPA's service, and Lynn Bloom, holder of the Aetna chair of writing at the University of Connecticut. Their national reputations in the profession and their having collaborated on numerous other reviews instilled confidence that the review would be well received.

The agenda for their 3-day visit was based on feedback from all the stakeholders. Meetings, interviews, meals, and receptions were scheduled that included the provost; the dean and his staff; CWP's director and staff; the Campus Writing Board, both as a whole and by sectors; IRC members; CWP's first director; WI faculty and students; representatives of the English Department; English 20 TAs; witing intensive TAs; CWP tutors; undergraduate deans and other administrators, plus anyone else who wanted to come. We advertised the review and various open meeting times so that virtually anyone who had an opinion could be heard. The openness and inclusiveness of the process contributed to the sense of trust and lack of apprehension that had accompanied the entire project. The external visit (intense and scheduled-to-the-minute though it was) was less a chore to endure than a learning opportunity to participate in.

Bloom and White's report was submitted exactly a year after the project started. Fourteen recommendations responded both to the questions we had posed and to issues they had identified. As with IRC's report, though, Bloom and White's recommendations were framed in ways that considered the context of our unique institutional realities. For example, the first, "Proceed to implement the second WI course" was qualified "with modifications" that included recertifying WI courses less frequently (we'd been doing it every semester), making WI course-approval criteria more flexible (our wording had been off-putting to those in the sciences), and encouraging even more than we had been the need for *voluntary* faculty participation. Another recommendation focused on improving the rewards and satisfactions of those teaching WI courses. Suggestions here included ensuring that faculty see WI teaching as valued by the institution, with the acknowledgement that the specifics for accomplishing this are "a matter of internal debate best resolved within schools and departments, perhaps even on a case-by-case basis"; maintaining TA support for WI faculty at the 20:1 ratio; and encouraging WI faculty to submit teaching portfolios in connection with annual merit reviews.

Perhaps the most surprising aspect of the report was the affirmation the campus received about the work we had been doing all along. Although we'd had a generalized sense that we'd been doing a good job with WAC, subjecting the program to the scrutiny of reviewers of Bloom and White's caliber and then reading "we make our recommendations in the context of an existing program of which any university could be proud, and which, in fact, could easily set the national standard for such programs" took many by surprise. Still, Bloom and White stressed during their visit that—as all compositionists know from teaching writing—the process is as important as the product. They suggested that their visit and report were ancillary to the process that MU had gone through in conducting the self-study. Having our assessment project formally "commissioned," though, validated it within the institutional community and gave us the opportunity to open doors, start conversations, ask questions, and get help that we otherwise might not have thought about.

OUTCOMES OF MU'S ASSESSMENT PROJECT

The outcomes of the project are numerous. Several of the changes we've made result from the continuous fine-tuning CWP does all the time, whereas others represent major shifts. It's difficult to differentiate between changes that would have occurred anyway from those we made as a result of the project, so ingrained is the project in our history. A partial list of results includes:

- MU implemented the second WI requirement for entering students in Fall 1993, the semester following the assessment. The Campus Writing Board amended the WI guidelines to accommodate writing assignments more appropriate to the natural and applied sciences, and it recertifies WI courses less often, though with safeguards built in to maintain the integrity of the process.
- We have become more proactive in seeking to improve the rewards and satisfaction of WI faculty. For example: We emphasize even more strongly the need for WI faculty to be voluntary, rather than "assigned" by departments. We offer stipends to faculty who repeat the faculty workshop as well as to first-time attendees. The Campus Writing Board has developed new guidelines for large-enrollment WI courses to ensure that departments are aware of faculty's increased responsibility. And we are studying—with the help of a WPA grant—the effects of WI teaching on pretenured faculty to determine whether this teaching has helped or hindered when going forward for tenure.
- We have strengthened TA training and TAs now receive stipends for attending workshops. Articulation between freshman composition and WI courses has been improved. CWP and the Department of English collaborate on A Guide to MU's Writing Requirements, a new publication for students and faculty.
- The Campus Writing Board strengthened its requirement that faculty participate in workshops before teaching their first WI course. We articulate CWP's mission to coincide with four of the University's central missions: undergraduate education, graduate education, faculty development, and research.

- General education and CWP faculty workshops are no longer scheduled simultaneously. Campus general education leaders refer to CWP as "successful, but still helping departments develop the second WI." Faculty continue to feel spread too thin, but one partial solution has been to urge departments to develop capstone courses (or cluster courses, or the sophomore seminar) that are also WI courses.
- As a result of new resources from MU administration (due in part to the positive review) we've been able to add three new full-time staff to assist with WI course development; increase the number of graduate TAs who assist with WI courses; increase TA stipends; upgrade computer equipment so that our tutors can tutor on-line; and move to larger, renovated space.
- Although it would be harder to document, I believe that our undertaking this project, which many would not have thought of as "assessment," has helped influence and ameliorate faculty attitudes toward assessment in general. MU's Assessment Task Force has successfully lobbied to replace a controversial and unpopular standardized test of general education, which included a poorly designed writing component, with assessment measures more appropriate to our campus. And, that group has become a standing committee with policy-making power.

CONCLUSION

We've made good progress integrating WAC into general education. The programs have come together well and ongoing assessment indicates that we're accomplishing what we intended with both. Most departments have developed the second level of WI courses that their majors need, and CWP is working with a few departments (mainly those with disproportionately large numbers of majors) to recruit sufficient volunteer faculty to offer the number of WI courses needed. WI course-development grants, funded jointly by the general education committee and CWP, are producing several new courses. One unexpected outcome of the project was MU's being cited as a university "that takes writing seriously" and CWP as one of few programs that has maintained an effective WI system in White's *Teaching and Assessing Writing* (pp. 161–164). Such citations help document the program's impact to administrators and off-campus sources. The university has used both this reference and the external report in response to Missouri's Coordinating Board of Higher Education calls for accountability and North Central Association's accrediting process. Admittedly, in doing the project some things "clicked" for us. Maybe the timing was "just right." Obviously not every project will produce the same results. And, we didn't answer *all* our questions. As Guba and Lincoln point out (and Bloom and White's report noted), assessment is a continuous process. Nonetheless, the self-study and external review process was a worthwhile undertaking, one that we would recommend to other WAC programs, especially if done within the social constructivist framework and using flexible practical guidelines. Without doubt, this assessment project called attention to WAC and solidified its place in MU's institutional culture even more fully.

REFERENCES

Guba, E. G., & Lincoln, Y. S. (1989). *Fourth generation evaluation*. Newbury Park, CA: Sage.

Townsend, M. A. (1991). Instituting changes in curriculum and teaching style in liberal arts programs: a study of nineteen Ford Foundation projects (Doctoral dissertation, Arizona State University, 1991). *Dissertation Abstracts International, 52,* 06A. (University Microfilms No. 91-34898)

White, E. M. (1994). *Teaching and assessing writing* (2nd ed., pp. 161–164). San Francisco: Jossey-Bass.

Weinberg, S. (June 16, 1993). Overcoming skepticism about writing across the curriculum. *The Chronicle of Higher Education*, B2–B3.

Chapter 11

.

Adventures in the WAC Assessment Trade: Reconsidering the Link Between Research and Consultation

Raymond Smith

Christine Farris

The studies we have conducted to assess WAC over the last 8 years at two large universities have raised a question about the researcher–subject relationship: Whose needs drive the inquiry—those of WAC programs, composition specialists, or faculty members teaching writing-intensive courses?

The observation that the writing-across-the-curriculum (WAC) "movement" has come in waves or phases has now achieved the status of trope (McLeod, 1989; Bazerman, 1991). During the first stage, many colleges and universities reformed curricula in order to improve students' sentence-level expression, to resuscitate the notion of a traditional liberal education at universities given over to credentialing, to promote the mental agility of students moving from discipline to discipline through the baccalaureate, and to engender "critical thinking," as rather broadly defined. These reforms came at considerable expense of effort and finances, often with disciplinary writing courses established within the curriculum and buttressed by institutional structures. After the initial struggles and successes of these new WAC reforms, however, there often came a period of contraction of university budgets and a concomitant (and perhaps welcome) demand for accountability that most readers of this text are familiar with—or will come to know. Not surprisingly, then, many colleges and universities launched assessment initiatives (occasionally at the request of accrediting agencies) that, though not devoted exclusively to examining the efficacy of WAC, nevertheless held WAC programs up to the light. Our involvement in one such institutionally motivated evaluation, dedicated to gauging so-called "student outcomes" relevant to WAC at the University of Missouri-Columbia, has led the

Campuswide Writing Program at Indiana University (IU), Bloomington—admittedly in a different institutional context—to attempt a more instructor-centered form of evaluation. These attempts, we maintain, will have immediate and long-lasting consequences for pedagogy on our campus and are born of our questions about the researcher–subject relationship; specifically, whose needs drive the inquiry: those of WAC programs, composition specialists, or faculty members teaching writing-intensive (WI) courses?

INSTITUTIONAL CONTEXTS

The Campus Writing Program at University of Missouri-Columbia, as Martha Townsend asserts in the previous chapter, is one of the more successful WAC programs at a large research institution. The creation of the program in 1985, like that of many others, was a result of the findings of a task force (chaired by Winifred B. Horner) charged by administrators with "improving student writing." Under the leadership of its first director, Douglas Hunt, and with significant institutional support, including the guidance of a hard-working faculty writing board, the program was offering within 3 years a number of courses sufficient to permit most undergraduates to graduate with the newly required "writing-intensive" course. Two such courses are now required.

Our study at Missouri, conducted from 1988 to 1989, was motivated mainly by the ideology of a WAC program with control over which courses would be approved as writing-intensive (WI) and, in some cases, which would receive additional financial support for writing instruction. At Missouri, faculty designed their own WI courses following the WAC program's guidelines and submitted their applications to the program's board, composed of faculty from many disciplines. The board, in disciplinary subcommittees, approved applications and reapplications. WAC program personnel functioned as agents, informing applicants of the committee's concerns and working closely with them on WI course designs that might better meet program guidelines or disciplinary needs. For classes over a certain size, funding for TA support was provided.

Our study of this program and larger matters relevant to WAC was in fact a response to a call for a standardized writing assessment of graduating seniors. We offered instead to investigate disciplinary and classroom contexts in which WI courses were taught, not just to combat value-added assessment, but also to pursue some of our own questions more formally. Faculty, writing lab tutors, and employers of graduates frequently told us that WI courses were indeed improving writing and critical thinking skills. These were pleasing reports, but they provided us with merely anecdotal and impressionistic evidence of the efficacy of WI courses. Our study was an attempt to gather data that would allow us to speak with more certainty about what classroom practices and assignment designs stretch the critical thinking of students. We were particularly interested in investigating the claim that the WAC movement frequently makes for writing in the disciplines (and one we had made in workshops)—that the incorporation of writing enables and strengthens independent, critical thinking in discipline-specific courses. As in other WAC programs, our intent had been to replace what Freire calls the "banking model" of education in which students passively receive, record, and return instructors' deposits of knowledge. Presumably, writing disrupts that conventional lecture–test–lecture pattern.

Guided by work in cognition and critical thinking, our program viewed WI courses not just as an obligation to demand a requisite number of pages and revisions, but also as an opportunity to encourage in students intellectual inquiry that cannot be engendered through the passive learning of conventional courses. Like other WAC advocates (Herrington), in workshops and consultations, we drew on Benjamin Bloom's (1956) taxonomy—recall, comprehension, analysis, synthesis, and evaluation—to get faculty to yoke assigned writing to the aims they have for student learning in their courses. We also made use of William Perry's (1970) scheme to encourage faculty to provide occasions for students to move beyond the dependence on authority and right–wrong dualisms that they presumably brought with them to college toward a tolerance for complexity and multiple perspectives.

Instructors who might once have provided "right answers" which students returned to them undamaged on multiple-choice exams were encouraged to design writing assignments that asked students to problematize issues, make connections between disciplinary knowledge and their own experience, weigh evidence, and reach informed and reasoned positions or interpretations. We therefore wanted to know if what faculty practiced after attending workshops and having their courses certified WI had anything to do with what we preached.

In our first study, we combined ethnographic "thick description" of classroom practices in introductory (100 to 200 level) WI courses in journalism, art appreciation, and human and family development with two other lines of investigation: Interviews with a sample of students before and after they took a WI course and ratings of those students' papers written for the course. Both the interview with students and their papers were rated on scales of critical thinking we derived from the intellectual development scale of William Perry (1970) and later the Reflective Judgment schema of Kitchener, King, Wood, and Davison (1987). We attempted to account for marked differences in base level critical thinking (as established in the interviews) and demonstrated critical thinking (as shown by the papers) through the thick description of the full context in which the WI courses were taught.

Discrepancies between the critical thinking that students seemed capa-

ble of in the interviews and their performance on the papers written for class
were the result for the most part of a failure to resolve instructors' two conflicting expectations of the use of writing: that students' personal responses
and experiences be validated and that they master basic disciplinary principles and conventions. Assignments were often not well integrated with the
purposes for the course and with the teaching strategies professors had
retained from years past—before writing was introduced. More often than
not, students' critical thinking was rated lower on the papers than in the
interviews. Students capable in interviews of recognizing that knowledge is a
construct and that theories are tools or lenses, not mirrors of reality, were
often unable to demonstrate that ability while writing papers that frequently demanded that they uncritically recall and reproduce course materials.

Particularly in the art appreciation course, students tended to resort to
either cut-and-pasted informational lecture notes on the one hand or idiosyncratic and unsupported assertions on the other. The thick description of
class meetings and teaching assistant (TA) grading sessions helped explain
the discrepancy by revealing the ways in which writing functioned as the
principal site of conflict in the instructor's goals. One goal was that students
be made aware of the possibility of multiple and individualistic responses to
works of art. In lecture, students were encouraged to share "how the work
made them feel." However, even in assignments that invited some personal
connections—for instance, "Make an argument to a roommate or relative
about the merits of a particular work of art or movement"—the art professor eclipsed students' fashioning a response into supported analysis by
reminding them to "actually write to me or your TA, someone knowledgeable in the field... using your class notes and textbook to cover the concepts
we have gone over in class so far." The writing was not helping students
move beyond the passive reception and regurgitation of knowledge held by
experts. At this point in the evolution of the course, writing was still an act
that occurred after learning had happened.

Like the art appreciation professor, the professor teaching the human
and family development course also saw value in having students make personal connections to the course material. He was somewhat more successful, however, in making students' personal experiences and beliefs a
meaningful context for applying and testing social theory. Nevertheless, ratings of papers, along with the thick description of class meetings, revealed a
subjective–objective split more than a developmental or dialectical process at
work in the course. The first two assignments required students to write
descriptive and narrative papers on gender and divorce. Because TA graders
stressed specific concrete detail, many students tended not to take a generalized or abstract approach to the topic, sticking with rich detail even to the
point of inventing fictional narratives. Although the later application-of-the-
ory-to-experience assignment was, on balance, a good one for stretching crit-

ical thinking and enhancing learning, the early emphasis on detail seemed to interfere with some students' ability later in the course to use theories and course concepts as lenses to interpret and illuminate their personal experience, in short, to engage in analysis and not description.

In the mass media course, however, where the discrepancy between interviews and papers was not as great, our field work nevertheless let us examine more closely our own complicity in tinkering with courses on our terms—something that was more difficult to recognize in art appreciation where there was clearly much pedagogical retooling that needed to be done. We were perhaps at first disappointed that the journalism professor assigned papers in which students were to report objectively on two sides of an issue and that his grading criteria focused on style, correctness, and proper citation of sources. We had hoped that papers on media ethics would encourage students to reach committed positions of their own. Journalism, after all, faces much controversy and ethical quandary about its responsibilities to bring "truth" to a democratic society. But journalism is also a set of writing skills and rhetorical strategies a professional must master to be successful and reach an audience. Although it at first appeared that the course might be plagued by a split similar to that evident in art appreciation and human and family development, the professor's approach to students' facing "ill-formed problems" and ethical dilemmas was in keeping with journalism's disciplinary conventions. Assignments asked that students objectively address two sides of an issue in the field rather than resorting to "what you think." We came to understand the professor's approach to ethical analysis (and to critical thinking) not as a move toward an individual committed position but a well-documented presentation of two sides of an issue by a technician.

We were also beginning to understand that we had been perhaps too concerned with our own agenda and not that of our colleagues. Admittedly, in the art appreciation course, we were also expecting the encouragement of original analyses and interpretations of works of art. Later, we came to take some of the responsibility for perhaps modeling and encouraging types of assignments that finally were not in keeping with instructors' deep-seated disciplinary and course goals for their students. The journalism professor was preparing his students to report on issues fairly and to check and cite their sources objectively and scrupulously. Art appreciation courses aim to introduce students to particular tools for heightened but amateur appreciation.

It would be several years before we would take our cue from what our fieldwork showed us rather than from what we learned from our ratings of critical thinking so as to go about our inquiry more holistically, coming to understand instructors, their courses, and their students' writing as located in "cultures" to be understood on their own terms. This is not to say that we were wrong in wanting to know if students who appeared to be "critical thinkers" in person were encouraged to write critically in their WI courses.

In retrospect, however, there may have been some bad faith at work. With WAC as our banner and bully pulpit, what we really wanted to know was whether faculty in other disciplines were using writing to retool their courses in the ways *we* thought were pedagogically sound. Further, we were tied in part to measures designed to assess students, not particular pedagogies or programs.

"Critical thinking," while a useful heuristic for getting faculty in workshops or consultations to think about what they would like to see more of and less of in their students' performances, could not, when used as a rating schema, contain or explain why a significant number of students venture a no-risk interpretation of a painting very like the one offered in lecture, or apply Erikson's theories of behavior to a childhood memory in predictable ways. Only time spent in the lived culture of the course, the interpretive community of the classroom, could tell us that. Although the rating schema provided us with reliable benchmarks for assessing student intellectual development, fieldwork told us more about what students must negotiate when faced, not just with the blank page and their own quandaries, but with an instructor's course goals, epistemological and ideological attitudes toward the course content, assignments, pep talks about writing, and red pen.

We were able on a daily basis to see how instructors tie writing to inquiry and course goals in the ways they assign it, share it, and evaluate it. We learned how students, in writing their papers, responded to the assumptions of the discipline and the beliefs and practices of their instructors. Finally, we concluded that writing assignments may foster skills or demand rhetorical moves different from those intended and desired by the WAC program or even articulated to us by WI instructors. At the time, still within the terms of the intellectual and ethical development schemes, we were able to conclude that most students' writing did not evidence critical thinking. The reasons why it did not were finally explained for us by the rhetoric of the classroom, by the ways that knowledge was negotiated, written about, and valued in the course. We also concluded that any investigation into the actual ways in which writing might enhance critical thinking must take into consideration more aspects of the disciplinary culture than students' written products or even an instructor's self-report on how writing functions in his or her discipline or how it will function in his or her courses. And, finally we have to question any claims for critical thinking in college that do not take into consideration the actual classroom cultures where students, teachers, ideology, and disciplinary norms intersect.

In the meantime, however, the findings proved valuable in ongoing consultation with the WI faculty involved in the study who wished to reapply for WI status. All three professors, with the help of the WAC program staff, devoted more time to developing assignments and assignment-specific criteria for papers that were tied to particular course goals, tightening the connection between writing and learning in their courses. Efforts were also made to connect personal experience and content knowledge more consistently in writing and in other aspects of the courses.

Although these were changes in their courses instructors were willing to make, the impetus was in part how to better meet WI guidelines and remain "worthy." What if instructors using writing both in WI courses and non-WI courses generated the research questions out of their own concerns? What if they determined more of the agenda and the WAC staff contributed writing expertise which would only be enhanced by further time spent "in the field"—theirs, not ours? Finally, what we sought was a closer connection between consulting and "research" with faculty sharing in the inquiry. Ethnographic fieldwork can do more in WAC programs than just reveal contradictions or construct a portrait of the "other." There is change that comes about—should come about—in the participant–observer as well.

These were conclusions that we took some time to reach, however. Like most WAC advocates, we saw ourselves as curricular reformers, a view ratified from the birth of the program by our colleagues and the administration, in the person of an energetic Dean of our College of Arts and Science, Milton Glick (1988). And there was, after all, a campuswide writing requirement to get off the ground and then maintain by recruiting additional faculty and employing thoughtful assessment practices. But the invocation—or even enforcement—of these writing guidelines is hardly unproblematic, and can, in fact, no matter how carefully crafted the guidelines, assume a Grand Unified Theory of Writing that fails to accommodate certain disciplinary differences or, at worst, flouts certain academic freedoms.

At some universities the WI requirement reflects (or misrepresents) a unanimity of faculty attitudes toward undergraduate writing and the reasons for requiring it. If, for example, one must in following WI guidelines invite students to write essays that treat issues on which reasonable people could disagree, then one is applying certain tenets of a traditional liberal education explicitly defended by Cardinal Newman and William G. Perry, Jr. If, to cite a more prevalent example, one must in following WI guidelines insist that students revise their essays, then one is perhaps of necessity foregrounding the emphasis of the past two decades or so on process in composition studies.

In short, WI guidelines, as enforced by WAC consultants or faculty committees, often assume and enforce certain curricular changes, changes that are almost certainly improvements on the lecture–test–lecture pedagogical patterns so often found at large research universities, but changes that for reasons political and pedagogical demand examination—thus the necessity of the assessment of WAC programs. Just what that assessment means, of course, is the question on which this volume is based. As one can infer from our description of our early efforts, there is often considerable local pressure to determine assessment—from administrators who demand gauges of the efficacy of what might be expensive programs and from faculty and from WAC consultants who are interested in promoting reflective practice. Typically, however, the efficacy of a program is determined solely by what have come to be known rather recently as "student outcomes," or the performance of students within these WI classes. We want to suggest here alternative means of assessment that have evolved, both in our own original tentative attempts at WAC assessment at Missouri and at IU, that is, two different, complementary, and faculty-centered strategies for measuring the effects of these courses and the programs that promote them.

TWO NEW STRATEGIES FOR WAC ASSESSMENT

One of the earliest WI courses we encountered at IU was a large class, enrolling approximately 175 students, entitled "The Legal Environment of Business," taught by an exceedingly well-regarded colleague. Business Law must be taken by all students aspiring to a degree in business; there is no major in business law, however. A service course, then, Business Law is taken with various degrees of enthusiasm by undergraduates, who could choose from various sections in a given semester. The section in question was the only one that demanded significant writing—4 short papers totaling about 2,000 words—and the instructor had been teaching the course in essentially the same fashion for some years, though recently our program had provided her with four graders. There is no formal WI requirement in IU's School of Business—though there is such a requirement in the College of Arts and Sciences. Nevertheless, the instructor, winner of more than one teaching award (and, not incidentally, a lawyer), thought that asking her students to do the types of writing and thinking demanded in legal briefs was essential to the way she wanted to teach the course. Not surprisingly, however, considering the workload, the instructor had begun to question the benefits of employing writing in teaching the course and evaluating the work of her students. She wondered about the costs (for her) and benefits (for her students) of offering the course in this incarnation. Though she had rather firm notions of the types of questions she wanted to ask of our course, she had little expertise in assessment methods. She came to the Writing Program. Her questions, in no particular order, were:

- Did my students' sentence-level proficiency improve over the course of the semester?
- Would a lay reader agree that my students' essays grew increasingly persuasive over the semester?

- Would an expert audience agree that over the semester my students demonstrated increasing sophistication in their application of the law and their use of certain legal writing conventions?
- Would both an expert and a lay audience agree that in revision my students' essays grew increasingly persuasive and that my students demonstrated more sophistication in their application of the law and in their use of certain legal writing conventions?

It should be emphasized here that these were the instructor's questions, not necessarily the ones that we might have chosen. And though these questions might seem at first glance only tangentially related, they revealed what we came to recognize as an enviably coherent pedagogy with its roots in two traditions sometimes at odds.

In consultations, the instructor had revealed that her overriding concern in the course was nudging her students toward a general understanding that legal thinking (and thus legal writing) was nonalgorithmic. There were at times no correct answers. Although certain protocols certainly exist in both legal thinking and writing (we are reluctant to make the distinction), by definition and in practice, legal rhetoric involves contending perspectives and sloppy human problems. At times during the semester, the course demanded a type of dialectic and critical thinking that one would not have been surprised to find in a curriculum dominated by Great Books, and the instructor quite self-consciously placed herself within this tradition. Her students were, she maintained, writing to learn and to develop a mental agility as they established their own opinions in light of those of experts. Surely a lay reader from English, say, would be able to help her determine whether or not her students were in fact more "agile" in this respect at the end of the semester than at the beginning?

At the same time, however, the course was being offered through a professional school. Although professional practice and the liberal arts are hardly irreconcilable, the instructor understandably felt some obligation to have her sophomore students write documents that judges would not be alarmed to find on their desks. Grammatical, mechanical, and orthographic errors in this "real world" setting would be found to be intolerable and perhaps even contemptuous of the discipline and the high seriousness of its concerns; consequently, there were significant penalties for these types of errors in the course. Did her students take her marginal admonitions and those of her graders (whom we had trained to read and mark with her criteria firmly in mind) to heart and reduce the number of errors over the semester?

Her other concerns—having to do with the efficacy of writing in improving her students' command of her subject and its disciplinary conventions and the benefits of demanding revision in an attempt to improve both their command of her subject and their abilities to deal with texts—were concerns closer to our own, for bureaucratic and disciplinary reasons. IU's writing program, in fact, is founded on the premise that, for numerous reasons, classes in which students write and revise in response to criticism are superior to classes that rely on other, perhaps more convenient, means of teaching and evaluating. So in this instance the instructor's concerns were most certainly our own: Did writing and revision "work" in this course, which was expensive in all senses of the word?

We addressed the four questions above in three ways that were sometimes necessarily unsophisticated because of the resources available to us: (a) Relying on studies by Connors and Lunsford (1988), Hairston (1981), and Williams (1981), we constructed a list of "status marker" sentence-level errors and read, blind, 25% of the essays (drafts and revisions) submitted for the course, counting those errors; (b) We also convened a small group of experienced teachers of English composition and asked them to rate drafts and revisions on the basis of certain criteria, including, most importantly, their overall impressions of the persuasiveness of these essays and (c) Finally, we compared the grades awarded on drafts to the grades awarded on revisions over the course of the semester—in short, we assumed that the grades for the course, awarded as they were by experienced graders–law students trained by the instructor, represented the opinions of an expert audience. These graders–law students were, of course, in grading revisions privy to the grades awarded on first drafts. Writing Program staff helped train the graders by providing "norming" sessions for each assignment, during which differences in grading and commentary on instructor-selected benchmark papers were negotiated and reduced.

The results can be summarized by saying simply that students' prose improved by virtually anyone's estimation over the semester or between initial submission and revision (Kurz & Smith, 1994). The number of sentence-level errors declined markedly over the semester and between drafts; revisions of a given assignment received higher rankings than earlier drafts from our compositionists; the grades awarded for revisions of a given assignment were higher than those awarded for earlier drafts of the same essays. More important than these results, however, was that the project served as a reminder: We were working for our business law colleague. In negotiating the nature of this research with the instructor–client, we came to conclusions perhaps unavailable to us in another university context. The class belonged to the instructor and her students; no other university entity had a proprietary interest in The Legal Environment of Business. We also came to realize the importance of considerations rarely taken into account in judging the effects and successes of WAC programs: (a) The educational epistemology of the instructor must be taken fully into account in course design, regardless of the dictates of WI guidelines or the differences that may exist between the pedagogies of the faculty member and the WAC consultants who work with him or her; (and b) Faculty "retention," that is, the likelihood that faculty members will persist in using writing to teach their courses, depends as heavily on the satisfaction of the faculty members as on any measure of student outcomes—though that satisfaction may be derived in part from the perception of those student outcomes.

As a practical matter, what has come out of our study of this course is a new, hybrid model of WAC assessment at IU. Our earliest efforts at Missouri, using Perry-style scales of intellectual and ethical development, were to compare student performance in focused interviews and in essays produced while they were enrolled in WI courses. We then moved to accounting for differences in these two modes of performance through an examination of classroom practice by means of ethnographic thick description. In both instances, of course, the emphasis was on student performance. We have since come to believe that new emphasis should be placed on the educational epistemology of WI instructors as expressed in Perry-style interviews ("expressed" pedagogy) against a backdrop of ethnographic descriptions of classroom practices and grader training ("revealed" pedagogy). Though considerable ink has been spilt on student performance as it pertains to writing and certainly on classroom practice as it relates to WAC or writing to learn, relatively little is known about the epistemological assumptions of those instructors who choose or, alternatively, reject the promise of curricular reform through using writing to teach in their corner of the academy.

Our new method, then, is to conduct Perry-style interviews of WI faculty and to observe their teaching while writing ethnographies of the culture that each class represents. In the process, we hope to be able to make useful generalizations in answer to two questions of central importance to our efforts as WAC consultants and to the long-term success of our program: What types of instructors are most likely to use writing successfully in their classes, and in what curricular contexts are these instructors most likely to use writing, by their own criteria, most successfully? This emphasis on gauging instructor satisfaction seems to us essential at the most pragmatic level. Finally, years after the WAC workshop revival meeting has left town, the faculty member is alone in the classroom or with a stack of papers, and with few psychic and palpable rewards for taking on what is invariably more work and frequently a more valuable and rigorous pedagogy—for students *and* teachers.

REFERENCES

Bazerman, C. (1991). The second stage in writing across the curriculum. *College English, 53,* 209–212.

Bloom, B. S. (Ed.) (1956). *Taxonomy of educational objectives. Vol. 1: Cognitive domain.* New York: McKay.

Connors, R., & Lunsford, A. (1988). Frequency of formal errors in current college writing, or ma and pa kettle do research. *College Composition and Communication, 39,* 395–409.

Farris, C., Wood, P., Smith, R., & Hunt, D. (1990). *Final report on critical thinking in writing intensive courses.* University of Missouri-Columbia, Office of the Provost.

Freire, P. (1970). *Pedagogy of the oppressed.* New York: Herder.

Glick, M. D. (1988, Spring). Writing across the curriculum: A dean's perspective. *WPA: Writing Program Administration, 11,* 53–57.

Hairston, M. (1981). Not all errors are created equal: Nonacademic readers in the professions respond to lapses in usage. *College Composition and Communication, 43,* 794–806.

Herrington, A. (1981). Writing to learn: Writing across the disciplines. *College English, 43,* 379–387.

Kitchener, K. S., King, P. M., Wood, P. K., & Davison, M. L. (1987). Sequentiality and consistency in the development of reflective judgment: A six-year longitudinal study. *Journal of Applied Developmental Psychology, 10,* 73–95.

Kurz, L., & Smith, R. (1994). *An assessment of student writing in L201.* Indiana University, Campuswide Writing Program.

McLeod, S. H. (1989). Writing across the curriculum: The second stage, and beyond. *College Composition and Communication, 40,* 337–343.

Perry, W. J., Jr. (1970). *Forms of intellectual and ethical development in the college years: A scheme.* New York: Holt.

Williams, J. (1981). The phenomenology of error. *College Composition and Communication, 32,* 152–168.

Chapter 12

·

Research and WAC Evaluation: An In-Progress Reflection

Paul Prior
Gail E. Hawisher
Sibylle Gruber
Nicole MacLaughlin

Writing across the curriculum (WAC), like most educational movements, is an umbrella label under which a wide variety of particular historically realized manifestations co-exist. This article discusses one program's evolving evaluation practices and our reflective understandings of those practices. We believe it is important to situate this discussion carefully in the particular historical contexts of our project, much as we believe it is useful to provide details of our research. The WAC Program at the University of Illinois, Urbana-Champaign, emerged from an institutional reevaluation begun in 1989 of undergraduate general education requirements. The first reform enacted by the General Education Board was a second composition requirement (Comp II), preferably fulfilled by taking a writing-intensive course in the major rather than through courses offered by the classical providers of writing instruction (mainly English and Speech Communication). To support this requirement, the university established an independent Center for Writing Studies (CWS) with three missions: (a) leadership in developing a WAC Program for faculty and teaching assistants (TAs); (b) provision of individual tutoring for students through a much expanded writing center (the Writers' Workshop); and (c) development of a cross-disciplinary graduate specialization in Writing Studies to support the first two missions.

This institutional history intersects with our own biographies in central ways. The establishment of the CWS led to the hiring of two of the coauthors (Gail Hawisher in 1990 as the Director of the Center/Associate Professor of English and Paul Prior in 1992 as the Director of Graduate Student WAC Programs/Assistant Professor of English). The graduate specialization attracted the other two co-authors (Sibylle Gruber as a doctoral student working on a dissertation that looks at the intersection of ethnicity, gender, writing, and technology, and Nicole MacLaughlin as one of the first cohort of Writing Studies students admitted to the Department of English in 1992). The Comp II requirement went into effect for the first-year class of 1991 (5,076 students who started graduating in 1995). The Center offered its first WAC seminars (one for faculty and one for graduate students) in May 1991. (These first seminars were led by Gail Hawisher and Michael Pemberton, who was also hired in 1990 as Associate Director of CWS/Director of the Writers' Workshop/Assistant Professor of English.) Prompted both by our own desire to evaluate and study the implementation of WAC activities and by an upcoming institutional review of the Center's work, we began to develop and pursue a research agenda in the 1993–1994 school year. It was at the end of that year that Gail and Paul presented some initial reflections at the CCCC Think-Tank on WAC evaluation. Since that session, our research activities have intensified, and our reflections on this process have continued. This article describes our in-progress evaluation of the Center's first mission— leadership in developing the WAC program for faculty and TAs at the University of Illinois, Urbana-Champaign—focusing particularly on how we have come to define and undertake our research activities.

THE RHETORIC OF EVALUATION/THE EVALUATION OF RHETORIC

When we began discussing program evaluation, we knew that we were entering unfamiliar territory. Evaluation would be a challenging mode of research for us in that although there is an established research literature on evaluation, none of us were particularly versed in its methods. As a category, then, evaluation seemed a mode of research not defined by the usual dimensions— not marked by a particular methodological orientation, disciplinary affiliation, or object of study. For us, evaluation could best be understood as a category defined in terms of the contexts of research: the goals that initiate the research, its projected use, and consequences. By their explicit connections to institutional decision making, evaluation research activities seemed to call attention to their own rhetorical situatedness, drawing even those researchers with strong positivistic leanings into questions of purposes, interests, audiences, and uses of the research. Another distinguishing characteristic proposed for evaluation is that it has stakeholders (interested parties whose futures may be affected by the research). Current reflections on research (e.g., Eisner & Peshkin, 1990; Haraway, 1991; Harding, 1991; Lather, 1991; Rosaldo, 1986) suggest, of course, that all research has stakeholders.[1] These were some of the thoughts we had as we began to consider why and how we should be involved in program evaluation.

To help us think through these issues as they related to our research, we generated a set of specific questions to help us identify the multiple institutional contexts for such research:

- What goals should guide our research?
- What activities are being assessed?
- Who is doing the assessment and who is being assessed?
- What audiences might this research address?
- What research strategies and resources are available to pursue these goals?
- How can we read our research data with different readers and goals in mind?
- How can we articulate relationships among goals, activities, audiences, resources, and research strategies?

As students of writing and rhetoric, we were comfortable with these questions. Focusing on purpose, audience, ethos, and means, we were working in effect to identify the rhetorical situations within which our research would be planned, conducted, written, and read. When we turned from institutional contexts to the object of study itself—the intersection of writing, learning, and disciplinarity—we again were on familiar ground. More than a decade of studies of writing in school, discipline, and workplace settings has provided us with rich conceptual and methodological resources for thinking through and undertaking a study of WAC implementation in a university setting. Thus, as we looked more closely at the unfamiliar territory of program evaluation, we found ourselves primarily in well-known territory: We recognized that we were situated in particular rhetorical, institutional, and material contexts, considering how to conduct research on writing.[2]

Within the dynamic confluence of the rhetorical situations of the research and the situated rhetorics of classroom writing, we were able to define four key contexts or domains of action (intersections of goals, objects of study, audiences, and available research strategies) that would motivate and shape our evaluation research:

---

[1] To take a well-known example, when longitudinal (basic) research on heart disease excluded women *a priori* from the subject pool, it is difficult to imagine a case with more stakeholders or more at stake.

[2] Our sense is that there are not hard boundaries between evaluation and basic research: All research is sociohistorically situated and interested. Thus, the questions that have come to be routine in evaluation research are increasingly being recognized as ones that also need to be asked in even the most scientific domains (see, e.g., Harding, 1991).

- WAC as an administrative and institutional enterprise
- WAC as a set of instructional activities and practices
- WAC as a set of student experiences with writing and the consequent learning
- WAC as a collective, cross-curricular university enterprise

First, WAC is an administrative and institutional enterprise subject to institutional review. It involves issues of funding, resource allocation, and curricular policy. In this domain, we see ourselves in the role of responsible advocates, working to participate actively in the review of our program. We first conceived of our audiences in local institutional terms (department heads, fellow faculty on key committees, deans, and the central administration of the university—chancellor, vice-chancellor, etc.).[3] Constructing busy administrative readers out of our experience, we asked what research questions and strategies would best address that audience. We thought first of broad-based quantitative measures to describe and evaluate the impact of the WAC program: descriptive statistics of the services provided to faculty and others, questionnaires that report on WAC seminar participants' satisfaction with WAC programs and implementation of WAC into disciplinary courses, and summary data connecting our WAC program to the development and implementation of writing intensive courses. However, we also imagined the value of using short cases, interview comments, and documents to give voice and substance to the quantitative data. In this domain, we envision products that mix quantitative and anecdotal information— essentially a multimodal approach.

Second, our WAC program (through workshops, consultation, and other activities) aims to promote a set of instructional practices across the curriculum (in both Comp II and other classes).[4] The central question is transmission—what kinds of linkages we find between the practices we promote in our WAC seminars and the instructional practices and beliefs imple-

---

[3] Although local administrators and faculty involved in governance are clearly a key audience, other participants in the Think-Tank discussion at the 1994 CCCC helped us see the broader public audiences (legislators, parents, students, the public) who also have a voice in setting institutional priorities and policies. We will later note one way we are working to address these audiences.

[4] We do not believe that the addition of a second required composition course alone can transform the overall educational experiences and outcomes of undergraduate students. What we are working for is a long-term, broader change in the culture of teaching and learning. Thus, we hope and expect that WAC activities and perspectives will not be limited to Comp II courses. We rely on faculty members and TAs working together in particular departments to change the institutional and instructional climates in small, but nevertheless important, ways. Eventually, these small shifts in practices and attitudes may effect, if not a sea change, at least a significant qualitative transformation of the undergraduate experience.

mented in courses. Given our growing understanding of the complexities of classroom environments and the literate activities found there (e.g., Casanave, 1995; Chin, 1994; Doheny-Farina, 1989; Herrington, 1985, 1988, 1992a; Nelson, 1990; Prior, 1991, 1994; Walvoord & McCarthy, 1990), the information required to study WAC implementation needs to be detailed and qualitative. Task labels are not adequate. We cannot simply ask whether instructors are "using" a WAC activity—say quick writes or peer groups or a structured process of drafting-response-revision—but, as Christine Farris and Raymond Smith demonstrate in the previous chapter, we must also explore how instructors are actually implementing those activities, why they are using them, and what consequences the activities are having.[5]

Several potential audiences exist for this information. Administrative and public audiences evaluating the Center's effectiveness (those of the first domain) would certainly have an interest in documenting transmission and perhaps even in anecdotal accounts of particular applications. We in the Center can use such information to assess and revise materials, methods, and strategies for the WAC program; to identify materials and practices we might present in future WAC seminars (e.g., examples of assignments with a strong emphasis on process); and to locate instructors that we might invite to discuss their use of WAC activities in those seminars. Instructors participating in future seminars stand as another potential audience for materials, examples, or presentations. Finally, detailed information on uses of WAC in classrooms fits well with current interests on writing in the disciplines, opening up the possibility of scholarly publication (cf. Herrington, 1988, 1992a; Walvoord & McCarthy, 1990). Our own potential roles (advocates, reflective practitioners, seminar leaders, WAC researchers) mirror these audiences. The products of research in this domain could, therefore, be quite diverse: quantitative summaries of coded data from interviews (e.g., number of interviewees whose course[s] clearly involved a structured writing process), detailed qualitative summaries of a particular writing task, changes in WAC seminar activities or materials, published research reports, invitations to instructors to present at a future WAC seminar, and so on.

The question of consequences for instruction leads to the third domain of action: student experiences with writing and their consequent learning. Ultimately, our work with instructors is designed to enhance students'

---

[5] Doyle (1983) defines academic tasks in terms of the products students produce, the operations they employ, and the resources available. He also stresses that idealized notions of the tasks are inadequate because "academic work is transformed fundamentally when it is placed in the complex social system of a classroom" (p. 185). The point here is that a writing task labeled as say, a microtheme, could vary not only in its social contextualization, but also in terms of the basic products, operations, and resources involved.

learning, particularly their development of needed or desired literate practices. In this context, it is necessary but not sufficient to document changes in instruction; information on student experiences and outcomes must also be generated. When we consider student outcomes, we find ourselves facing a particularly thorny set of rhetorical, theoretical, and methodological issues. The set of audiences and roles match well with those of the second domain; however, dominant definitions of writing that we see as radically reductive place us in the difficult role of working against powerful commonplaces. Writing is often understood primarily as transcription (Brodkey, 1987; Witte, 1985), attenuating severely an understanding of the processes that come into play when writing. Moreover, as Kaufer and Young (1993) have pointed out, writing is still often viewed—particularly in scientific and technical fields—as a generic language skill, sharply distinguished from content (a representation they trace back to the rhetoric of Ramus). In contrast, we see writing as a complexly situated literate activity that involves reading and writing, speaking and listening, observing and acting, knowing and learning with particular semiotic and material tools in particular sites. With this understanding of writing as an ensemble of situated practices, we want to avoid reductive, pre-post testing schemes for assessing "generic" student writing. However, when we imagine richer, more qualitative descriptions of students' writing, we quickly run not only into the wall of limited resources (as described below), but also into the very unsettled territory of writing assessment.[6]

Fourth, we see WAC as a collective cross-curricular enterprise; the vast majority of which is located outside the official WAC program. We believe instructors in the disciplines and their students should not be viewed simply as passive recipients of our methods and beliefs, but rather as valuable sources of knowledge in their own right, people who have things to teach us as well as to learn from us. Thus, another key goal of our assessment is to explore how literate activity in the academy intersects with content instruction, disciplinary enculturation, and personal development. In other words, we must undertake research not only, or even mainly, to evaluate transmission of our ideas and practices, but rather to deepen our understanding of our colleagues' ideas and practices. Although this second-generation WAC goal is not well represented in reports of WAC evaluation, we believe that it is a crucial component to our program—an approach that will help us avoid

---

[6] Complex issues of reliability and validity have been raised with regard to holistic assessment of writing (see, e.g., Charney, 1984, Freedman, 1984; Huot, 1990). These questions are further complicated by such issues as how writing should be defined, how disciplinary values are inscribed in assessment criteria, and how writing assessment serves social and institutional functions (Williamson, 1993).

the limitations of evangelical first generation WAC (see Jones & Comprone, 1993; Kaufer & Young, 1993). In this collective enterprise, one of our research roles is to "capture" local and often tacit practices so that they can be reflected on more explicitly and communicated to others. In some cases, these practices may be broadly applicable in diverse settings or narrowly be applicable in very similar settings. In other cases, they may simply serve as provocative cases that help others to see and think about related issues in their own settings. More generally, to transform the teaching and learning practices of our local academic community, we see a pressing need for dialogic interactions among instructors across disciplinary and departmental boundaries.

With these four domains in mind, we formulated four key guidelines that express our sense of what we need to do and of what we hope to gain.

1. The research must provide desired information to the varied audiences that influence institutional and administrative decisions on funding, resource allocation, and curricular policy.
2. The research must examine the implementation of WAC in sufficient detail to allow for a reasonable evaluation of the program's transmission of practices and to facilitate the revision of its activities, materials, and methods.
3. The research must seek qualitative and longitudinal data on students' writing development to assess the impact, not only of Comp II courses, but also of the broader WAC movement on campus.
4. Because we view WAC as a two-way, cross-curricular enterprise, the research must go beyond questions of transmission: it must engage in an open-ended exploration of writing, teaching, and knowledge-making practices in the disciplines of our university.

At this point in the process, our evaluation of the first mission of the Center (the WAC program for faculty and TAs) has focused on the second and fourth domains of action, that is, on how WAC faculty and TAs who have been through our seminars have been implementing WAC in Comp II and other courses. To illustrate the concrete connections between our goals and research strategies, we will present extracts from data (class handouts, interview transcripts) collected by Sibylle and Nicole as part of the first phase of WAC research at the University of Illinois. We will explore how we can read and understand such data, what questions we should ask about them, what uses we might make of them, and what kinds of further information we might want to seek. However, before we turn to that data, we will first provide background information on the WAC program and the research itself.

SETTING THE CONTEXT: THE WAC PROGRAM

The Center offers varied forms of support for WAC activities on campus. However, two key forums are the Faculty Seminars and the Graduate Student Seminars. Four-day seminars for faculty are held annually in May (during intersession), for which the faculty participants receive a stipend. Two-day seminars for TAs are offered in the May intersession and in August, just before the start of Fall semester. Starting in 1994, the Center also began offering one-day seminars for TAs in January before the start of Spring semester. TAs also receive a stipend for their participation. The faculty seminars are led by Gail, Michael Pemberton, and Paul; the TA seminars by Paul and Gail.

Many participants enter the seminars with reductive models of writing as a skill. These models—often grounded in their own experiences of current–traditional rhetoric in composition courses—emphasize the basics of correctness and conformity and are driven by a sense of deficit and crisis. Pedagogically, these models are typically expressed in notions of frequent practice, transmission of rules for writing, and correction of errors. Our seminars are designed in large part to supplant those models with a richer notion of writing as a complex mode of thinking, learning, and communicating. While we also emphasize the value of regular practice, our pedagogical model emphasizes (a) dialogue, (b) enriching resources for invention and revision, (c) acknowledgment of the difficulty of writing and inquiry, and (d) concern for motivational and affective issues. Fortunately, for most seminar participants, their own experiences as writers resonate more with the models we hope to promote than with the one drawn from their experiences of composition instruction. In this way, our work consists mainly of drawing connections between instructors' own experiences as writers and students' experiences as writers in their classes.

Some of the basic themes we stress in the WAC seminars are:

- Writing is part of a complex literate activity that also involves reading, talk, observation and action.
- Writing is a tool in making, unmaking, and negotiating knowledge within disciplines.
- Writing conventions and values are diverse, shaped by fields of specialization.
- Writing should be an object and mode of instruction, not a constant test.
- Writing should help students improve their writing, learn content, and generate meaning; it should contribute positively to their overall development as students.

Table 12.1 provides a more detailed representation of how we translate these broad principles into specific pedagogical issues and practices that we

Table 12.1. Key Practices and Issues Emphasized in WAC Seminars

Informal Writing/Writing to learn
- Quick writing, various kinds of logs and journals, microthemes
- Writing as a tool to support and enhance class discussion and reading

Process
- Multiple opportunities, i.e., multiple drafts or repeated tasks
- Shorter, more frequent writing (perhaps, breaking up larger tasks into shorter steps)
- Structured occasions for in-progress invention and response from self, peers, instructors.
- Structuring student processes through intermediate steps
- Memos (e.g., paper proposals, in-progress reports, cover letters)

Assignments
- Being aware of and addressing issues of task representation
- Considering student interest or motivation
- Building process into individual tasks and sequencing tasks
- Structuring a resource-rich environment to support student writing and learning
- Integrating writing with disciplinary conventions, course content and student evaluation

Response and Evaluation
- Responding in progress
  substantive, preferably ungraded, response by instructors
  fit response to stage in the process (e.g., don't proofread first drafts)
  peer and self response (with models of some sort provided)
  the value of students' seeing one another's writing
- Minimal response as an option for some kinds of writing (e.g., quick writing, journal assignments, responses to peers)
- The value of positive/substantive response at all stages
- Considering alternative audiences (public, external professional, other students)
- Written response as a problematic form of text (i.e., considering the clarity and adequacy of written response text itself)
  paradoxical comments (be clear, elaborate, don't use contractions)
  underspecified rules (do not change tenses, do not use "I," consider your audience)
  unclear response jargon (awk, log, dev)
- Including process components in grading (i.e., counting engagement in the process)
- Making evaluation broader or more substantive (e.g., portfolios, primary trait scales)

encourage instructors to consider. We also ask participants to read articles on writing and response.[7] These articles are often tied to specific activities in the seminar. We mix written activities, small group discussion, whole group discussion, and presentation. As is typical of other WAC programs, we attempt to model the active learning strategies we are suggesting in the way we structure the workshop, and we especially work to relate participants' own writing and response experiences to their students' experiences. After discussing the methodological contexts and strategies for our research, we

---

[7] The core texts that we have turned to repeatedly include Bartholomae (1985), Bean, Drenk, and Lee (1982), Elbow (1993), Griffin (1983), Herrrington (1992b), Kiniry and Strenski (1985), and Sommers (1982).

will look at some data that explore how one activity in the seminar was taken up and applied in a particular course to illustrate the complex issues that arise as we trace the effects of WAC seminars on instruction.

THE RESEARCH: STANCES, RESOURCES, AND STRATEGIES

Stances

From a traditional empirical perspective, the multiplicity of our roles (particularly as we alternate between the evaluated and the evaluators) would be seen as problematic—a conflict of interests that would threaten the objectivity of our research. However, the objectivist stance of disinterested research is itself in serious doubt (e.g., Roman & Apple, 1990; Haraway, 1991; Harding, 1991; Lather, 1991; Lincoln & Guba, 1985; Rosaldo, 1986). The question is not whether researchers are interested cultural agents, but rather what kind of interested agents the researchers are. Empirical research has traditionally constructed its objectivity by constituting the researchers and the objects of study as existing on two distinct planes (de Certeau, 1984). Unlike this sort of research, we see ourselves and our "subjects" as occupying a single plane. In practice, our roles as practitioners are not sharply distinguished from our roles as researchers. Because of this stance, we see our multiple roles as sources of synergy as well as conflict— more as resources than as obstacles.

For example, in January of 1994, we were invited to participate in a faculty–TA meeting in the Department of History. The meeting was set up to review implementation of WAC in history Comp II courses. As we listened to the TAs, a supervising faculty member, and the head of the department discuss how they had implemented WAC and what successes they had experienced, we became truly excited. The writing and teaching activities they described were clearly designed in light of practices we had promoted in the WAC seminar. We were particularly interested to discover that TAs who had not attended the seminar were also familiar with the philosophy, practices, and even readings that we had introduced there. They, along with the seminar participants, seemed to have adopted WAC instructional practices, transforming them in the process. What we saw that day was an institutionalization of WAC—a phenomenon we were naturally very interested in understanding.

That meeting led to several outcomes. First, we decided to be sure that some history TAs were among the first instructors we would contact for research interviews. Second, Gail contacted a university newspaper to suggest that it do a story on Comp II courses in history. (The result was a very favorable story on Comp II published that Spring.) Third, as we listened to the TAs that day, we also heard a theme emerging that we had not suggested in the seminar. Several TAs had developed activities that involved using primary sources and imaginative scenarios to introduce students to the work of making history and to encourage the development of what they all called "the historical imagination." Because we believed that these kinds of imaginative tasks could be useful for others as well, a month later we gave a TA workshop on imaginative writing assignments. (Appendix E is a handout developed for that workshop; the first example bears witness to our debt to the history TA meeting we attended.) After that meeting, we learned more about these assignments from our research interviews, but we had already taken up the idea when those interviews were scheduled. Finally, the meeting reinforced our belief that we have much to learn from our colleagues in looking at WAC at departmental and institutional levels as well as in particular courses. Were Gail and Paul researchers or practitioners the day they participated in that seminar? Clearly, that distinction is blurred in this case. We feel comfortable with a mode of research as practical action, with not attempting to construct epistemic firewalls that break (or more likely suppress) the connections among our roles.[8]

With others in our field (e.g., Bazerman, 1991, Farris & Smith, 1992; Jones & Comprone, 1993; Kaufer & Young, 1993; Russell, 1991), we see research and evaluation as central to WAC practice. It is an activity we would pursue in some form without any institutional demand. The data we are collecting provide a multifunctional resource base that can be activated in multiple ways to achieve diverse ends. Because our notion of evaluation is informed by a strong rhetorical perspective, we should perhaps specify our notion of rhetoric further. Informed by feminist rhetorics, we certainly do not understand rhetoric as a militaristic marshaling of forces for persuasion. Instead, we see our research and analysis as rhetorical in the sense that it is a form of communicative praxis that helps us understand and foster growth in our academic community. The research merges with our practice— together they push us to remain deeply and dialogically engaged with others in an evolving, learning community.

---

[8] Even constructivist, hermeneutic discussions of evaluation (e.g., Guba & Lincoln, 1989) continue to assume that evaluation is a bounded focal activity initiated by a managerial client and that the roles of evaluator and evaluated do not coincide (i.e., evaluators are outsiders). Although some elements of our evaluation research (e.g., the institutional review) may fit that model, much of our activity falls outside such models because we see evaluation as an ongoing activity that we engage in as reflective practitioners.

Resources

Although in many respects our program has been well funded and supported, we nevertheless find the resources available for evaluation research
quite limited, particularly given the scale of WAC activities on campus. Gail
and Paul have administrative release time (Gail, two courses, and Paul, one),
but evaluation is only one of the activities that the release time is intended
to support. Indeed, the bulk of the release time is for administering the varied tasks of the Center and for delivering the WAC program itself (WAC seminars, retreats, shorter departmental workshops, individual consultation).
Sibylle's research assistantship involves several tasks, so only a part of her
appointment is directed at evaluation. Nicole's one third time appointment
this year has been solely dedicated to WAC evaluation. The potential scope
of our evaluation research, on the other hand, is wide. Since May of 1991,
169 professors and 297 TAs have participated in the formal WAC seminars.
Counting participation in shorter departmental and all-campus workshops,
along with the annual WAC Retreat, boosts the number of faculty and TAs
by approximately another 50%. As of April 1995, 77 Comp II courses (a number of which have multiple sections) have been certified, and so far those
courses have enrolled approximately 9,000 "students" (the actual number
may be smaller because some might take more than one Comp II course). In
addition, some of the faculty and TAs involved in Comp II have not attended the seminars, and many instructors who have participated have incorporated WAC activities in other (non-Comp II) courses.

Our collection of data began in 1993–1994, when Sibylle piloted semi-
structured interviews with several TAs. From 1994–1995, Sibylle and Nicole
intensified data collection, and the four of us, Nicole and Paul particularly,
began to work on initial analyses of those data. As Gail and Paul worked
with Nicole and Sibylle during this period, the value of the Center's third
mission, the graduate specialization in Writing Studies, became apparent.
Our first attempt to study WAC implementation was made in 1992–1993;
however, with only a recently established specialization in Writing Studies,
the first research assistants did not have the background to participate in
planning, conducting, or analyzing writing research. One of the RAs conducted a limited observational study of WAC in an engineering course, but
the information gathered proved only minimally useful. In contrast, as Gail
and Paul considered potential research assistants for 1994–1995, they
looked to a group of active graduate students well prepared to undertake
this kind of research.

In the intersection of our goals and resources, we have initiated only
part of a broader program of research. The development of a questionnaire—one of the broad quantitative measures we relate most to the institutional review—is temporarily on hold. Those measures will be developed

in collaboration with a team composed of internal and external reviewers and the Office of the Dean of Liberal Arts and Sciences (LAS).[9] In conjunction with the university's procedure to recertify Comp II courses, the General Education Board is developing a questionnaire that asks students to characterize and evaluate their experiences of writing in Comp II courses.[10] However, the widest gap between the kind of research we envision and our resources is in the domain of student writing. We would like to conduct in-depth longitudinal research to explore the kinds of writing students are being assigned, of processes students report engaging in, of understandings of writing students are forging through these experiences, and of learning that appears to be associated with the writing. The pursuit of such research, however, even with only a sample of students is a daunting prospect at present. Instead, our current understanding of student outcomes is inferred from instructor's descriptions or gleaned from the occasional examples of student texts and reflective introductions to portfolios that we have collected in the interviews. The limitations on the evaluation are not so much financial as human. Despite the importance of using student data to inform the evaluation, at the moment there are simply not enough faculty and graduate students available to conduct large-scale qualitative research.

With the available resources, we are developing an initial image of WAC implementation across campus. The first phase of the research involves interviews with faculty and TAs, most of whom have participated in the WAC seminars. As we analyze the data gathered through these interviews, we are looking at the transmission and transformation of WAC activities and seeking to learn about writing practices in the disciplines of the University community. We also see these interviews as an important basis for selecting issues and sites for more in-depth study in the next phases of the research (which will include focused qualitative study of students' writing experiences and learning outcomes).

Strategies

A key strategy in qualitative research is triangulation, that is, the deliberate attempt to see a phenomenon from multiple perspectives. Triangulation

---

[9] Although the core faculty of the CWS hold tenure and tenure-lines in English and Speech Communication, the Center itself is a separate academic unit within the College of Liberal Arts and Sciences (LAS) under the auspices of Jesse Delia, the Dean of LAS.

[10] The questionnaire itself is being developed by the Office of Instructional Resources (OIR), which is responsible for teacher and course evaluations in general. However, OIR has received input on question design from the General Education Board and the Campus Advisory Committee of the Center for Writing Studies (which consists largely of faculty who have participated in WAC seminars and includes CWS faculty as *ex officio* members).

involves seeking multiple sources of information using multiple methods at multiple times and having the data analyzed through multiple theoretical lenses by multiple people (Denzin, 1989). The multiple perspectives of triangulation decenter dominant perspectives and disrupt easy answers. Thus, triangulation supports grounded interpretation and thickly textured description. At this point in our research, we are relying on one set of sources (instructors) and one basic method (interviewing). We plan to diversify sources and methods over time.

However, we have worked to build in several forms of triangulation within our interviews with instructors. First, we decided this year to set up interviews with departmental groupings of faculty and TAs (differently situated instructors). This strategy not only provides us with a more complete institutional picture of WAC implementation (one grounded in particular departmental contexts), but also offers us multiple perspectives on writing in the relevant discipline, on WAC implementation in key courses, and on relations of TAs and faculty (an institutional issue that has increasingly attracted our attention). Second, we ask instructors to bring course materials (syllabi, assignment sheets, handouts, student papers) with them to the interviews. When instructors comply with this request (and they often do), Sibylle and Nicole can shift from semi-structured to text-based interviewing. With the stimulation of specific documents, text-based interviews often allow for a more in-depth dialogue on issues (cf. Odell, Goswami, & Herrington, 1983; Prior, 1991, 1995). General representations of tasks or practices can be pushed into specific clarifying representations, and new questions can be developed on the spot. Third, collecting copies of such course materials provides us with another source of data—data that might normally be collected from observational methods. Finally, working as a team, we bring multiple perspectives to bear not only on analysis, but also on planning and conducting the research.

We ask faculty and TAs who have been through our seminars (or who have not, but are teaching Comp II courses) to participate in the research. In the initial contact letter (see Appendix A), we introduce the research but then follow up with phone calls to set up the interviews. Asking people to respond through the mail seems less effective than a letter with a phone follow up to request participation.[11] The contact letter mentions our request that instructors bring syllabi, assignments, sample papers, and handouts to the interview, and that request is repeated in the phone conversation when

---

[11] As of April 1995, 12 of 14 professors contacted agreed to participate in interviews and 11 of 21 TAs. The lower percentage for TAs reflects several factors: four TAs had left the university by the time we contacted them, two had never taught a writing intensive course, and three were no longer doing so. Turnover and changes in teaching assignments among TAs are, thus, clearly visible in these figures, an important finding in itself.

Table 12.2. General Interview Protocol for TAs

Background
- How did you get involved in the course(s) that you are teaching?
- Who are you working with? (professors, other graduate students, etc.)
- What role are you playing in the class? (grader, discussion leader, etc.)

Structure
- Use syllabus, assignments, etc.
- What kinds of writing are you having students do?
    How is it working?
    What are the problems? Are there problems?
    How did you address the problems?
    Do you do any other kind of writing besides what is listed in the syllabus?
    (How do you structure the task?)
- How are you responding to/evaluating student writing?
    Do you respond to drafts?
    Do you use peer response? What is the structure of the peer response (do you use
        models, response sheets, how do you incorporate them when you evaluate student
        writing?)

Questions on WAC
- Are you using any of the techniques you are using in your writing intensive course in
    other classes? (assignments, how you respond to papers, etc.)
- Were the WAC seminars useful? What techniques/ideas are you using that came from
    WAC?
- Has teaching the course and going to WAC seminars been a good experience? Why or
    why not?
- Are there any issues or problems that we haven't talked about that you want to bring up?

---

people agree to an interview. Because we have envisioned several potential uses for the interview comments and for any documents collected, we have fashioned an informed consent form (see Appendix B) that provides a map of possible uses to clarify for participants and ourselves whether we have permission to use the information in a particular context or fashion.

The interview is semistructured, guided loosely by the set of questions. Table 12.2 presents a general set of questions used for TA interviews.[12] As previously mentioned, when instructors bring instructional documents to the interviews, those texts are used to elicit more specific information and to develop questions on the spot. The kind of detail that is typical of interviews with such texts is illustrated in Appendix C (an extract from an interview Nicole did with a political science TA, Jeff Roberg). Looking at his syllabus description of the assignment appears to have prompted Jeff to provide fairly rich descriptions, not only of the policy paper task and the structured process, but also of his rationales and expectations for this work.

---

[12] Before interviews, we also discuss whether there are specific questions to pursue. These discussions often take place on an electronic bulletin board (PacerForum software) set up for the four of us to facilitate the research.

In addition to a syllabus, Jeff brought a handout that listed topics for the policy paper. Using that text, Nicole formulated a question on the task (this exchange follows those seen in Appendix C).

Nicole: OK, well, I 'd like to delve into this assignment a bit... and talk about.. I wonder if you could just take one of these sample topics (indicates assignment sheet) and tell me a little bit about how you perceive a paper written on one of these topics, like what it would look like, just the bare bones of what it might look like, keeping in mind a couple of things. One thing we're trying to find out what sorts of things teachers are trying to get students to do in these papers. And you've told me a little bit about that, but it might be a little bit more clear with an example. And the other thing I'm really interested in is you having them pick a particular audience for the paper, and I'm wondering how that, if you can give an example of how that audience might influence the text, what the text actually ends up looking like.

Jeff: OK. Pick your topic. I haven't looked at that list in some time. This could be humorous.

Nicole: OK. Let's say-how about US assistance to Eastern Europe and the Soviet Union? Is that a good one?

Jeff: Sure. There's obviously numerous ways to go about this. Let's take the usual one, which would be, just that—U.S. assistance—so we're looking at, let's say advising the President, and I'll take the role of the Secretary of State. Now as the Secretary of State I have certain obligations to pursue, and I'm going to want the most bang for my buck in terms of presenting, or for giving money to these states. So the first thing I have to do is I have to argue, why do we even need to give help to these states? Which is something the President wants to know, because he has to go before—or she as it happens—has to go before the public. So why is it, what's the problem? The problem is that these states are going through changes. If we've spent 45 years fighting the evil empire and "communism," in quotes, we must now try and supplement and help their transition to a market economy. I won't be so bold to say capitalist, so that's more presumptuous. So that's the first thing. Now as Secretary of State, I not only am worrying about the United States, but I have things I worry about as a member of the State Department. The State Department has a different way of looking at things than the Defense Department. So that, if I'm the State Department I have to worry about relations. I can't just give weapons let's say to one state, without worrying about what's going to happen in these other states. And I'm worrying about this on a political level, where the Defense Department, the Defense Secretary might be worrying about this on a military level. So that's the importance of the adviser, and who it is you represent, who it is you're advising.

This thread of the interview continues for another 60 lines of transcript. Nicole's concrete question leads Jeff to provide a rich account of his expectations and rationales for the task. An interesting feature of this account is his specification of particular disciplinary and professional audiences and topics (cf. Miller & Selzer, 1985). In other words, in these interviews, the texts function both as aids to memory and as resources for increasing dialogue.

When collecting extensive qualitative data, one of the challenges is to enhance access to that data. Appendix D provides our interview cover sheet—one of the key tools that we have developed for enhancing access and for identifying central themes. The cover sheet includes a listing of topics that amounts to a topical map of issues we might want to attend to—issues that grew out of the seminars and the interviews themselves. The development of this topical map has also been a valuable part of the analysis. An initial version of the cover sheet was generated through discussion, written up by Nicole, responded to, and revised. As Nicole coded and Nicole and Paul read through the coded interviews, gaps became apparent. For example, the categories listed as "writing assignments—functions" were all added after Paul realized that several of the assignments that instructors discussed were means to other ends (e.g., better discussion, better reading) and that those functions were stressed in WAC seminar handouts and discussions. Recently, Nicole noted that she was generating a lot of additional categories (listed at the bottom of the cover sheet) and that many of those categories had to do with the way the writing process was structured, again an issue we focus on in our WAC seminars. This led to the addition of the writing process categories seen in Appendix D. We have also added topics, however, to reflect our own goals. For example, in discussions with campus administrators, Gail has encountered the view that because faculty are paid a stipend for attending the WAC seminars, they should all be developing, proposing, and teaching Comp II courses. After hearing from administrators that approximately a quarter of the faculty participants in our seminars had proposed Comp II courses, we were somewhat surprised that the numbers were so high whereas some suggested that the numbers were too low.[13] However, we decided that we should particularly watch for faculty discussions of why they had chosen or not chosen to propose Comp II. Our sense from informal discussions with faculty was that a complex configuration of institutional rewards and contexts were shaping that decision. In addition to adding this category to the cover sheet, we also decided that Nicole and Sibylle should be alert for this topic in interviews and be sure to probe why faculty decided to propose or not propose Comp II courses. Here again, the

---

[13] Our WAC program, though strongly connected to Comp II, is a full WAC program, open to any interested faculty. For example, a number of faculty from foreign language departments have participated in our WAC seminars because of an interest in using these approaches to teach composition, culture, and literature. However, courses in a foreign language are not eligible for Comp II status, so few have proposed Comp II courses. We also see faculty in the WAC seminars who are teaching Comp II courses already on the books. And, of course, there are those who leave the seminar without any interest in teaching writing-intensive courses but are genuinely interested in using writing more productively in other classes.

goals of the research and the research instruments have been shaped by our reading of the rhetorical situation and the interests of administrators—one group of stakeholders.

Experimental research might question trying to make the data work for multiple purposes and multiple audiences. The problem is seen as one of fit, the notion that data are collected and analyzed to answer specific research questions and, thus, that using that data to address other questions results in slippage. Our sense of the research process, however, is more emergent, flexible, and exploratory—consistent with ethnographic and qualitative methodology. We are comfortable following the data and reading it interpretively for multiple meanings rather than assuming that a particular set of data has only one story to tell and can be resolved into a monovocal interpretation. Because we understand the interviews themselves as multivoiced and multifunctional, it would be problematic for us to privilege any single reading of an interview as its final and full meaning.

TRANSMISSION AND BEYOND: TRACKING, AND LEARNING FROM, THE IMPLEMENTATION OF WAC

In our initial readings of the various interviews, we have been struck by several themes. One is that we have seen signs of transmission, of activities and issues covered in WAC seminars turning up not only in interview responses, but also in course artifacts (syllabi, assignments, handouts, student papers). We have also been struck by the diverse ways "our" WAC activities and ideas have been translated and taken up, and see the beginnings of the process of transformation. For example, though many participants in our workshops have picked up the notion of "microthemes" from Bean, Drenk, and Lee (1982), we have seen that label applied to an almost bewildering variety of activities. "Microthemes" may include writing done at home or in class. They might be limited to a paragraph or several pages in length. Much of the in-class writing some of the instructors call microthemes is what we would identify as quickwrites, that is, 5 or 10 minute responses. In some cases, microthemes have appeared in the form of extended (20 to 30 minute) informal, in-class writing, a practice we had not recommended and didn't know would develop. Reading the data for transmission is, thus, no easy matter. Without additional contextual specification, course materials and task labels are often deeply ambiguous. To explore the complexity of identifying both transmission and transformation, we first describe in some detail one particular activity from the seminar and then examine some research artifacts to consider how they can be read.

One activity in the seminars for faculty and TAs is built around Kiniry and Strenski's (1985) article. The article presents a taxonomy of tasks based loosely on Bloom's hierarchy of cognitive operations. In the seminar we give participants a list of eight writing prompts from the article, including:

Define what is meant by bilingual education;
Compare the respiratory systems of amphibians and reptiles; and
During what periods of American history have critics of capital punishment helped to decrease its popularity, and what forces have usually brought it back in favor?

Working in pairs, the participants rank the prompts from most demanding to least demanding. Lively discussions ensue, involving both substantive debates over which tasks are easiest and reflective complaints about the task itself. We then discuss the rankings and the problems with doing the ranking itself without greater attention to context. The upshot is usually the recognition that the tasks and key terms for operations, like "define," need to be contextualized to be understood. For example, defining bilingual education might involve nothing more than giving a textbook definition in an introductory course, making it a very undemanding task, but it could also serve as a preliminary examination question for a doctoral candidate in applied linguistics, thus making it a highly demanding task. This discussion then reinvokes an issue participants have already discussed by this point in the seminar, the complexity of task representation.

Next we ask participants to use the key words (list, define, argue, etc.) to develop writing tasks for a class they are teaching in. After they have developed their tasks, we have several participants read their tasks aloud. Participants often find that working through this heuristic for a specific class results in usable assignments that they would not otherwise have considered. In other words, while we end up critiquing rather than endorsing a predictable hierarchy of cognitive operations, this activity does suggest the value of thinking through the sequencing of tasks, of considering the complexity often buried in operational terms like "analyze," and, more generally, of attending carefully to the development of writing tasks.

Table 12.3 is a written assignment we received from a history TA, Toby Higbie. Does this text provide evidence of transmission of WAC practices and notions from our seminar? The assignment's overall structure (goals, terms, and questions) is not one that we proposed or discussed. The three-task scheme of summary, analysis, and academic argument is again not one we used (though naturally we did talk about summary, analysis, and argument). Much of the content of this assignment seems to be a mix of history (e.g., "The process of analyzing a historical document....") and fairly standard notions of writing (e.g., development of a narrow thesis). The specific texts are very historical. The assignment specifies no structured writing process, and its mode seems to be primarily presentational (not a mode we particularly encourage).

On the other hand, the assignment could be read as displaying some features triggered by our WAC seminar. The assignment sheet provides a goal, and we do argue in the seminar for letting students in on the rationales for our pedagogies. The focus on explaining terms could have been prompted by discussion of task representation. As we noted in describing the activity in the WAC seminar built around Kiniry and Strenski's (1985) article, one outcome we hope for and usually "see" is an enhanced awareness that task terms are not transparent. In fact, we argue that teaching students what it means to argue persuasively or analyze well in history or sociology or biology is an integral part of learning those fields of inquiry. In addition, although the three-part scheme is not one we would claim as ours, it does involve sequencing. Standing alone, this course handout is not only ambiguous on the question of transmission, but it also leaves us with mixed feelings. Should we be happy with this handout? Are we looking at a text that is open-

Table 12.3. History assignment provided by Toby Higbie (TA)

History 152 Writing Intensive

Goal: To understand three important writing tasks—"summary," "analysis," and "argument"—each of which is vital to good historical writing.

Terms

Summarizing can be as simple as listing, but usually requires that you be able to pick apart a text, a set of statistics, or an image.

Analyzing is similar to summarizing in that it demands breaking down the text or phenomenon into constituent parts of causes. The process of analyzing an historical document or event may require you to summarize constituent parts, compare and/or contrast the document or event with other similar subjects, and above all, place the subject in historical context. The context for the subject of analysis comes from contemporary historical (primary) sources, and information in secondary sources, lectures, and discussion sections. An effective analysis will both isolate, define, and explain specific attributes of the subject under analysis (the particular), and will also link the subject under analysis to the wider historical context of causation and inter-related meanings (the general).

Academic Argument. To make an effective argument you will need to draw on analysis more than summary. Which things you choose to analyze will be guided by the nature of your argument or thesis. In an argumentative essay, you should draw primarily on information from the course rather than general knowledge or value judgements (although these may help you direct your argument). An effective argument will coherently integrate several analyses, each of which support a central thesis.

Questions

1. Summarize the main points in Booker T. Washington's Atlanta Exposition Address (Source 12 in Wheeler and Becker). Compare his ideas to those of W. J. Whipper who fought the disenfranchisement of African Americans in the South Carolina constitutional convention ("Black Leaders Fight Disenfranchisement, 1895" in the coursepack, pp. 1–2). Also look at the document titled, "The Supreme Court Upholds 'Separate-but-equal,' 1896" (coursepack, p. 3)

Analyze the social and political plight of African Americans in the context of segregation and disenfranchisement. What was the relation between social segregation and political disenfranchisement?

ing up disciplinary secrets, inviting reflective interpretations of tasks, and moving writing from its typical status as test to a site for teaching (Herrington, 1992a)? Or are we looking at a disciplinary version of the kind of product-oriented, presentational prescription that most current writing pedagogies have defined themselves against?

The addition of data from the interview with Toby helps us to disambiguate both the task and our evaluation of it:

Toby: ...one thing that I found I needed to do after assessing writing and feedback from last, my first time doing it (i.e., teaching a Comp II course) and also from the students as I was working with it, there were certain writing skills we were really interested in having them learn, specifically how to analyze historical documents and to critically analyze these things, and look at who wrote the document and who produced it, what kind of biases they might have because of their position in society, or institution or anything like that. And I discovered that critically analyzing things is not something that everybody is born with and, you know, that's pretty obvious, and I tried to think of how I learned, and I am not sure if I could say how I ever learned, but so I tried to come up with some things that I modeled off the articles in the course pack of the WAC orientation.

Sibylle: Do you remember what article that was?

Toby: No, but if I saw the course pack I could find it. It's the one that deals with, it talks about listing, analysis, argument, and things like that, it has this sort of hierarchy of tasks that are meant to lead people to more and more complex forms of thinking and writing. So what I did, it had about 10 of these tasks, so I decided I would just boil them down to the ones I was really interested in. What I found was, when I asked people to analyze things, often they were summarizing. And so I made up a lesson plan that tried to describe what summarizing was and what analyzing was, and then what arguing was.

Sibylle: Did you give a lecture on that or did you hand out some copies to your students?

Toby: I handed out a lesson plan to the students (showed lesson plan; see Table 12.3). This lesson plan was the first time I tried to do something like that, and I would preface it by saying this is a fine example of when you try to do too much. It was more than could be done in one lesson period. And we had the problem of having to cover a lot of material, so once you have attempted this, which is specifically geared toward historical context, there was no way to move, to go back to it, really. I had to do a similar thing with another time period.... this lesson plan starts with a goal, and the goal was to understand important writing tasks, summary, analysis, and argument, and so I had to read this, and then I talked about some of the differences and I tried to model them on what was summarized and analyzed...and we had a course pack of mostly primary documents dealing with the issues of agrarian populism and African Americans in the South during the latter times of the 19th century....We broke them into I think it's four groups and each group had a task, and this task was to analyze these documents, and so they would summarize the main points of Booker T Washington's Atlanta Exposition, and that, I think people could do that very well.

Sibylle: To analyze or to summarize?

Toby: To summarize it. There wasn't too much of a problem, and then I thought, but I realized that one of the ways that you analyze is by comparing, look at the differences, so that's how I asked them to compare Booker T. Washington to this other guy who was, who comes from a very different, also an African American, but who came from a different political background. He was a delegate to the Florida Populist Convention, or something like that, we pulled this document out of some public book about, so. Right, but so for instance, I mean in nuts and bolts terms, let's see, ok, so they had to look at two documents that are produced by African Americans, African American men, roughly about the same time, and then this Plessy v. Ferguson Supreme Court decision, and then, ideally, if there was enough time they would have summaries of all 3, and then the final product would be to analyze the social and political context. And this is a kind of conceptual leap that they didn't make at that point, but made it later on.... and then they were supposed to do all that and, partially, what else did they have to do? I think that I asked them at the end of the class to write a thesis statement based on their analysis.

Adding Toby's interview comments on the course handout clarifies much. First, transmission is displayed much more clearly. Toby alludes to the Kiniry and Strenski (1985) article and the WAC seminar activity around that article in unmistakable terms. He also connects task representations (e.g., what it means to analyze) directly to disciplinary socialization (what it means to think like a historian), another point we make explicitly in the seminar. In addition, we see that this handout was used as a structured, in-class activity, with students reading, talking, and writing in groups as they worked through a sequence of summarizing primary documents, comparatively analyzing them, and then developing a thesis from them. This specification of how the handout figured in situated practices leaves us clearer about this task: It was not realized in the predominantly presentational mode.

Finally, it is also interesting to see features of the task that did not derive from transmission, but that adapted and transformed the ideas presented in the WAC seminar. The selection of operations (summary, analysis, and argument), the particularly disciplinary values those operations invoke, and the role of primary documents are all features of this task that we did not imagine when we led the WAC seminar. From observing these transformations, we have learned more about what WAC might mean in history, what kinds of disciplinary issues WAC might be associated with. (Of course, we also wish here for the additional contextualizations that observation of such lessons, interviews with students, and analysis of student texts could offer.). Nevertheless, we do see a dialogic blend of WAC practices and notions we meant to convey to participants in the seminars and of practices and notions that Toby and his colleagues brought with them as historians.

FINAL REFLECTIONS

Judging from recent articles reflecting on the state of WAC in university settings (e.g., Jones & Comprone, 1993), it appears that the WAC movement is struggling to sustain momentum. Although the number of WAC programs is clearly increasing (McLeod, 1992), the depth and impact of WAC may be running into institutional walls. It is possible that the missionary fervor of writing to learn and process movements has swept up the usual suspects—those most concerned with undergraduate instruction and most attuned by personal and disciplinary orientations to these practices—but has left much of the academy unaffected. One of the most exciting things about the 1994 CCCC Think-Tank mentioned earlier and this volume is the clear sense that many WAC professionals see evaluation research as an activity they own and operate, at least partly, for their own purposes. The desire to evangelize WAC and convert colleagues in other departments is diminishing, and in its place is emerging an interest in understanding and learning from those in other disciplinary cultures and in engaging in cooperative action and dialogue with them to enrich the experiences of students and instructors in our universities. We see the evaluation research we have initiated in this light, as a crucial complement of our practical engagement in writing across the curriculum.

REFERENCES

Bartholomae, D. (1985). Inventing the university. In M. Rose (Ed.), *When a writer can't write.* (pp. 134–165). New York: Guilford.

Bazerman, C. (1991). The second stage in writing across the curriculum. *College English, 53,* 209–212.

Bean, J., Drenk, D., & Lee, F. (1982). Microtheme strategies for developing cognitive skills. In C.W. Williams (Ed.), *Teaching writing in all disciplines* (pp. 27–38). San Francisco: Jossey-Bass.

Brodkey, L. (1987). *Academic writing as social practice.* Philadelphia: Temple University Press.

Casanave, C. P. (1995). Local interactions: Constructing contexts for composing in a graduate sociology program. In D. Belcher & G. Braine (Eds.), *Academic writing in a second language: Essays on research and pedagogy* (pp. 83–110). Norwood, NJ: Ablex.

de Certeau, M. (1984). *The practice of everyday life.* (Trans. S. Rendall.) Berkeley, CA: University of California Press.

Charney, D. (1984). The validity of using holistic scoring to evaluate writing: A critical overview. *Research in the Teaching of English, 18,* 65–81.

Chin, E. (1994). Redefining "context" in research and writing. *Written Communication, 11,* 445–482.

Chiseri-Strater, E. (1991). *Academic literacies: The public and private discourse of university students*. Portsmouth, NH: Boyton/Cook.

Denzin, N. (1989). *The research act: A theoretical introduction to sociological methods*. (3rd ed.) Englewood Cliffs, NJ: Prentice Hall.

Doheny-Farina, S. (1989). A case study of one adult writing in academic and nonacademic discourse communities. In C. B. Matalene (Ed.), *Worlds of writing: Teaching and learning in discourse communities of work* (pp. 17–42). New York: Random House.

Doyle, W. (1983). Academic work. *Review of Educational Research, 53,* 159–199.

Eisner, E., & Peshkin, A. (Eds.). (1990). *Qualitative inquiry in education: The continuing debate* (pp. 38–73). New York: Teachers College Press.

Elbow, P. (1993). Ranking, evaluating, and liking: Sorting out three forms of judgment. *College English, 55,* 187–206.

Farris, C., & Smith, R. (1992). Writing intensive courses: Tools for curricular change. In S. McLeod & M. Soven (Eds.), *Writing across the curriculum: A guide to developing programs* (pp. 71–86). Newbury Park, CA: Sage.

Freedman, S. (1984). The registers of student and professional expository writing: Influences on teachers' responses. In R. Beach & L.S. Bridwell (Eds.), *New directions in composition research* (362–380). New York: Guilford.

Griffin, C.W. (1983). Using writing to teach many disciplines. *Improving College and University Teaching, 31,* 121–128.

Guba, E. & Lincoln, Y. (1989). *Fourth generation evaluation*. Newbury Park: Sage.

Haraway, D. (1991). *Simians, cyborgs, and women: The reinvention of nature*. New York: Routledge.

Harding, S. (1991). *Whose science? Whose knowledge? Thinking from women's lives*. Ithaca, NY: Cornell University Press.

Herrington, A. (1985). Writing in academic settings: A study of the contexts for writing in two college chemical engineering courses. *Research in the Teaching of English, 19,* 331–359.

Herrington, A. (1988). Teaching, writing, and learning. In D. Jolliffe (Ed.), *Writing in Academic Disciplines: Vol. 2 of Advances in Writing Research* (pp. 133–166). Norwood, NJ: Ablex.

Herrington, A. (1992a). Composing one's self in a discipline: Students' and teachers' negotiations. In M. Secor & D. Charney (Eds.), *Constructing rhetorical education* (pp. 91–115). Carbondale, IL: Southern Illinois University Press.

Herrington, A. (1992b). Assignment and response: Teaching with writing across the disciplines. In S. Witte, N. Nakadate, & R. Cherry (Eds.), *A rhetoric of doing: Essays on written discourse in honor of James L. Kinneavy* (pp. 244–260.). Carbondale, IL: Southern Illinois University Press.

Huot, B. (1990). The literature of direct writing assessment: Major concerns and prevailing trends. *Review of Educational Research, 60,* 237–263.

Jones, R., & Comprone, J. (1993). Where do we go next in Writing across the Curriculum? *College Composition and Communication, 44,* 59–68.

Kaufer, D., & Young, R. (1993). Writing in the content areas: Some theoretical complexities. In L. Odell (Ed.), *Theory and practice in the teaching of writing: Rethinking the discipline* (pp. 71–104). Carbondale: SIU Press.

Kiniry, M., & Strenski, E. (1985). Sequencing expository writing. *College*

Composition and Communication, 36, 191–202.

Lather, P. (1991). *Getting smart: Feminist research and pedagogy with/in the postmodern.* New York: Routledge.

Lincoln, Y., & Guba, E. (1985). *Naturalistic inquiry.* Beverly Hills, CA: Sage.

McLeod, S. (1992). Writing across the curriculum: An introduction. In S. McLeod & M. Soven (Eds.), *Writing across the curriculum: A guide to developing programs* (pp. 1–11). Newbury Park: Sage.

Miller, C.R., & Selzer, J. (1985). Special topics of argument in engineering reports. In L. Odell & D. Goswami (Eds.), *Writing in nonacademic settings* (pp. 309–341). New York: Guilford.

Odell, L., Goswami, D., & Herrington, A. (1983). The discourse-based interview: A procedure for exploring the tacit knowledge of writers in non-academic settings. In P. Mosenthal, L. Tamor, & S. Walmsley (Eds.), *Research on Writing* (pp. 221–236). New York: Longman.

Nelson, J. (1990). This was an easy assignment: Examining how students interpret academic writing tasks. *Research in the Teaching of English, 24,* 362–396.

Prior, P. (1995). Tracing authoritative and internally persuasive discourses: A case study of response, revision, and disciplinary enculturation. *Research in the Teaching of English, 29,* 288–325.

Prior, P. (1994). Response, revision, disciplinarity: A microhistory of a dissertation prospectus in sociology." *Written Communication, 11,* 483–533.

Prior, P. (1991). Contextualizing writing and response in a graduate seminar. *Written Communication, 8,* 267–310.

Roman, L., & Apple, M. (1990). Is naturalism a move away from positivism? Materialistic and feminist approaches to subjectivity. In E. Eisner & A. Peshkin (Eds.), *Qualitative inquiry in education: The continuing debate* (pp. 38–73). New York: Teachers College Press.

Rosaldo, R. (1986). From the door of his tent: The fieldworker and the inquisitor. In J. Clifford & G. Marcus (Eds.), *Writing culture: The poetics and politics of ethnography* (pp. 77–97). Berkeley: University of California Press.

Russell, D. (1991). *Writing in the academic disciplines, 1870–1990: A curricular history.* Carbondale, IL: Southern Illinois University Press.

Sommers, N. (1982). Responding to student writing. *College Composition and Communication, 33,* 148–56.

Walvoord, B., & McCarthy, L. (1990). *Thinking and writing in college: A naturalistic study of students in four disciplines.* Urbana, IL: NCTE.

Williamson, M. (1993). An introduction to holistic scoring: The social, historical, and theoretical context for writing assessment. In M. Williamson & B. Huot (Eds.), *Validating holistic scoring: Theoretical and empirical evaluations* (pp. 1–43). Cresskill, NJ: Hampton Press.

Witte, S. (1985). Revising, composing, theory, and research design. In S. Freedman (Ed.), *The acquisition of written language: Revision and response* (pp. 250–284). Norwood, NJ: Ablex.

APPENDIX A. INITIAL CONTACT LETTER

17 November, 1994

Cindy Magic
Sociology
422 Lincoln Hall
MC-111

Dear Cindy,

   We are writing to request your cooperation in the Center's on-going evaluation of WAC activities at the University of Illinois. We are interested in finding out what kinds of writing activities are being incorporated into courses throughout the curriculum and how those activities are working, not working, or being creatively modified in particular courses and disciplines. Besides the general goal of evaluating the Center's work, we also anticipate finding useful stories and materials that will help us refine our WAC workshops and seminars.

   Specifically, we hope you will agree to participate in a short interview about your use of writing activities in courses you teach/have taught, particularly Comp II and other writing intensive courses. For the interview, we will ask you to bring copies of any materials you have available (e.g., syllabi, samples of student writing). The minimum time for an interview will be about 20 minutes; however, if you are willing to provide more time we would appreciate it.

   We will be contacting you by phone shortly to see if you are able to schedule an interview. Your participation in our efforts to improve the WAC program are much appreciated.

   Thank you for your time and consideration.

Sincerely,

Paul Prior   Sibylle Gruber
Director of Graduate Student WAC   Assistant to the Director of Writing Studies
Programs   e-mail: s-gruber@uiuc.edu
e-mail: p-prior@uiuc.edu

APPENDIX B. INTERVIEW CONSENT FORM

The Center for Writing Studies is conducting research to evaluate and facilitate both the Center's work and the implementation of writing activities in courses across the UIUC campus. Thank you for agreeing to participate in this interview.

Please review and check off the options below to ensure that the Center's staff knows how it may use the information you provide. If you have any questions, please feel free to ask the interviewer.

• I agree that this interview (on_____, 199__) can be audiotape-recorded (Yes____ No____). (I understand that the tape will be reviewed and possibly transcribed by Center staff.)

• Comments from this interview
    1. may be quoted in evaluation reports (Yes____ No____) or WAC instructional materials (Yes____ No____).
    2. may be paraphrased or referred to in evaluation reports (Yes____ No____) or WAC instructional materials (Yes____ No____).

• The texts that I have provided (e.g., syllabi, assignments, response sheets, evaluation forms)
    1. may be quoted in evaluation reports (Yes____ No____) or WAC instructional materials (Yes____ No____).
    2. may be paraphrased or referred to in evaluation reports (Yes____ No____) or WAC instructional materials (Yes____ No____).

• In using the information gathered in this interview, the Center may identify me by name (Yes____ No____), the course by name (yes____ No____), and the department by name (Yes ____ No____).

[Note: If you have answered no to any of the last three questions but have agreed that the Center may use your interview comments or texts you have provided, then we should remind you that when specific responses to interviews or extracts from course materials are used (even without identification), you may be identifiable to others who are familiar with you or the course.]

If you have any questions or concerns, please call: Paul Prior at 333-3024 or 333-4346.

Your signature indicates that you have read the information above and have decided to participate. You may withdraw at any time after signing this form should you choose to discontinue participation in this evaluation research.

_____   _____

(signature)   (date)

_____

(signature of interviewer)

APPENDIX C. ROBERG INTERVIEW

Nicole: Um, let's talk a little bit about how you used writing in your classroom. Why don't we start out by talking about the writing assignments that are sort of the big things that are on the syllabus here?

Jeff: Well, as you see, there were a few things that were mandatory. Um the first one has to do with... Well, there was a policy paper that was due at the end of the semester. Uh, as a way of making sure that people were progressing on their topics and understood where they were going, uh, I had them write, first of all a topic statement on that, which was essentially "What is is that you're thinking of doing? What's the big question you're looking at? What are some of the sources that you might use on that? And in the most briefest possibility, what is it that... The policy paper is that you had to present a policy. There's a problem, let's say uh, how to stop drugs from entering the United States, something like that. OK, how is it, what are some alternative policies? How do you stop it? We know what's going on now, but I ask them to present three alternative policies for stopping this. And so the topic statement in the most basic sense was, in the most basic sense, was asked to present those tentative policy options for how to go about that. Didn't necessarily have to back it up, just a brief statement so I can see kind of where you're headed. So they turned that in, and then I gave them feedback on that, sources that they could follow up on. Grammar did count but not heavily. It was only I think a ten point assignment....

Nicole: ...OK. Where do we go from there?

Jeff: From there then, in terms of assignments, in terms of formal assignments, uh, we go to an outline. And the outline, of course, was something much more in depth. And you'll see in the syllabus, uh I've got, I'm asking several things. First of all, that there be a proper, a full-paragraph introduction, what it is that your paper is going to try and what are the options you're going to present, and so, "Tell me what you're going to tell me"... the standard format... "Tell me what you're.. Tell me.. Tell me what you told me." So in the outline, I wanted them to identify what the problem is, uh, what 's the background of the problem, some of the research they've already done, what are the policy alternatives they've come up with. By this time, because this was already around the ninth week or so, if memory serves, they should, or actually I guess it was earlier than that, they should have had in their mind the policies and have developed the realization.. whether it's possible to put these into effect. For instance, I could say " One policy to stop the drug problem is to increase border protection." OK, great, which is fine for the topic statement, but for the outline what I want to know is how. Tell me why you want to do this, tell me how you want to do this. What are the positives and the negatives of doing this? And when you weigh out the positives and negatives for each policy alternative, which is your best one to pick? So rather than your traditional research paper, which is "Here's your problem.. go out and tell me all about it, and then bring it back.." I wanted it to be more of a thinking paper. So that they would have to stretch their minds, stretch their imaginations in some cases, for solving these problems, which is something we do every day in our lives anyways. So that's, and then, of course the fourth part of the outline is, after you've presented these policies, you've got to pick one. You must recommend a policy and tell me why you recommended it. So that's in the outline. And the outline , from my perspective, if you did a good outline like you should have, there shouldn't be that much more to do to make it a paper....

Nicole: ...it seems like it has some elements of a first draft.

Jeff: That's right., That's exactly how I conceived of it. And the other thing that I asked them to do, in terms of the outline, was, you had to pick who you were proposing to. Would it be the President of the US, the Secretary of state, the President of a third world country? Because I wanted them to realize, who you decided to advise was going to influence heavily on what policy options you could pick.... and so then what we did was we took that, and before I had them write a final paper, but close to it, I spent a period of three weeks on this, we set aside time every day in class to have oral presentations. Because it's one thing to write up a paper, and some of the topics and alternatives may be rather imaginative, uh, but you have to be able to stand by what you write, and stick by your opinion. And some of the times when people did immigrations papers, and some other topics that were quite hotly debated, it was fun. Because what I asked them to do was do a five minute presentation in class. So you've only got a bare minimum amount of time to lay forth your argument. But what made it interesting is that I assigned in every class three people to play critic. And those three people would give oral criticism and written criticism, because I made them write down their criticisms, of the presenter, of the argument, not.. I didn't care how it was presented, in terms of good oral voice, bad oral voice, but rather the substance and what.. You know, are there any problems with (???), are there any (???), these types of things. And then I asked the critiquers to hand in their critiques to me and then I handed them to the presenter the following class day. I wanted a chance to read over the critiques, make sure they were not out of line, and I stressed to the class several times... I said "Look, this this not by way of public flogging. This is to help people write better papers. I want you to keep that in mind." And that worked, it seemed to work quite well.

APPENDIX D. WAC EVALUATION INTERVIEW COVER SHEET

Interviewer:

Interviewee:

Departmental Affiliation/Position:

Date of interview: Time:

Time length: Page length:

Attachments:

Give a brief summary/description of the interview:

Note page numbers of the transcript where the following topics are addressed:

Comp II courses: general
Comp II: proposals
Comp II: institutional support
Comp II: courses—institutional constraints

evaluation: general
evaluation: out of class drafts
evaluation: out of class final papers
evaluation: lab reports
evaluation: microthemes
evaluation: grading
evaluation: comments

learning through writing
learning through grades
learning through peer response
learning through instructor response

instructor/professor/TA duties: general
instructor/professor/TA duties: assigning
instructor/ professor/ TA duties: responding
instructor/ professor/ TA duties: evaluating

problems using writing: general
problems using writing: increased workload
problems using writing: incorporation into existing curriculum

response: general
response: content
response: length
response: placement
response: peer

writing assignments: general
writing assignments: microthemes
writing assignments: other genres
writing assignments: collaborative writing
writing assignments: long-term projects involving writing
writing assignments: lab reports
writing assignments: research projects
writing assignments: disciplinary
writing assignments: (functions) general

writing assignments: (functions) support discussion
writing assignments: (functions) support reading
writing assignments: (functions) assess content knowledge
writing assignments: (functions) testing

student writing: quality
student writing: improvement/changes
student writing: content
student writing: grammar, style

writing conventions/ expectations: disciplinary
writing conventions/ expectations: general

writing process: general
writing process: in-progress planning/ monitoring/ negotiations
writing process: sequencing assignments
writing process: drafts
writing process: resources
writing process: instructor response
writing process: peer response

WAC: general feedback
WAC seminars/workshops: techniques learned
WAC seminars and workshops: benefits
WAC seminars and workshops: criticisms
WAC: effects on instruction/ personal/professional practices

List other topics addressed and page numbers in the transcript:

APPENDIX E. IMAGINATIVE WRITING ASSIGNMENTS

A. Creating an assignment

By imaginative writing assignments, we mean writing assignments that ask students to actively use their imaginations. These assignments may ask students to imagine themselves or others in other identities or worlds. They may be highly realistic (e.g., a business case study involving a real corporation and considerable documentation) or highly fantastic (e.g., a first-person narrative of a highly intelligent silicon-based life form on the fourth planet of the Alpha Centauri system).

Examples

1. In a history course, students are asked to imagine themselves in some particular role during an event (e.g., the Tet offensive during the Vietnam War) and to write a letter to a friend or family member describing their perceptions, opinions, and feelings about what is happening. (Obviously, there are many possible variations on this task. Roles may be assigned and common, assigned and different, chosen

from a particular set, or completely open. Roles might be well known public figures or private individuals—historical or imagined. Students might be asked to take up two roles embodying very different perspectives.)

2. In a landscape design course, students are asked to quickwrite a vivid detailed narrative of a person visiting a site that they are developing a design for. They are asked to describe the perceptions, feelings, and thoughts of the person and how the site environment affects the person. (As a follow-up assignment, students reflect on the narrative and consider whether any specific design changes might be suggested.)

3. Students in a geography course are asked to write a first person narrative of a water molecule as it travels through the hydrological cycle.

4. In an extended scenario/role play for an Environmental Studies course, groups of students take on different institutional roles (governmental—state and federal EPA, federal court, local city government; corporate; and organizational—Greenpeace, a corporate PAC) for a 2-week negotiation around the siting of a toxic waste dump. Each group has to produce internal documents (e.g., memos) and external documents (e.g., press releases; testimony for EPA review; letters to other groups).

5. Students in an American literature course are asked to rewrite a part of Hawthorne's *Scarlet Letter,* altering some feature of it (e.g., the actions of a particular character, the gender of a character, a particular event in the novel, the historical context—perhaps placing it in the 1990s, the author—perhaps as Mark Twain would have written it, or the genre—perhaps as the script for a TV show) and exploring the consequences of that alteration.

6. Students in a chemistry class are asked to rewrite the procedures and results of their last lab experiment as if it had been done in the microgravity of a spacelab on the Discovery.

B. Goals, resources, and responses

In designing an imaginative writing assignment, three key issues should be considered: goals, resources and response.

1. What goals does the assignment address? The assignment might rehearse content, support other writing assignments or in-class work, prepare students for tests, develop problem-solving skills, develop inquiry and communication processes, appeal to student interest, facilitate personal connections to course materials, and so on.

2. What resources are needed to enable and enrich the assignment? Resources might include actual or hypothetical background knowledge, actual or hypothetical documents, pictures or other graphic images, personal experiences, models, access to information, and so on.

3. How should such assignments be responded to? Should they be graded or simply counted? Should they be read by peers or outside audiences as well as the instructor? To what extent should response focus on content, creativity, or form?

Chapter 13

·

WAC Assessment and Internal Audiences: A Dialogue

Richard Haswell

Susan McLeod

It started in spring (1995). At first, it was a query in passing. "What's up? You know what they want?" But it quickly evolved into a series of sit downs, with caffeine and working papers between us—on the one side, Rich, campus coordinator of writing assessment; on the other side, Susan, associate Dean of Liberal Arts. The last of the dialogue—at least for the time being—was the conversation transcribed later in this article. We knew what we were talking *about* from the beginning: a request from central administration for a status report on our university's rising-junior writing assessment. But what we were *talking* about dawned on us only gradually: the rhetorical nature of writing program assessment within an academic institution. This article uses the report as an example. But our principal topic is the institutional realities of such a report.

THE RHETORIC OF ASSESSMENT

We list below some assumptions readily made about the rhetorical nature of writing-across-the-curriculum (WAC) assessment. These assumptions are easy to make but, for evaluators, easier to forget than put into practice. First, the need for assessment arises out of both a general and a particular context. The general context is provided by institutions of higher learning, which are large, complex, and thoroughly stratified. The particular context is complex and is also continually changing. It follows that the rhetorical participants in a WAC assessment will be varied. Even when there is only one evaluator (which is rarely the case), there will be multiple readers, multiple stakeholders. Further, each of these participants will have different relationships, purposes, and needs for the evaluation. The two main participants—faculty evaluator and administrative reader—often assume diverse motives and roles. This means that WAC assessment provides ample grounds for communicative conflict, clashes that stem from misunderstandings and which can lead to further misunderstandings. In short, the rhetorical nature of WAC evaluation tests all that the evaluator knows about rhetorical purpose, context, kairos, and audience.

This article explores the rhetoric of WAC assessment in a very pragmatic way. It stresses—realistically, we hope—the crucial fact of multiple purpose and multiple audience. WAC directors, for instance, need information from ongoing assessment in order to know how their programs are working and where they might need to fine tune. In such situations, the WAC director herself is the audience, and the purpose is formative. Oftentimes, however, the WAC director is asked to assess the program for some other audience: a central administrator, a Board of Regents, or a legislator. The purpose in such a case may be summative or outright political, assuring the reader of the program's overall worth. This chapter focuses on situations where readers stand outside the WAC program. We take the perspective of what Michael Patton calls "utilization-focused evaluation"—a perspective that foregrounds the needs of the decision makers who have asked for or will be using the results of the assessment. Our pragmatic approach assumes that all elements of assessment have constitutive links with sociopolitical action, from value-construction (Swidler), validity (Messick), and methodology (Smith), to the evaluator's concerns about personal reputation (Gomm). We agree with these authors that program assessment is a negotiative process among stakeholders, a way of organizing and valuing experience with institutional and personal consequences.

Pragmatically put, our goal is to arrive at some recommendations to help WAC evaluators write reports that will achieve their own goals. Our route is fairly straightforward. We begin by contrasting the typical roles and motives of evaluator and administrator, because these two groups form the rhetorical core of an assessment report, writer and reader, and because clashes between their respective roles and motives lead to some of the most common rhetorical failures in WAC evaluation. We then describe our own particular situation of Spring 1995, in much detail, in order to argue that rhetorically WAC assessment is always particular, always sui generis, and always complex. We do so with our dialogue between a WAC coordinator evaluating his own program for an outside audience and an administrator who knows both the program and the outside audience and its needs. The dialogue mode is appropriate because it models the ideal spirit in which we believe program assessment should be undertaken. Dialogue, in a very real sense, is both the nature of WAC evaluation and the solution to its rhetorical problems. From this specific case, we then extract some general ways that evaluators and administrators tend to clash, because we believe that it is often with attention to these conflicting perspectives that functional evaluation arises within an academic institution. We have found that it is out of the specific history of particular WAC assessments on the one hand, and out of general notions of conflicting perspective between evaluator and audience on the other hand, that good rhetorical advice for WAC evaluation emerges.

ROLES OF THE WAC EVALUATOR

Typically, the roles of WAC coordinators who are evaluating their own program arise out of a matrix of professional experience different from that of administrators. This is an obvious but crucial point. WAC coordinators–evaluators are entangled, in a direct and ongoing way, with the very programs and personnel that they are evaluating. They may be teaching one or more of the WAC courses that are being scrutinized. Or they may be managing a testing office responsible for both the cross-campus assessment procedures and the validation of those procedures. They may even have helped design the courses, the assessments, and the validation studies. Certainly they are experiencing daily and front-line encounters with the people who are most immediately affected (and sometimes confused) by WAC programs: students and their relatives, advisors, teachers, department chairs, and clerical staff. They spend more time than they would like in meetings with statisticians, oversight committees, and technology teams from the computing center. And because they are at once teachers and researchers as well as evaluators, they usually persist in the endless task of reading the professional literature, conducting workshops, and writing, presenting, and publishing their own scholarship.

   This might seem an impossible melange of experience in which any one individual could find reasonable roles, but in fact out of this primordial soup a certain number of roles emerge for the WAC evaluator. The catalyst is the end of WAC evaluation for the evaluator. That primary motivation—to describe and assess the WAC program in order to better it—synthesizes the variety of drives and impulses into a few overriding motives. It is, of course, these motives that shape and fuel the roles that the evaluator will assume.

   What are those basic motives?

- The first is intellectual curiosity, i.e., the simple need to learn the truth. Are teachers really following the procedures recommended by the program and reading drafts of student writing? Do students really appreciate or even understand the principles that govern WAC initiatives? WAC evaluators want to sound out these and other mysteries. Indeed, sounding out stands as a core impulse behind any WAC evaluation.
- A second basic motive, which is sometimes at odds with the first, is self-defense. Evaluators—caught up in the formation and implementation of

WAC programs—need to defend their positions. They need to justify both the educational practices in the program they are assessing and the assessment procedures they are using—and in the process to demonstrate their expertise.

- A third motive is to maintain social groups. WAC evaluation may help unify coworkers in the assessment office, bind together a cohort of WAC teachers through self-understanding, or support the self-image of an entire faculty by making programmatic outcomes public. The motivation to further social groups lies behind a spectrum of evaluator actions, from placating oversight boards to gaining budgetary support.
- A final basic motive is to better the educational process. WAC evaluation may satisfy some quite self-serving ends of the evaluator, but it never fully lacks—at least for WAC evaluators it never fully loses—that essential yearning to find a better way for students and teachers.

These motives establish ends to be achieved, and expose the need for evaluators to take on certain roles. Because we will be comparing the roles of the WAC evaluator with those of the academic administrator, we will start with the roles for the WAC evaluator.

1. *Expert*: One who knows what has been done and what can be done in terms of assessment.
2. *Interpreter*: One who serves a constituency outside the program (e.g., administrators) by explaining how things operate and fare from the inside. Or one who serves an internal group (e.g., a WAC seminar or an assessment office) by conveying and explaining the position from outside (e.g., the university budgetary office).
3. *Educator:* One whose final allegiance is the learning and welfare of students.
4. *Scientist-Researcher*: One whose final allegiance is to the truth as far as it can be determined; one who will uphold assessment standards of reliability, validity, and fairness.
5. *Team Worker*: One who will maintain and further the cohesion and viability of a group, be it validation team, testing office, or WAC faculty.
6. *Apologist*: One whose duty it is to defend historically and theoretically an enterprise, be it a validation process, a WAC initiative, or an inter-disciplinary writing workshop.

ROLES OF THE ADMINISTRATOR

It is part of academic culture to grouse about administrators, to classify them as "other," to blame them for the day-to-day inconveniences and stupidities of university life. After all, they set and enforce policies and procedures; ipso facto, they are the focal point for dissatisfaction about such issues. The two of us have done our share of such recreational grousing. However, in order to write an effective assessment of a WAC program, we need to think carefully about administrators as audience—what they do, what they want, and what kind of information they might need from evaluators in order to do their job.

Administrators have different motives than WAC coordinators–evaluators. The primary motive of administrators, unlike evaluators, is to decide where the WAC program fits in the institutional priorities so that decisions can be made about it. Administrators are not devoid of intellectual curiosity and the need to discover the truth, but those motives are always secondary to a primary need: to make decisions about allocation of resources. As the academic equivalent of managers in a corporation, it is their job to maintain the quality of the institution while dealing with budgets (these days ever-shrinking). Administrators are busy people. They work on long-range planning for the institution, articulate and enforce policies, monitor (and worry about) such things as enrollments, faculty hiring and retention, and outside perceptions of the university. Like WAC evaluators, they too have particular roles to play.

1. *Generalist*: One who knows a good deal about several different disciplines by virtue of being in charge of all departmental units, but who is not an expert in any discipline but his or her own, and who is usually not an expert in assessment. The description of administrative knowledge, "a mile wide and an inch deep," is useful to keep in mind.
2. *Mediator–Problem-solver*: One who explains various groups in the university hierarchy to each other, conveying the wishes and needs of those above (trustees, legislators) to those below, and in return representing the needs and desires of those below to those above. Mediation often includes resolving conflicts (for example, between faculty who feel over-worked and legislators who think that the number of hours in a faculty teaching load is equivalent to the number of hours in that faculty's work week).
3. *Manager–Team Leader*: One whose final allegiance is to the health and welfare of the institution or the unit which he/she heads.
4. *Steward*: One who is charged with upholding standards and maintaining quality control, of using resources in accordance with institutional priorities.
5. *Entrepreneur*: One who is expected to meet with possible donors to the institution, to be involved in fundraising.
6. *Spokesperson–PR Specialist*: One whose duty it is to publicly defend the institution or a piece of it by highlighting its quality and its success.

In summary, on one side the evaluator tends to operate as an expert researcher and educator with commitments to the truth, to student learning, and to various circumscribed groups within the institution, guiding those groups by interpreting the larger academic community and informing the community by defending theoretically and pragmatically the groups. On the other side, the administrator tends to operate as a steward and manager with commitments outside the institution to efficiency and to public standards, creating and enforcing policy, solving problems, gaining funding, and in other diplomatic ways mediating between academic groups for the benefit of the whole institution.

Listing their roles helps identify one major conflict in the ways that evaluators and administrators see and utilize assessment. When evaluators assess their own WAC programs, they look toward improvement in the program. But administrators, though not unconcerned about improving WAC programs, are more concerned about the health of the entire institution. They look toward quality assurance, accountability, and public relations. The WAC assessment thus must give administrators *only* the particular data that will fill their needs. An unexpected outcome ripe for further research, for instance—an evaluator's plum—is of no interest to the administrator unless it demonstrates the ongoing health of the program.

Our listing of the different roles suggests many further areas of conflict and potential misunderstanding between evaluator and administrator. Conflicts will arise, however, not simply out of a clash between two divergent academic functions, but complexly out of the particular situation at hand. They will depend on the history of the program and the institution, on the current political and economic forces at play, on the organizational channels in operation, on the personnel in place, and on a wealth of other contingencies. By definition, WAC programs are complex, and many of them are youthful and still in development. It is not that some general areas of conflict cannot be extracted; we plan to end this article by doing just that. It is just that the very nature of the conflicts—the fact that they exist *as* dialogue among the participants (or lack of dialogue)—recommends that they be conceived in context. An understanding of misunderstanding between evaluator and administrator requires a look at its local, messy venue.

A DIALOGUE ABOUT REPORTING ASSESSMENT RESULTS

To illustrate the interaction of all these roles, we present here a dialogue between an administrator, Susan, and an evaluator, Rich. This dialogue will illustrate two things: (a) the potential for misunderstanding which we have just discussed and (b) the advantages when the administrator occupies a middle ground between the intended audience and the WAC program. Susan happens to occupy this middle ground, although she is certainly not unique in this advantage. As we have said, this particular dialogue was occasioned by one particular WAC assessment initiative, dating from Spring 1995. Two years earlier, as part of an ambitious WAC program, upper-division students at Washington State University had begun taking a new writing portfolio examination, our version of a "rising junior" writing assessment instrument (see Haswell, Johnson-Shull, & Wyche-Smith; Haswell & Wyche-Smith 1996). For their University Writing Portfolio of five pieces, all undergraduates had been submitting three pieces of writing from previous courses and then composing two essays under timed conditions. Their completed portfolio, once evaluated, either deemed them as qualified for upper-division writing intensive courses in their major or required that they take further writing instruction.

In 2 years the examination had produced results and data that told us some interesting things about the institution: Besides the rates of "pass" versus "needs work" assigned to the portfolios, we could track which departments assigned a good deal of writing, which teachers within those departments assigned the most writing, and which groups of students (e.g., transfers, biology majors, internationals) received the highest and the lowest evaluations on their portfolios. By the spring, the central administration (that is, the provost, who is the chief academic officer of the university, and the vice provost) indicated that they were looking for a report on these results. What eventually ensued was that the Coordinator of Writing Assessment (Rich Haswell) produced, in fact, not one but four reports: chronologically,

1. A four-page "stopgap" informational report issued 5 weeks into the Spring semester, directed to the Director of General Education and sent on to the Provost, to whom he reports.
2. A 5-minute oral report, delivered to the Board of Regents during their annual meeting at commencement, with the Vice Provost, the Provost, and the President in attendance.
3. A six-page "progress" report to the Provost and Vice Provost, via the Director of General Education, sent a month after the end of the spring semester.
4. A long, formal "internal" report issued at the end of the summer, sent to the Director of General Education with copies to the chair of the All-University Writing Committee (AUWC) and Director of University Assessment.

The following dialogue occurred between the two of us in June, after the first two reports had been issued, but while the third, the "progress" report, was still being written. The dialogue is both a reminiscence of the circumstances that occasioned the first two reports and a working session adding finishing details to the third.

Rich Haswell, as the Director of Writing Assessment, was the principal designer, administrator, and now the evaluator of the campus-wide junior Writing Portfolio. Susan McLeod had left her position as Director of Composition to become the Associate Dean of the College of Liberal Arts, and was thus well positioned to know the campus-wide writing program as well as the administrators to which this report will go and the decisions they might make as a result. Both of us had thought a good deal about writing assessment.[1] Here we are, looking at the raw data out of which this third report will be shaped: a list of teachers who have signed off on papers that went into the portfolios and the departments from which the papers came; statistics on how many students fell into which category in the readings ("pass," "pass with distinction," "needs work") and what majors those students have declared; statistics on other populations, such as males and females, transfer students, students who have identified themselves as first-language or ESL writers.

Eventually, out of this data we will create the rest of the reports. The report under construction, the third, has multiple audiences. Besides the usual routing (to the provost and vice provost via the general education director), other readers may be the AUWC, the dean of the college of liberal arts (in whose area most of the writing courses reside), the president, the board of regents, and the higher education coordinating board (a statewide oversight body which looks at all of higher education in the state). The reports may also come into the hands of a stray legislator or two, as well as a local reporter who thinks of himself as "investigative" and seems convinced that the university is hiding important secrets from the public.[2] Indeed, it was an awareness of the diversity of needs among these readers that led to the splitting of one report into four.

Rich: This January I heard that the central administration was itchy for a formal account of the Portfolio. That caught me by surprise me because the exam is only 2 years old and not yet at full steam. From the start I have sent results of student performance (the percentage of "pass with distinction," "pass," and "needs work") to people who needed them at the moment, such as the AUWC, the director of general education, the director of assessment, various department chairs, the director of composition, and the student

---

[1] See Richard Haswell and Susan Wyche-Smith, 1994; Haswell, *Gaining Ground*, Ch. 14; Susan McLeod, 1992.

[2] A recent headline from this reporter read, "University President Lives Like A King at Taxpayer's Expense." The story had to do with the President's relatively modest budget for entertainment, all of which comes from donations to the institution, not from taxes.

advising and learning center. Of course I thought that sooner or later there would be a validation study, but I didn't imagine the kind of accountability report the administrators wanted. Do you know what lay behind that want?

Susan: Yes. I remember that the biennial budget was coming due, and every time that the university's budget request comes before the legislature, there are questions about accountability: What are we spending the state's money on, and what kind of bang we are getting for their buck, what's working, what isn't. The administration needs data, evidence of quality for the budget hearings, to justify the newest request. I think the other driver was the Higher Education Coordinating Board. The HEC Board, like its counterparts in other states, is heavily invested in outcomes assessment statewide.

Rich: My first response was what we are calling the stopgap report. The name reflects my mood at the time. In it I asked six questions, which reflect problem areas, and gave whatever statistics or data I had as answers to these questions. Looking back, would you say this was wise?

Susan: Were they questions or problem areas that you had been asked about, or were they ones you just saw in the material?

Rich: Both. I saw that I had answers to questions that I was interested in, and there were questions that had come out in some conversations that I had with the AUWC. Like this whole issue of performance: at what rate are we giving out ratings of "needs work" and "pass with distinction"? The issue of how well transfer students do is a question that the general education director has brought up several times. Now in the subsequent report to the regents, I took a considerably different approach, highlighting positive outcomes of the exam and mentioning no areas in need of action. Won't such a radical change of format and content make administrators suspicious?

Susan: No, because the two reports have different purposes. Earlier in the spring the pressure was to give a preliminary report, and it looks to me that there were some very specific questions that people wanted to know the answers to—for instance the success of the transfer students. In fact, one way to approach a report like this is simply to contact the administrator who requested it and ask, "What do you want to know?" Then frame the report as you did, using the questions they want answered. It's a way of getting a quick outline. Administrators don't have a lot of time to answer questions they are being asked by their constituencies—they much prefer that the expert craft answers for them. But the presentation to the Regents—well, the regents want to hear that the program is working. They are here for just one day, and they have a lot to absorb. That doesn't give us much time for subtleties.

Rich: That brings up the question of what they mean by "working." Everyone seems to have a different take on the outcomes. For instance, after the director of general education saw the stopgap report, he told me that the figure of 10% of exam takers put into the "needs work" category was low. He said that he thought 20% was more "accurate." On the other hand, the dean of liberal arts thought that 10% was a good sign, showing that undergraduates are writing well here, better than expected.

Susan: There will be some readers of all your reports who think that undergraduates write very badly, but that notion is based on some comparison with what they remember as the golden days of their undergraduate years. I think of this as a "Paradise Lost" mindset, and it is perhaps more prevalent than you and me might like to believe. What they think they should see and what the report says may be two different things, and we need to be honest.

Rich: Well, *what's honest* has about the same rhetorical status as *what works*— both are equally problematical, though from different sides of the fence. One of the learning moments in all of this was when I first talked with a central administrator about my oral report to the regents. On the phone he said that—he was looking at this "stopgap" report —"you have some good data here, could you give me five minutes at that meeting?" And then he was very careful, and he said, "Vanilla, nothing fancy." So from that I put together some stuff, most of it positive. But at the time I asked him would it be all right to report the poor performance of the transfer ESL students and the comparative performance of colleges, and he hesitated. Then he said, "Yes, if you want to." Then at the meeting itself, I quickly saw that he was giving me good advice about audience and kairos—what was being reported by other presenters was truly nothing but vanilla.

Susan: Right. The regents technically are at the top of the University's organizational chart—the deans and the general education director and the vice provost report to the provost, the provost reports to the president, the president to the regents. The regents are appointed by the governor; they are bright, well-educated people who are deeply concerned about the institution, but they are more of a ceremonial body. They must approve all tenure decisions, for example, but that approval is really a rubber-stamp. This is not to say they are not an important audience—they are in fact influential in the state and quite shrewd, and they have a veto power they are not afraid to use. But they don't have the decision-making power that the provost has at the local level. They are interested in the overall picture. They are like the President—more external, more involved in liaison efforts between the university and the legislature.

Rich: As I was giving this oral report to the regents, there was one piece of data that they reacted to much more than to the others. It was when I said that portfolio papers had been submitted from "880 different teachers in 660 different courses in 63 different departments." That seemed to be very impressive to them. You could hear the intake of breath. Why do you think it was?

Susan: You said generally that there was widespread compliance. But when you started talking about actual numbers, I think that makes it real to them. They are thinking, wow, this is a big operation. Until you hear those numbers, you don't realize the sheer size of it. That is precisely the sort of fact that the Provost will want to quote in his various public presentations, for good public relations. It gives people an idea of how hard we are working.

Rich: There is also something about the picture that those numbers give of the whole university that was impressive to them, too.

Susan: I think so. They probably had the notion, based perhaps on the "why-Johnny-can't-write" articles in the newspaper, that teachers nowadays aren't assigning writing, or not as many as when they went to school (that

"Paradise Lost" mindset), and I think that those numbers gave them a different picture of the institution—that there are a lot of conscientious teachers out there who care about writing and are assigning papers to their students. To put it in very simplistic terms, the regents wanted some kind of evidence that WSU was doing something about the literacy crisis, and they got it.

Rich: As I said, at the regents' meeting I saw they were truly getting vanilla. And so as reports of others kept coming in, I kept marking stuff to leave out of mine. I left out that data on transfer ESL students. I did mention that the portfolio was having a good cross-curricular effect, that a number of departments are doing exceptionally well, and I named them. But I did not name the departments that are having trouble.

Susan: I think that was a really wise strategy, because you were talking to regents, who want to hear only about what's working. But the provost and vice provost need to have a more complete picture, because they are the chief academic officers of the institution. Quality control is their job.

Rich: So we are back to what's working. What is the vice provost's take?

Susan: He is first and foremost interested in academic quality. That is his definition of "working." As vice provost for academic affairs, he is responsible for the day-to-day quality control of academic programs. He is the provost's right hand person and feeds him information. As one of the very first participants in the original WAC seminar I ran in 1986, and as a fine teacher who has always required writing in his anthropology classes, he is very supportive of anything having to do with the writing effort. He has read Boyer's book, College: The Undergraduate Experience, and firmly believes that communication skills are the key to a successful undergraduate experience. He will define "working" as "improving the quality of our product"—student writing.

Rich: How will he use the progress reports?

Susan: To show the folks above him in the administrative hierarchy who hold him accountable—the provost, the president, the regents, the HEC board, and the legislators—that the university is doing a good job with writing on the undergraduate level.

Rich: So that is why you insist that, even with him, we need to emphasize the positive?

Susan: Yes. Not that we don't want to think about how the program can be improved, but things that we can improve ourselves are not his concern.

Rich: What about the provost? Is he different from the vice provost in how he defines what is working?

Susan: Yes, but mostly in the way he wants that information given to him. He is a hard scientist—where the vice provost is used to ethnographic studies (because that is how he writes up his own research), the provost wants clean facts, to show quality and cost effectiveness. One of the ways I get at the question of readers is to look at the documents they themselves have produced. And, if you look at what the provost produces for other people in the university to consume, it is a very short amount of text with a series of bullets, one right after another. Like many public figures, that's also the way he talks, in sound bites, giving nuggets of information. One of the things we want to do with this report is to provide something that then he could translate very easily into one of the overhead transparencies that he is uses in his presentations to show what the institution is doing.

Rich: Is that why you recommended in the progress report an executive summary of no more than a page?

Susan: Yes, and not just because the bullets and executive summary are parts of his own administrative style. That format will help him get the gist of the report quickly, and he will appreciate that because he has so much paper to go through. Administrators are overwhelmed by paper—there's always a stack to be read and translated into action. They don't have much time to ponder and reflect.

Rich: Which of these bullets will most attract his attention?

Susan: I think the fact that students are complying with the portfolio requirement in good order, especially with the legislature asking about efficiency and time to graduation. They want to be sure that this new writing requirement isn't holding students back. Also the fact that students are doing writing in all corners of the campus—that teachers as well as students are complying. The numbers will also attract him. He wants data and statistics, and it is not just a characteristic of the provost. Decisions at the university are data driven. Administrators all have to have some kind of data-based justification, not just whim or gut reaction. The bullet giving the ESL data will be particularly interesting because I think there is a general feeling on campus that ESL students have writing difficulties but no one quite knows what to do about the problem. I'm sure you are going to hear about this figure, that 36% of transfer students who identified themselves as ESL received the "needs work" designation. That's going to be pulled out immediately. And this bullet, "By all signs the portfolio examination is entrenched and healthy," ought to be pulled out and put at the very beginning. And this final bullet, "Areas in need of further study and improvement," needs to be changed to "Recommendations." What we want them to do with this report is not just learn about what we are doing, but take some action.

Rich: Now the provost will be the one who finally makes the decision to take action. What kinds of action do you think he will take?

Susan: It depends on what the data show, and we need to foreground the data that we think are most suggestive of the action that the provost has the power to take. The data show pretty convincingly that ESL students need support, and at the moment we have no area in the university with the expertise to provide that help. So we may want to recommend that a specialist in ESL be hired to provide us with that expertise. University administrators are problem solvers; we can help them solve those problems by suggesting solutions.

Rich: Well, because I leave most of the negative information about departments out of this progress report, how is the provost to learn about it? About a month ago, after I had written the stopgap report, we talked and decided that for the "final" product I should in fact write two different accounts, this short progress report and then a longer internal report with the data in full—each college and each department and how well they are doing in terms of their students' performance and of their faculty's compliance with assigning writing in their classes. Your suggestion was that the progress report should go up the administrative line, while the internal report should go to the AUWC, and they should decide what should be done with it. Why do you think that is better than sending negative information directly to the vice provost and the provost?

Susan: Because the AUWC has been the body working directly with individual faculty members on writing-in-the-major courses and on issues of faculty compliance with assigning writing in their classes. The provost and vice provost are decision makers, but on a day-to-day basis the university committee structure is the machinery by which we get things done. Rather than forwarding what could be damaging information to the provost and putting the provost in a position of needing to reward or punish departments or colleges through his decisions, it would be much better politically to have the AUWC look at this material and say to the committee's representative from Business, "Your area is not doing well—your faculty are not assigning writing, as far as we can tell from the portfolios, and a larger percentage of your students get the 'needs work' designation, perhaps as a result of the fact that they do not do much writing in your college. What do you suggest we should be do about this situation? We don't want to embarrass your college. How could we work with your faculty so that they are in better compliance, and so that your students' writing ability improves?"

Rich: So because the AUWC is representative, their decision to do something about it can be more effective.

Susan: They can do something about it in a formative way by working with faculty who are their colleagues, rather than in a punitive way, as the provost might be pressured to do.

Rich: And that would take the heat off of me. And keep people from saying, well, he's from English, and of course he has something against Business, so all he wants to do is humiliate my college and colleagues publicly.

Susan: Right.

Rich: Early on you said that we should not discuss anything that had to do with our startup problems in the reports that went up the line to the administration. Why was that?

Susan: Because administrators are interested not in startup but bottom-line issues, ones they can do something about. I hear that phrase "bottom line" a lot. Administrators have to make decisions. The issue of startup or pilot difficulties is of interest to those of us who administer the exam; we want to understand, for example, why the percentage of "pass with distinction" ratings was higher during the first year of the portfolio's existence. Was it due to the raters' inexperience, or perhaps our training methods? What we found was that the better writing students, for instance those in the Honors Program, tended to take the exam early. As the less motivated (or less organized) students were brought into the exam, the "pass with distinction" ratings dropped. But administrators are interested only in final implications, not in interesting little blips in the data that intrigue us as researchers.

Rich: So the question is always, what will administrators make of this data, what will they do with it?

Susan: Absolutely. Administrators are always under pressure in terms of resources and are always looking for reasons to reallocate those resources. The only reason to give them negative information about the workings of the program is if the program really isn't working over all and should be discontinued, or if we thought they should do something about the problem by allocating more resources. For example, in our ESL situation, we have a clear problem and we can't solve it. The administration can help solve the problem by allocating resources (hiring an expert in this area). But if it is a problem we can correct, they don't need to know about it, or if they do, just enough to know that we are correcting it. Any negative information in an otherwise positive report can be easily misunderstood and misused by those who have their own agendas. What would happen if we said in our report that rater reliability could be improved? Administrators might respond by saying, "OK—then we will discontinue the Portfolio and put in a machine-scored multiple choice test, which will be reliable." Ouch. We have to be honest in the overall picture, of course. If a program is not doing what we thought it would, we need to come clean.

Rich: So it's a matter of including in a report only the information that administrators can use, can show to their constituencies or take particular action that we can't take.

Susan: Yes, utilization-focused assessment.

Rich: With the progress report, you recommended showing the various departments that Portfolio raters came from. Why did you think this information would be useful to administrators?

Susan: I want to make sure that they understood that this is not an English Department operation, that it is a broad-based assessment effort involving people from all disciplines on campus. I think that this is important politically.

Rich: You mean as a general perception on campus?

Susan: Yes. Because you have been so proactive in getting people from all different disciplines involved in the reading of the portfolios, the word has spread among faculty that this is an effort that includes all who wish to be involved. But administrators tend to be isolated from such general campus understandings. It's hard for them even to attend faculty meetings in the departments with which they are officially affiliated. Administrators have to be careful about their understanding of what is really happening, because so many times they hear only from the squeaky wheels. When things are going well, they tend not to hear about it. Your report then serves an important informational function; you are telling them what the general campus already knows.

Rich: And telling them in a substantive form, with figures, so they can test the information against what they have heard.

Susan: Yes, so if Professor Indignant marches in and says "This is an English Department plot against the rest of us!" the administrator can pull out the report and say, "Well that's not what these figures show."

Rich: As I was preparing the stopgap report, there was one area where I began to sense that I had a different concept of this assessment than the central administrators did. I have always thought of the portfolio as instructional, as a diagnostic tool to get students the help they need in order to succeed at the upper-division level. But administrators seem to see the Portfolio as a test, a hurdle demonstrating quality control. Two clashing notions of the basic motive behind the portfolio—and a good candidate for misunderstandings.

Susan: I think that as long as the people in charge of the portfolio understand that its function is diagnostic rather than punitive, there's no need to explain the niceties of that distinction to the administration. Administrators are involved in two things that may make it better for them to think of this as a test: quality control and public relations. Their job is to let people know that yes, we have standards and we are doing something about student writing. We're testing it. And furthermore, no institution of our size has been able to make this sort of test work but (trumpets, please) we are. I don't think we need to be overly concerned about the distinction between our professional "expert" conception of what we are doing and their more general understanding. The portfolio does finally function, after all, as a quality control device, and also as a way to improve student writing. We're just not doing it in a sheep–goats sort of way.

Rich: So this is one area in which the display of data can get around those conceptual issues.

Susan: Yes. And that understanding of the portfolio as a test might even work in their favor—when they are talking to legislators, or potential donors, or to the regents or the HEC board. Some segments of the public have a rather punitive notion of what education is all about, and the notion of a test might fit their schema of an institution with high standards.

Rich: To what degree should I think about any of these reports I have been writing as public?

Susan: Once it is out of your hands, it is a public document. Anyone can ask for it, including reporters from the local newspaper. A report that goes to an administrator has the potential for a very long life and many different readers. This is a thought to make even the most reckless person cautious about any information in the reports that could be misinterpreted or misrepresented.

Rich: Let's talk a little about length. You advise that this progress report should be no more than three or four pages. It's now six pages, and I worry that it is too long.

Susan: Right—you don't want to include everything. Besides an executive summary, one way to deal with the issue of length is to have a short document with appendices, which readers can refer to if necessary. It is a mistake to send a comprehensive report to an administrator and expect him or her to extract important information from it. Sometimes people think of reports on assessment as analogous to reports sent to granting agencies, who want to know every nuance. That is not the case with administrators, who want to know specific things—as we have said before, quality assurance issues, possible PR opportunities, and information that will help them make decisions about resources. I said earlier that in this progress report instead of a list of "issues for further study," you should have a list of "recommendations." One thing that I always have to remind myself when I'm writing up a report for the administration is that I'm not writing a research report or journal article. The administrators are not necessarily interested in a detailed discussion of methodology; for example—what they want are the results of our study, the answers to particular questions that they might have or that their various constituencies or the people they report to might have.

Rich: One last question: It was my idea to make this progress report the first of a sequence, 1 every 2 years. Does that make sense?

Susan: Yes. You have managed to coordinate it with the biennial budget request that the director of general education has to send forward. You want to make sure that if you are asking administrators to do something with the information you give them, then you do it at a time when they have the resources. It's very savvy of you to know what the budget cycle is and coordinate your report and accompanying recommendations with that cycle.

Rich: So 2 more years and another progress report?

Susan: The administration will hope so. Administrators are always being held accountable by all of their constituencies—above and below them. The information we give them is information that they want to use. Especially these days when authority of any sort is under fire, they are constantly scrambling to find data that show the university is really doing its job—that professors are not just a bunch of drones and that we are teaching students something useful. They are eager for information, especially when we have programs that are really working and can prove that they are.

CONFLICTS BETWEEN EVALUATOR AND ADMINISTRATOR

As we hope our dialogue shows, there are numerous possibilities for conflicts between WAC evaluators and administrators. Within the arena of WAC programs, there are six common conflicts that warrant isolation. These conflicts may appear to be simplifications and even abstractions, but they have served to help troubleshoot or clarify encounters between WAC evaluators and administrators in the past. An understanding of these conflicts should serve to ameliorate such encounters in the future.

1. *The clash between a vision of a part and a vision of the whole.* Almost by definition, evaluation of a program requires a restricted gaze. An evaluator who studies an upper-division writing-intensive program, for example, is constantly tempted to disregard the relevance of that program to the university as a whole. The attention is given to certain courses, certain teachers and students, and certain outcomes. The nature of empirical testing and inferential statistics further circumscribes that

attention, and the evaluator may investigate only a sample of sections and test for a small selection of outcomes. When all is done, it is hard to resist speaking in the time-honored words of many a validation study and refuse to vouch for the implications of the conclusions beyond the few variables measured. But the administrator, however sympathetic, needs to go beyond. Decisions need to be made about the entire program, with constant attention to the ramifications of those decisions in terms of the university as a whole.

2. *The clash between description and action.* Indeed, when administrators rightly complain that the evaluation report lacks clear relevance to the formation of policy or fails to recommend a clear course of action, the evaluator may easily fall back on the researcher's defense that the study is purely descriptive and that others must decide on its implications. Descriptive findings, however, can be more or less useful. The evaluator can measure the number of pages submitted in writing-intensive courses, from which it is difficult to recommend further action, or to assess the value of the writing from the students' and the teachers' point of view, from which point recommendations for change are more readily seen. A wise evaluator will design the need for final recommendations right from the start.

3. *The clash between problem discovery and problem solving.* It is a temptation for program evaluators to think of assessment as a search for problems. Comparison of syllabi from writing-intensive courses across disciplines should show some departments weaker than others in the integration of writing assignments with subject matter. This is a problem for which the administrator will wish the evaluator had included other findings indicating a solution. Of more use to the administrator might be the identification of especially successful teachers and techniques within disciplines, in which case recommendation for improvement is clearer. Again, evaluators could well be aware of the need to shape evaluation toward solutions from the beginning.

4. *The clash between expert and public understanding.* Evaluation of human performance has become a highly technical field in that every part of it has a professional history of unresolved debate. It is easy for knowledgeable evaluators (the more knowledgeable, the easier) to direct their reports to their own kind. Administrators need to send evaluation findings to persons and groups who may have little professional understanding of evaluation and even personal bias against aspects of it such as data collection and statistical analysis.

5. *The clash between the need for truth and the need for usefulness.* By nature and certainly by the creed and procedures of assessment methodology, the evaluator will present all the findings, the whole findings, and nothing but the findings, no matter how negative, discouraging, or con-

founding. There is even a commitment to report conclusions of the evaluation that suggest the evaluation itself was flawed. It is often very difficult for the administrator to make use of such an approach. Some of the most difficult standoffs between evaluator and administrator occur because of the imperative of one to report negative findings and the need of the other to have findings that are convincing, supportive, or persuasive for a particular constituency.

6. *The clash between abstractions and personalities.* Formal assessment asks that the evaluator move toward objectivity and abstractions whenever possible. The evaluator is looking for generalities that lie underneath the confusion of surface input, and is trying to set the eccentricities and individual agendas of the individuals involved in assessment—students and teachers—aside. The administrator, on the other hand, must deal directly with personalities because they are a means by which and an avenue through which things in a complex organization are accomplished. And the administrator must deal with them on a sui generis basis, knowing that each person is unique and that uniqueness often is the key to successful action through that person.

RECOMMENDATIONS

Having presented our own dialogue, which illustrates some of these clashes, we would like to follow our own advice and close with some recommendations for those asked to produce evaluations of WAC programs.

1. Ask as many questions as you politely can about the needs of your primary audience (who may or may not be the person requesting the assessment report). Who is your most important reader, and why does that person or committee want this evaluation? Is the purpose to find out how well the program works? To find out how cost efficient it is? To justify additional funding for (or slashing of) the program? Then sketch out as much as you can about this primary audience and their intended utilization of the evaluation report. Your report (or as in our case, reports) will no doubt have multiple audiences, and you should not ignore them, but you should focus on the primary audience, usually central administrators, and the use they will make of the report.

2. Examine the sorts of documents that are consumed and produced by the office to which your report ultimately will go. Use these documents as models.

3. If at all possible, as you draft your report , carry on your own dialogue with an administrator who knows all the stakeholders and is willing to help you think through all the issues we have raised here. This dia-

logue will work best, we think, if that person is a mid-level administrator, not someone to whom the report will go, but someone who knows the personalities and their motives and who has experience writing similar reports and can help you phrase things where necessary in administrationese.

4. Focus on recommendations and action. Administrators rarely ask for reports so that they can file them—they are decision makers. They need evidence that they have made good decisions and evidence on which to base new ones. Think carefully about what you want to happen as a result of the information that you are presenting. Do the data suggest that you need a bigger budget for the program? Is the program growing at such a rate that you need a new computer to track it? Do you need (as it seems we do) some expertise to provide support for students whose first language is not English? Don't expect administrators to figure out what you need. Tell them the problems your data illuminate and then suggest a solution. For this audience, do not ignore the need for public relations. As members of the academic community, we tend to scorn self-promotion (although of course we can see that vice clearly in some of our colleagues). But public relations are an important part of any administrator's job. It is wise to offer a few choice sound bites to tout your program (if indeed it is toutable).

5. Find out about the budget cycle at your institution and what relationship your report might have to that cycle. Unless we have been involved with administration at the chair's level or above, most of us have little knowledge of how the budget process actually works. If we want resources for our program, we have to tie our evaluations and subsequent recommendations to the budget process.

If we may return to our opening point, writing an assessment of a WAC program tests all that the evaluator knows about rhetoric. We should take the advice we give our students: to figure out who the audience is, what the purpose and situation are, what the audience will do with what we send them; to tailor the format to meet the audience's needs, to use models to guide us, to ask for feedback on our drafts. This is less difficult than it may seem. After all, the distance between evaluator and administrator is not that great. Although we have contrasted their motives and roles, we also think it instructive to remember that both usually started out with the same experiences, as faculty. Where there are commonalties in experience, there are ways to communicate. We have presented our own dialogue as a model of the process, but as we have pointed out, rhetorical contexts for WAC programs differ markedly from institution to institution. Our final products may turn out useful at our university, but probably not at yours. To those WAC evaluators just starting, our final recommendation is to find someone at your institution with whom you can discuss your evaluation and carry out your own dialogue.

REFERENCES

Gomm, R. (1981). Salvage evaluation. In D. Smetherham (Ed.), Practising evaluation (pp. 127-144). Chester, England: Bemrose Press.

Haswell, R. (1991). Gaining ground in college writing. Dallas: Southern Methodist University Press.

Haswell, R., Johnson-Shull L., & Wyche-Smith, S. (1994). Shooting Niagara: Making portfolio assessment serve instruction at a state university. WPA: Writing Program Administration, 18, 44-53.

Haswell, R., & Wyche-Smith, S. (1994). Adventuring into writing assessment. College Composition and Communication 45(2), 220-236.

Haswell, R., & Wyche-Smith, S. (1996). A two-tiered rating procedure for placement essays. In T. Banta (Ed.), Assessment strategies that work (pp. 204-207). San Francisco: Jossey-Bass.

McLeod, S. (1992). Evaluating writing programs: Paradigms, problems, possibilities. Journal of Advanced Composition, 12(2), 373-382.

Messick, S. (1989). Meaning and values in test validation: The science and ethics of assessment. Educational Researcher, 18(2), 5-11.

Patton, M. (1986). Utilization-focused evaluation (2nd ed). Newbury Park, CA: Sage.

Smith, M. L. (1986). The whole is greater: Combining qualitative and quantitative approaches in evaluation studies. In D. D. Williams (Ed.), Naturalistic evaluation. New Directions for Program Evaluation (Vol. 31, pp. 37-54). San Francisco: Jossey-Bass.

Swidler, A. (1986). Culture in action: Symbols and strategies. American Sociological Review, 51, 273-286.

Chapter 14

·

Pragmatism, Positivism, and Program Evaluation

Michael M. Williamson

As Paul Taylor notes, our teaching and research has taught us that the social and psychological processes involved with writing, writing pedagogy, and writing assessment are not necessarily logical, rational, or orderly. We have come to see writing, in research and teaching, as constructed through the efforts of the community of researchers, teachers, and students. We have worked very hard at developing theories of writing based on both empirical and theoretical research. In writing assessment, we have challenged narrowly defined uses of psychometric theory to the extent these approaches have been scientistic or have remained strictly positivistic in their orientation. In notable contrast to the picture painted by Taylor, positivist approaches to research rest in the belief that science can uncover the essentially rational and orderly processes of the natural and social world by using scientific, logical research methodology.

In attempting to develop a sensible approach to writing assessment, we have argued that writing is an extremely complex phenomenon that can only be understood through such "messy" assessment techniques as holistic scoring and portfolio assessment. In contrast to multiple-choice tests which provide only a limited view of some of the knowledge that is required to participate in a discourse community, holistic scoring can provide a snapshot of each student's composing processes because such assessments require students to produce a text to be rated. Portfolios have the potential for an even greater view of students' ability to write because they can provide a sense of the range of students' writing interests, their differing approaches to writing, and their reflections on the meaning of literacy that each of the texts in the portfolio has for them. The richer assessment techniques, although messy to collect and evaluate, make much more sense than the more orderly multiple-choice tests of writing ability precisely because of the richness of the information they reveal to both researchers and teachers. In addition to the obvious limitations of multiple-choice tests of writing in terms of what they can tell us about our students, most of us who teach writing worry about the effects that multiple-choice tests have on our pedagogies. In particular, multiple-choice tests seem to compel teachers to focus their efforts on students' accuracy with the prestige dialect of Standard Written English to the exclusion of the richer aspects of literacy and the more complex problems faced by writers as they attempt to understand that literacy involves participation in a community of writers. Unfortunately, as Roger Cherry and Paul Meyer suggest, our arguments continue to fly in the face of the logic of such theoretical categories from the psychometric literature as reliability and validity, as they are conventionally, and thus, narrowly defined.

Our research and our teaching may acknowledge the complexity of writing. However, when faced with evaluation of a writing-across-the-curriculum (WAC) program, the pragmatic aspects of assessing the results of our efforts can lead us to behave as though we were examining an orderly and logical situation, in contrast to our perspective on research and teaching. This chapter explores the difficulties of living up to our constructivist views of research and teaching in curriculum and program assessment and evaluation. Part of the problem emerges from our own biases. For the most part, our daily activities seem quite orderly and rational to us. On the other hand, we may be forced into adversarial relationships when our institutions are making hard decisions about limited funding. In such situations, other participants in our institutions may create an environment that does not lend itself readily to our presentation of the complexity of our curricula and our students' learning. Thus, we can be deflected from our hard-won understanding that truth is a multifaceted construction, contingent on the concerted activities of all those who participate in the community.

Although it is played out in a practical as opposed to a theoretical arena, this situation is not unlike the theoretical conflict between positivism and constructivism. Positivism views truth as independent of particular contexts and observers, relying on scientific methods to provide access to truth through their logical and orderly structure. Positivism also denies other avenues to truth than the strictly objectivist stance of the traditional scientist, thus making holding our ground difficult for those of us who would like to admit that the community in which we participate is composed of a broader constituency with a diversity of views. This difficulty exists, of course, when any ideology demands that it be held as the single acceptable approach taken by members of the community. Besides, in a very real sense, a pragmatic epistemology based on an informal positivism is a pervasive aspect of American culture. The media, for instance, represent events as single-sided. We tend to value explicit demonstrations of knowledge, as illustrated in our "seeing is believing" attitude, and, despite a general commitment to democracy, by the current public commitment by the ruling party in Congress to root out the evil ways of the other party suggests that a plurality of views is only valuable as an ideological touchstone, rather than as a routine mode of operation.

WHAT IS PROGRAM EVALUATION?

I will be using the terms curriculum and program and the terms assessment and evaluation as synonyms. A description of the curriculum is part of a WAC program. The curriculum, then, is represented in any document that makes claims for the purposes of a WAC program—both by setting goals and prescribing or suggesting sequences of experiences that teachers provide to students. A program involves all of the participants and stakeholders involved with that program. Curriculum statements are only a limited part of a program in this strict sense. However, curriculum and program are often used interchangeably in the broader sense of the word program.

An evaluation is a distinct form of programmatic or curriculum assessment. Assessment is nothing more than gathering information useful to describe the operations of a program or curriculum. Evaluation, on the other hand, involves ascribing merit based on the information gathered in an assessment. The phrase "program evaluation" has a competitiveness and accountability for those of us who have been involved with federal educational program evaluation. Continued funding often depends on demonstrating that one program has greater merit than others like it. Program evaluation also has the sense of an audit because it provides funding authorities with an accounting of how their money was spent and an analysis of the benefits that accrued from the activity that was funded. I will use the term program as shorthand for program and curriculum, and the term assessment as shorthand for assessment and evaluation, because "program and curriculum assessment and evaluation" is cumbersome.

Program evaluation is a very different kind of research than the study of writing or the teaching of writing in contexts which are intended to focus on making a contribution to the broader field. Program evaluation may make a contribution to the field, but it usually begins with the concerns of one or more participants in a particular program about the program's future. As W. James Popham notes, quantitative approaches to program evaluation typically define program evaluation research as decision oriented. In this context, evaluation is supported by an institution in order to make a decision about some aspect of a program or curriculum. One of the most common forms of decisions to be made about a program is whether it is cost effective. University-wide administrators are almost always curious about this issue, whether it is a clearly articulated goal of an evaluation study or not. On the other hand, teachers in a WAC program are almost always curious about whether they need to make curricular or instructional changes in the program to meet the ever-changing needs of an ever-changing student population. They also wish to know more about their students.

Thus, the basis for research and scholarship is different than the basis for program evaluation. While the decision-oriented approach to program evaluation is unnecessary, it should be clear that the participants in a program are interested in an evaluation study because they want to make decisions about how to conduct themselves as they plan for the future of the program. After some experience with program evaluation at several institutions, as both an internal and an external evaluation consultant, I have come to see that participants in educational programs—including students, teachers, and administrators—are likely to engage the belief systems of their everyday lives in the process. This means that though we may accept the multifaceted reality of writing and the teaching of writing, we often find ourselves in adversarial relationships as we participate in evaluations. Thus, we find ourselves having to define "the truth" as opposed to helping community members construct a truth from the evaluation study processes.

The purpose of this chapter is not to challenge the basic endeavor of writing program assessment in WAC programs. Indeed, the other authors in this book present approaches to writing program evaluation that address the problems I will be raising. However, in program and curriculum research we are likely to find ourselves in contexts for making decisions in which the stakeholders for our evaluation reports are pragmatically logical. They are frequently concerned with the value added to students' learning by our writing programs or with the costs of our programs assessed against the benefits to our institutions. University administrators trained in higher education administration, in particular, are typically inculcated in social science research methodologies, which are primarily quantitative. Thus, methodological pressure similar to positivism that has influenced our research and scholarship—which we have continued to resist in that context—influences the practical work of our institutional lives as members of college and university English departments in general, and as WAC program administrators in particular. Furthermore, given that other stakeholders—our students and our colleagues—expect logic and order in our administration and assessment procedures, we have additional pressure to conform to their expectations about the conduct of our evaluation research studies.

In addition, many of us are likely to revert to a kind of practical positivism in program evaluation for two other reasons. First, as I have noted, our culture promotes a sense of the singleness of truth. Second, it is difficult to translate complex theories of writing and assessment into actual writing curricula and programmatic evaluation processes of those curricula. It is also difficult to balance competing institutional demands with the complexity of theory and research. However, if conducted appropriately, program evaluation can provide the tools of inquiry to help us design the most appropriate program of assessment for our institutions.

Ultimately, program evaluation has to be seen as an extension of the commitment that we have made to classroom-centered and teacher research; a form of self study of pedagogy, a way of researching our teaching and our students' learning. The primary goal of this chapter is to expose the sources of pressure I have been describing and to suggest that we must continue to resist any pressure that moves us away from the core of what we have learned about the complexity of writing and the teaching and learning of writing. Subtle institutional pressures and our tendency to be pragmatic about program evaluation can undermine our efforts. I will illustrate my point by the following story.

A WRITING PROGRAM EVALUATION

Several years ago, I was engaged by a college English department to conduct a writing program evaluation project as a member of a team of six researchers and teachers at a university I will call Altamont. The university as a whole and members of the English Department in particular were interested in understanding more about the status of their writing program and were beginning to plan for the future, as an aging faculty began retiring. There was clearly an interest among university administrators and several members of the department in planning for the kind of change that would be occurring. By the end of the project, the institution had invested approximately $60,000 in personnel and material costs to fund the evaluation research project, not to mention the countless hours volunteered by researchers, writing teachers, and students to develop, administer, and complete the various writing tasks and other assessment instruments which were not figured into the direct personnel costs of the evaluation. The evaluation team, with the assistance of the faculty, collected pretest data on every entering student in a three-course writing program which included a basic writing course and a two-semester long first-year composition sequence. In addition, we collected data in the introductory literature course for nonmajors because students' writing development was one of its stated objectives. We also followed up with post tests at the end of each student's first course (either basic writing or the first-semester writing course). We also followed up with a second post test at the end of each student's second-semester writing course (either first-semester composition or the second-semester writing course). Students in the introduction to literature courses were also pre and post-tested. In addition, we developed a qualitative data collection strand that involved an advanced doctoral student as a participant observer in each of three first-semester writing classes and a basic writing class. That researcher attended all sessions of each of the classes, took the examinations, and completed all writing assignments. In total, we had data for the entire year from more than 1,400 students and single-semester data from more than 3,000 students, as well as countless hours of observational data in the form of participant observer notes and behavioral surveys.

A very important problem emerged even before we began to consider the problems of research design, however. The evaluation team was unable to uncover any stated goals for the writing program or the writing in the literature course. The lack of goals arose, I think, in part from the theoretical orientation of the English Department toward writing. Because nearly every member of the department was trained in the tradition of belles lettres (rather than rhetoric), they all believed that they could recognize good writing and that they could teach willing and able students to write. For the most part, however, their definitions of good writing were pragmatic and pretheoretical. Their experience with holistic scoring under a previous, apparently paternalistic director of composition had provided them with opportunities to explore their communal sense of texts through frequent discussion of student texts as part of that regular departmental assessment process. Without education in teaching student writers, however, few had developed pedagogies from explicitly stated models of student writing, as opposed to models of writing based on literary authors. Furthermore, few had explicitly stated models of developmental processes for student writers, leaving them, for the most part, without an explicit rationale for their pedagogies.

In addition to a lack of an explicitly stated pedagogy, there was a tendency to polarize in the process of making decisions, leaving the department with the ability to only make minimal statements about the amount of work required of students in their writing courses and one or two specific, but minimal specifications for pedagogy, such as the number of papers that a student should writing in English 101 and that none of the writing should be about literature. In retrospect, it was unfortunate that no member of the research team considered tapping the interpretive community that had grown up among the members of the department though their collective experience with holistic scoring, departmental meetings, and coffee room discussion of students' writing.

The research consultants on the evaluation team made two crucial mistakes. The first involved a decision about the lack of goals for the program, and the second involved a decision about the perspective we would take on the data. The consultants spent considerable time debating, among ourselves, the lack of clear goals for the program. Our mistake lay in deciding, independently of consultation with the teachers on the team and other teachers in the department, to design an evaluation study that examined the growth of students as writers. Despite their lack of training and difficulty in articulating their pedagogies, many of the teachers had been developing those pedagogies for more than a quarter of a century. Viewed in retrospect, I believe that we imposed a growth model on the program without a concern for the genuine needs of the participating teachers and students. I cannot say that it was lack of a feeling of concern for the participants' views, although we systematically ignored them by not inviting them to our discussions. Nor can I say that it was a lack of concern for the growing complexity of the task, as the extent of the data collection strategies should indicate. For instance, getting a second post test from every student in the second-semester writing course required a member of the research team working full time for one semester. Nothing would have simplified our task more than to get a clear-cut, collective statement of goals for the program from the department to help us in designing our research plan. Without this guidance, we ended up collecting mountains of data—both quantitative and qualitative. Although this data was highly informative, we lacked an interpretive context for understanding what we had found, in terms of the participating teachers' views of their program.

I believe that the primary motivation of the researchers emerged from our own unexamined orientation toward program evaluation. Because educational evaluation is most often conducted in the context of a value-added orientation toward educational programs, we adopted a pre/post test design. This design also suits a growth model of student learning that was dominant in the curriculum and evaluation literature in all disciplines at the time over a decade ago.

We decided to use a mixed research design because the literature suggested that each approach to data collection could provide estimates of different aspects of the writing program. The quantitative data collection strategies were designed to give us an estimate of the extent of growth of the students as writers which was of primary interest to the broader institution in terms of future policy decisions. The qualitative data collection strategies were designed to help us understand how the three basic types of pedagogical approaches, uncovered in a survey of the faculty, led to that growth. The qualitative data were designed to be informative to the teachers in the program and program administrator, in particular, because they would provide the basis for planning modifications to the curriculum and suggest needed future support for the changes that would come among the faculty as new people joined the department to fill retirements.

In retrospect I have to confess that the research consultants seem to have adopted the role of missionaries in that we seemed like writing experts who arrived on campus to rescue the lost souls who, we believed, knew nothing about the teaching of writing, despite their obvious commitment and energy for the task. Ultimately, the chutzpa characterizing our task as enlightening primitives was the cause of our second, and arguably our most catastrophic error.[1]

Most of the faculty were committed to a fairly traditional view of writing and the teaching of writing. We assumed that our education had provided us with a superior vantage point for understanding what student writers at the university needed and how best to teach them to write. Thus, our evaluation report became a matter of telling the truth *as we saw it*. Our epistemological position was that the truth—as defined by our thoroughly designed and carefully balanced data collection and analysis—existed prior to our arrival on campus. A more constructivist position, in two senses of the word, would have been to attempt to define the program from within the perspective of the community and to help them locate their own senses of the strengths and weaknesses of the program as they sought to define growth areas for themselves and the program for the future.

By taking the position that we were there to tell people what was going on, rather than helping them see what they were doing more clearly, we, in effect, invited them to reject our findings and our recommendations. We made the evaluation findings "unusable" by the participants, to a very large extent.[2]

LESSONS LEARNED

I relearned, in a very hard way, two lessons that 10 years of prior training and work in educational evaluation had taught me and that I also carefully

---

[1] See Wendy Bishop's *Something Old, Something New* for an examination of this tendency in our field.

[2] After 2 years of work in the department, the researchers on the team presented the findings to the department at a public meeting. The findings were quite strong. We found that students at the end of the first-semester course made statistically and educationally significant gains in their writing ability, as measured by a comparison of pre/post test, holistically scored essays. Our recommendations involved extensive training to update the faculty on contemporary methods of instruction in composition, as the qualitative results suggested that the majority of the faculty were using current-traditional methodologies. In particular, the qualitative results suggested that one of the best teachers in the department was giving problematic instruction because he was using a current-traditional approach. This finding was stated in the final report despite the fact that the growth of the writers in that teacher's class were, measured quantitatively, one of the two best in the department.

Despite the involvement by the department chair and other key senior faculty in the department in the planning and implementation of the study, the meeting turned into a session where several senior members of the department acted in confrontational ways that went beyond anything I have ever experienced. All of the teachers on the team distanced themselves from the report and the criticism quite explicitly. It was not a pleasant experience, and, as I have suggested, was one that could have been avoided by more careful listening at the outset of the study. The researchers would have also had to lose their attitude about the superiority of their approach to teaching writing.

ignored as the missionary zeal increased among the researchers on the team. The first lesson is that evaluation research must serve the purposes of the participants in the writing program being examined. The second lesson involves the stance of anyone who proposes to assume the role of "evaluator" of an educational project. Program evaluation cannot be turned into *conversion experience*. Although we developed a state of the art evaluation program based on a mix of qualitative and quantitative types of data, we failed to serve our basic constituency, the participants in the program, because we caused them to reject much in the report of the study.

The study of writing has developed considerably since that time. Constructivism, an emergent ideology at the time of the evaluation program I have just described, has clearly taken a central position in challenging the predominantly cognitive and quantitative models of writing and program evaluation that we were using as the basis for our work. Thus, some interpretation of my experience is possible only in retrospect. However, I had 10 years of experience in educational evaluation projects in which I had learned to be more respectful of program participants. I think that the missionary zeal that I displayed in the project emerges from two important places. The first is the study of writing itself. As I have suggested, Wendy Bishop has described the proponents of "new paradigm" writing pedagogy in terms that are quite like the zeal of the missionary out to convert the heathens to the "correct" view of the field. I think that I have made this particular sin of pride explicit in my narrative.

However, in this chapter, I am more interested in the historical conditioning of educational evaluation by its antecedent discipline, educational research methodologies, and the contexts which led to a sense that educational programs needed evaluation at all. The arrogance of experts, including our own, is something that many of us must face in our professional lives. However, I think that the systemic problems resulting from the historical antecedents of our activities are much harder to understand because they do not always remain accessible in contemporary theory. Thus, I want to describe the origins of program evaluation in educational research methodologies as a way of demonstrating why, even if we had not been filled with the conceit of a superior sense of knowledge, my researcher colleagues and I who were involved with the English department evaluation described above would probably have been doomed to the same result.

LOGICAL POSITIVISM AS THE BASIS FOR A SCIENCE OF EDUCATION

Writing in 1917, Walter Scott Monroe looked for the development of "standards of measurement which will do for education what has been done for agriculture as a result of the application of scientific knowledge and scientific methods to farming" (p. vii). In the social and intellectual context of the turn of the century, logical positivism appeared to promise that science would allow men, thorough rational and orderly scientific enquiry, to determine the fundamental nature of phenomena and thus, to control the future. Monroe is referring directly to Fisherian experimental research design models that had helped to develop a science of agriculture, which resulted in considerably greater crop yields and increasingly disease- and pest-resistant strains of basic food sources. Reading Monroe and other educational and psychological measurement specialists of the time reveals the optimism that was at the heart of logical positivism as it was emerging in natural sciences in terms of its potential application to the social sciences and education. This optimism was the basis for a Utopian view of the future; a future when science would solve all problems faced by humans as they became increasingly able to control their environment and protect themselves against the future in terms of both the natural and cultural ecology.

However, as viewed today, the rhetoric of this perspective seems condescendingly paternalistic and dangerously deterministic. I say nothing new when I observe that logical positivism, at least in its radically deterministic form, is not seriously maintained by scientists in any field today. Although both natural and social sciences remain empirical in their basic methodologies, few natural or social scientists currently look toward the time when their fields can provide solutions to the problems they face in explaining the phenomena of their disciplines, much less to the problems of allied fields.

If, as I will attempt to demonstrate, evaluation research emerges from educational research methodology, then the conceit of the positivist expert results in precisely the paternalist attitude that my colleagues and I displayed in our stance toward the English department we evaluated. English literature of the 19th century is filled with the descriptions of such attitudes, which are based on the sense of superiority of the emerging sciences, based in positivism. The condescending superiority of Sherlock Holmes, for instance, who demeans the intuitive methodologies of the police compared to his scientific approach to solving crime, is a good example. While Sir Arthur Conan Doyle portrays Holmes as a flawed character because of his cocaine addiction, he certainly seems to hold him up as an example of the possibilities that the future holds if only we have enough sense to let science take its course. More importantly, Holmes' flaws seem to suggest that his scientific methodology is more superior because it can be applied by imperfect humans to achieve infallible results.

However, the Utopia that was promised by logical positivism remains highly problematic. For instance, agricultural researchers have found that increased crop yields can exhaust farm land so that it is no longer useful, even as pasture land. Thus, the search for crops that are permanently disease- and pest-resistant has proved to be a dream. Researchers continue to struggle to keep ahead of diseases and pests that mutate nearly as rapidly as new, resistant strains of agricultural crops are developed. Thus, science can never provide a "finished product" that will allow humans to rest in the comfort of a utopia where science has answered all the questions and solved all of the problems.

Another promised Utopia of positivist experimental methodology emerged in medical research. The miracle antibiotic drugs invented in this century suggested that we would soon be able to conquer disease. Cures or prophylactic practices that seemed to defeat the most pernicious and perpetual diseases plaguing humans—syphilis and other sexually transmitted diseases, tuberculosis, polio, whooping cough, plague, among many others— were uncovered by biomedical research based in the same experimental research methodology used in agriculture. Recent developments, such as AIDS and the Eubola virus, however, have confounded the optimism of medical scientists who struggle to define and contain these epidemics. At the same time, the miracle drugs of the 1940s and 1950s are less efficacious with repeated use. Strains of diseases such as tuberculosis which are resistant to older antibiotics suggest that human diseases, like agricultural diseases, can mutate to forms that cannot be controlled without continual research into new forms of antibiotics.

In social sciences, B. F. Skinner promised a social Utopia in his book *Walden Two,* based on his theory of human behavior. His book, like Conan Doyle's, explores, through literary form, the results he imagines of his theory of operant conditioning as applied to educational and other political institutions. His optimistic promises reflect the power of positivism as late as the 1960s to give social scientists a very powerful sense of the possibility of providing a Utopic future. The problems with his theory and the practical limits of operant conditioning were clearly defined by linguists such as Noam Chomsky and cognitive psychologists such as Howard Gardiner.

The fact that science can never be conclusive does not provide a necessary condition for repudiation of its aims and methodologies, however. It would be easy to accept a revision to positivism that would see the need for continuing struggle with basic explanations of phenomena and technological manipulation of the human natural and cultural ecology as a substitution of a more realistic pragmatism for the earlier Utopic optimism. Most contemporary scientists seem to have made this transition quite easily. I suspect that this position is dominant in most scientific fields. In social sciences, and in evaluation research in particular, Egon Guba has continually challenged such a revised view of science by pointing out that the truth itself represents a socially constructed view. To understand that science is socially constructed also suggests that it must be viewed in the same terms as other cultural artifacts. Thus, disciplines are not orderly structures, built on a logical foundation; instead, they are quite chaotic and are based on the particular problems or problem sets that have been of interest to a particular disciplinary community over the course of the history of the discipline. (The recognition that science is not the salvation of humans might be a greater cause for humility, but the rhetoric of expertise does not seem to have changed greatly.)

However, there are two important problems that still remain with positivism as an orientation toward research methodology. The first problem is not part of the epistemology of positivism, but is at the heart of the logical structure of positivist approaches to science. It was quickly realized that phenomena were too complex to study in vivo. This difficulty led to research methodologies that used segmentation of scientific problems into manageable sets. Because science involves segmentation of problems into parts that can be subjected to experimental methodologies involving control and manipulation of those parts, researchers have tended to ignore problems not directly related to their immediate concerns. Thus, DDT became a widely used pesticide, until in *Silent Spring* Rachel Carson sounded the alarm about its effects on the environment. Failure to understand the consequences of manipulating the natural and human social ecology is one of the main practical failures of positivist science and represents the failure of scientists to engage in critical examinations of the foundations of their disciplines, which would have led them to raise questions about the interrelatedness of knowledge and possible collateral consequences of their work. Lack of critical examination can also lead to failure to consider the moral and ethical responsibilities inherent in any research methodology, including the moral and ethical responsibilities for potential uses of research results. This is the case with atomic physics. For instance, there seemed to be a clear sense of the military potential of nuclear fission, but several prominent scientists ignored the problem in their excitement about answering basic questions in the field.

The second problem arises from an epistemological perspective. The basic goal of positivism was to discover the logical framework that would provide explanations for the phenomena in various fields. Research programs were based on a belief that science was intended to discover "context free" laws that determined the basic functioning of the natural and social world. Egon Guba uses this term to describe the positivist's view resulting from the epistemological principle of objectivity. The laws that scientists aimed to discover were considered objective because they were thought to have existed prior to the attempt to discover them and were thus independent of the cultural context of the observer. As a result, scientists had to use methodological approaches that took them outside of their subjective experience with the natural and social world in the process of discovering those laws. Hence, methodology becomes the driving force in science.

Furthermore, mathematics was considered to be a logical system independent of human subjectivity because, given certain assumptions, it could be shown to provide a rational and consistent logical model of phenomena. The more abstract a science, the more it relied on mathematical models for its methodology.

THE CHALLENGE TO POSITIVISM

Many social scientists and educational researchers, writing specialists among them, have disavowed positivism. Indeed, the very assumptions of all science have been shaken by questions about the foundations of science in both social and natural sciences. Thus, the theory underlying most disciplines has been severely challenged by, for instance, social constructionist and feminist perspectives. However, western European and northern American culture retains, at its very roots, an essential pragmatism that is founded in empiricism (the belief that seeing is believing), and the faith that logic and order—when viewed from our perspective—will prevail over disorder and chaos.

Writing in 1976, William Cooley and Paul Lohnes located the importance of seeing, particularly as one aspect of the state of evaluation research in education:

> There is debate today over who should be conducting evaluation studies. Some claim that developers of new educational means should not be engaged in evaluating the effectiveness of those means because of their obvious bias in favor of them. This is like saying that Priestly's experiments on oxygen should not be believed because he was biased against the phlogiston theory of burning.... What tends to keep researchers honest is the publicly available record of what they did and what they found and not a godlike objectivity which some people seem to feel those doing evaluation should exhibit.

Thus, after almost 80 years after Monroe, we can see that basic notions of the science of education have begun to change. Objectivity as an epistemological principle is replaced by a recognition that researchers have a vested interest in their research. Implicit in Cooley and Lohnes' statement is the belief that the discussion about research among the community of researchers will tend to make explicit the positioning of authors as they report on their research.

I want to argue that this position, published in 1976, but written some 10 years earlier according to Lohnes, is a precursor of a postmodern view of science—a view that admits the embeddedness of any researcher, but in particular the evaluation researcher, in a social context. Furthermore, it admits that evaluation researchers not only do have, but should have, a commitment to the programs they are evaluating. It is interesting that sitting on the lowest rung on the hierarchial ladder of science, program evaluators should be among the first to raise important questions about the notion of objectivity—the central epistemological tenet of positivism. Egon Guba and Yvonna Lincoln, two other noted educational evaluators, go into a much more developed series of positions on the problems of positivism and its application, not just to evaluation research, but in any scientific research methodology.

EVALUATION RESEARCH

Cooley and Lohnes began to explore the problem of objectivity at about the same time the federal government began pouring massive amounts of money into education. Educational program assessment emerged in the historical context of the development of federal entitlement programs for education. The primary problem for any centralized attempt to alter educational practices in the United States is that education is funded and directed locally through the collection of local taxes and the election of school board members. State governments exert differing amounts of control over school districts, but ultimately, the legal and fiscal responsibility for each school district lies with its school board.

Both state and federal funding became one method for centralizing control over the independence of schools, because it let school districts pay part of the costs of their programs without increasing local taxes. Of course, school districts seeking funds are subject to conformity with federal and state guidelines. An evaluation of the way funds are used by local boards becomes important; because the money made available to educational programs by government funding agencies has never been sufficient to fund all requests for assistance, those agencies began demanding both an accounting of the manner in which the money was spent and a report of the value returned for the investment of capital in educational programs. Thus, evaluation became the operative word in program and curriculum assessment. Furthermore, the funding made available to local education agencies, such as school boards, was designed to promote particular kinds of programs, thus leading to the need for objective evaluators. Here, objective means evaluators that would not have a vested interest in the local program, but would provide an external accounting of the conformity of the program under study to the funding guidelines that made it possible. However, it ought to be clear that evaluators did have a vested interest in the program continuing because it provided them with consulting fees, a definite source of income. Thus, it is unlikely that any external evaluator can be seen to be entirely objective. However, as Cooley and Lohnes note, the report of the evaluation study should contain sufficient information to make the results of any special bias explicit.

It is tempting for those in higher education to say that government regulation is not a problem. However, one only has to look at the regulation of higher education that currently exists to understand that all of our curricula may come under the same legislative pressure that has been placed on the public schools. Any university receiving funds from the federal government, for instance, must conform to Title IX guidelines for gender equity in athletics. Furthermore, a number of policies mandating ethical review of research using animals and human subjects have affected the process by which researchers at universities plan their work. (It is worth noting that these two kinds of policies in particular were written in response to perceptions that discriminatory or unethical behavior was widespread.)

Calls for more uniform college curricula have already been seen in several states, such as Florida, where the College Level Assessment Program is used to regulate writing curricula at public universities. Furthermore, given that the first WAC programs were created through funding from the National Endowment for the Humanities, government intervention is explicitly connected to WAC.

In the context of government funding and regulation, evaluation, as it is typically used in education, involves using assessment as a basis for judging the relative merit or value of individuals within a group. It also involves evaluation of the conformity of the program to the funding guidelines. Thus, evaluation research uses assessment as the basis for making judgments about the relative merit of programs and assures federal and state funding agencies and institutional administrators that their money is, indeed, causing education to move in the direction that they intended when they made it available. In the same way that teachers often grade students with indices of the relative merit of their achievement, educational program research was intended to provide an index that would allow those in charge of funding to understand the relative merit of the expenditures they approved.

Given this goal for educational evaluation research, it is easy to see how the emphasis on the use of standardized tests, with nationally established norms, emerged. The worth of a particular educational project was established if it could show that it induced unusual gains in standardized test scores or if it caused a movement of a particular reference group in the population of students to higher levels than had been observed in the past. For instance, if a WAC program, which involves three writing-intensive courses, produces gains on a standardized test of writing ability that indicated students in the college grew from below average on the test at the beginning of their college careers to well above average at graduation, the program could claim to be particularly successful. Unfortunately, there are no such tests or any such norms for the college student population.

The federal and state funding agencies required that evaluation research projects be conducted by third parties contracting with the recipient of the funding. The intent of this requirement was to provide the funding agencies, and ultimately the legislative body that appropriated tax money as the funding source, with reasonable assurances that the research procedures were not designed to provide only self-serving information at the same time evaluation reports provided a demonstration of the effectiveness of control over the directions that education would lead. Herein lies the objectivity in evaluation studies to which Cooley and Lohnes refer. As W. James Popham, a noted educational evaluation expert, puts it,

> local educators had to evaluate a given year's...projects if they wished to continue to receive the subsequent year's...money. And money, as we know, represents an exceptionally powerful incentive for getting people to modify their behavior. (p. 4)

The closest analogy to this kind of evaluation research is the financial audit that is common in both the public and the private sectors. External accountants come into a business or public agency and certify that the bookkeeping practices are honest and that all assets and liabilities are appropriately accounted for. Of course, the licensure process for certified public accountants provides a basis for establishing their credibility as auditors.

In education, there have never been any such certification or licensure processes for individuals who conduct assessment and evaluation projects. Of course, the earned doctorate in a field provides some assurance of the quality of an individual's work, but in a field such as writing, the variability of expertise in writing assessment among holders of the doctorate in rhetoric, composition, and English teacher education suggests that not all recipients are equally or similarly qualified to conduct evaluation research. Furthermore, at the time evaluation research was emerging in education, psychometricians like Cooley and Lohnes had a lock on perceptions of expertise in educational research, at least among the politicians, bureaucrats, and educators that ran funding agencies. In an effort to assist recipients of funding, money was provided to set up a series of regional educational laboratories. These regional laboratories were not unlike the current funding made available to the Center for the Study of Reading at the University of Illinois. The difference is that the prevailing model at the time the regional labs were set up suggested that all knowledge and pedagogy in all disciplines shared some common properties. Thus, language learning and teaching were considered to be similar in fundamental ways to the teaching and learning in science, social science, and mathematics.

The current state of the art in writing assessment is due partly to these developments. And there is another factor: the tools these evaluators used. Because third-party evaluators required assessment tools, educational institutions and evaluators found them readily available "off the shelf" from such vendors as Educational Testing Service and the Psychological Corporation.

Such tools readily provided the normative data necessary for "objective" evaluation research. Unfortunately, although these tools were well-suited to large scale assessment, they were not as well suited to the assessment of individual achievement. Furthermore, the assessment tools had to be cost effective to norm reference through the use of large random samples of students enrolled in schools. Although local development and administration costs are about the same for either multiple-choice or holistic scoring assessments, the costs of norming research are proportionally quite different to conduct. Thus, multiple-choice tests of writing, which could be easily administered and scored clearly, won the contest.

Because educational assessment is considered a costly endeavor under any circumstances, the most cost-effective thing to do was to have assessment tools serve two purposes: program and student evaluation (see Williamson, 1994 for more in-depth discussion of the importance of efficiency in educational assessment). Thus, we have the needs of the individual subsumed by the needs of the institution.

One practical result of the perceived need for objectivity in evaluating an educational program is the third-party evaluator. This kind of perspective in an evaluation study is precisely what Cooley and Lohnes are disputing. Most federal government educational funding mandates an independent evaluation of the program, hence the use of third-party evaluators. This model persists in writing program assessment in the model used by the Writing Program Administration (WPA) when they offer evaluation consulting. However, although it involves on-site observation, such consultation does not typically involve the methodological rigor mandated by federal guidelines. WPA consultants can provide assurance to college or university administrators that their local program expert is working at professionally acceptable standards. But, the extent of formal self-study that precedes the visit of evaluation consultants determines how much impact they can have on the day-to-day workings of a WAC program.

WAC PROGRAM EVALUATION

It is important to remember that WAC programs got their start with federal funding. The federal money made available through the National Endowment for the Humanities and the Fund for the Improvement of Post Secondary Education that helped several of the very early programs to operate in innovative ways may very well be why program assessment and evaluation is foregrounded for participants in WAC programs, compared to other college writing programs. However, literacy seems to be a special problem in higher education, because writing programs are much more likely to be the target of assessment and evaluation schemes. Few people call for assessment of students' ability in biology or chemistry, for instance, even though there has been a fairly consistent sense that there is a problem in science education since the Russian's launched Sputnik in advance of America's first attempt to get a satellite orbiting around the earth.

I do not have sufficient space to develop an argument about the reason for public concern and scrutiny of literacy education. It is probably sufficient to say that an individual's literacy is directly related to his or her educational achievement and limits. Thus, the teaching of literacy has special sociopolitical implications that cause people from across the range of the American political spectrum to take a special interest in what is taught in any writing class at American universities and how it is taught. It is clear that the future is likely to bring more, as opposed to less, regulation, thus leading to increasing requirements for assessment and evaluation. As a result, participants in WAC programs are increasingly likely to face both internal and external review.

SOME PRACTICAL CONSIDERATIONS FOR WAC EVALUATION

I hope that my story and discussion illustrate clearly the first and most important consideration in any evaluation process. The parties to the process have to sit down and provide an explicit basis for undertaking the evaluation. All stakeholders for the evaluation report have to be considered at this point. It is not necessary, however, to see a mandated, external evaluation as a necessarily bad medicine that has to be suffered. In my experience, university English departments are all too likely to see such a mandate as merely a product-oriented matter that has to be suffered through to satisfy some internal or external bureaucracy. I would argue that even a mandated external evaluation can be co-opted by a department that is willing to accept the invitation to examine itself with an eye to improving its understanding of its program. Thus, the time, effort, and money spent on evaluation need not be wasted in gestures, but can be put to some real use by participants in WAC programs.

However, a sense of how to use an evaluation process to learn more about oneself and to look for needed changes only begins with a shared sense that the purpose of the evaluation reflects the stakeholders' sense of the program and how they should study themselves or be studied by outsiders. My narrative in this chapter demonstrates what happens when evaluators usurp for themselves the process of developing decisions involved with both the goals of the program and the design of the evaluation itself. This process should have involved as broad a representation of the community within and without the department as possible.

Of course, the program needs to have clearly defined goals. The unfortunate situation that confronted the English department I worked with rarely faces WAC programs, I suspect. The more clearly defined goals of WAC programs derive from WAC program administrators' understanding that they have to work with several other programs and departments in the course of helping students learn to write "across the curriculum." There is no substitute, however, for linking the discussions about why an evaluation should be undertaken with a clarification of the goal statements that exist, because goals may have been approved some years earlier and may not be retrievable in written form or have been changed considerably by changes in the institution, without subsequent processing through the mandated approval processes.

I know of one WAC program that was mandated by a college dean, for instance, because he wanted his institution to be sure to participate in one of the most important new options that could be used to sell it to prospective students and parents. Faculty at that university complained that no new funds were made available to support a program. Furthermore, course descriptions were pressed through the curriculum review process to get them on line as quickly as possible, with little regard for their academic credibility. So, even WAC programs are not immune to failure to establish goals or to program drift.

Another danger in program evaluation lies with evaluation consultants who adopt a single approach to design and attempt to fit any program into their preconceived designs. Our adoption of a pre/post test design at Altamont resulted from the training of two of the evaluation consultants at an institution where the dominant orientation toward curriculum research was "experimental," specifically multivariate, repeated measures designs. We had studied with one of the international figures in the field and had internalized his approach to research design, not as one option to be used in an appropriate setting, but as *the only choice we were able to define for ourselves at the time*. I have also worked on evaluation studies that began with the kind of process that I have been advocating here. In planning the study, the research design grew organically out of the requirements of the external funding agencies and the needs that were articulated by the participants in the program. Unfortunately, few evaluation studies are published in the literature. One that is was authored by Linda Hollandsworth; her carefully designed study at a university in South Carolina presents a highly focused picture of the needs of students entering the writing program—one aspect of evaluating a writing program.[3]

---

[3] One of the best published examples of a qualitative study that used an organic approach to research design was recently completed by Gail Okawa. Although this study is not an example of evaluation work, it does provide an excellent view of her thinking as she developed a design to examine influences on the career paths of faculty of color in college and university English departments. Thus, it provides a model for others who would follow.

Another important aspect of conducting an evaluation study is maintaining communication with stakeholders throughout the evaluation process. While we did not fail to stay in contact with the stakeholders at Altamont, we did begin the project with a fundamental failure to establish communications about certain aspects of the evaluation. Professional pride, in particular, caused us to fail to imagine that the teacher participants would have any useful perspective on the evaluative stance we took toward the program. However, it is equally important to remain in contact with the stakeholders throughout the program through some form of regular communication that avoids the problems generated by the rumor mill. Evaluation is a particularly stressful time for teachers and program administrators. It may cause them to expose themselves to outsiders who are not likely to engage in a similar kind of exposure until the end of the process. All of us who have had observers in our writing classrooms—regardless of the extent of our experience, the cooperativeness of the students, and the disposition of the observer—can understand that fear of being exposed.

Most importantly, communication among all the participants in a WAC program during an evaluation gives everyone a sense of ownership of the evaluation. If, as was the case at Altamont, evaluators set themselves up as external experts, the result is that the teachers in the program may reject the results of the evaluation as something done to them, not something done with them. It is this sense of ownership that is also crucial to an assessment that produces the kind of complex and contextualized picture of WAC programs compelled by our research and our teaching. Including all perspectives in an evaluation study guarantees, it seems to me, both that the participants will feel included and that the complexity of perspectives on the program will be represented in the report of the evaluation.

CONCLUSION

I have always believed that program assessment can be one of the most important steps that we take to understand our professional lives and our teaching. It can provide an opportunity for us to sit back and reflect on what we are doing in our classes and how effectively we seem to be meeting the needs of our students. Unfortunately, program evaluation, as I have attempted to show, has emerged as a form of accountability. We have to be very careful when we undertake an assessment of our work that we do not find ourselves co-opted by individuals who fail to understand either the complexity of our work or the problematic origins of evaluation studies themselves. When our attempts to obtain descriptions of our work are undermined, we are robbed of the most valuable thing that any teacher can be given: the opportunity to reflect on our work. I count reflection as especially important to my own teaching because it is what keeps me from giving up on the frustrations of teaching. Taking the time to reflect on a carefully prepared description of my teaching allows me to see my strengths and weakness and allows me to understand how I might change to improve my work. Because teaching involves learning to address the needs of an ever-changing group of students with changing needs, change is both a survival skill and a necessary tool for success. Continued frustration is precisely what burns out writing teachers, and the frustration of whole groups of teachers is what causes programs to fail.

Finally, then, program assessment is a matter of continuing professional health for individual teachers and the programs that they comprise, but only if it is conducted in ways that are sensitive to the needs of the particular context in which they teach and in which their students learn.

REFERENCES

Bishop, W. (1990). *Something old, something new*. Carbondale and Edwardsville, IL: SIU.

Cherry, R., & Meyer, P. In Michael M. Williamson and Brian A. Huot, 109-141.

Chomsky, N. (1959). A review of B. F. Skinner's *verbal behavior*. *Language, 35*, 26-58.

Conan Doyle, Sir Arthur. (1930). *The adventures of Sherlock Holmes*. New York: Harper.

Cooley, W. W., & Lohnes, P. R. (1976). *Evaluation research in education: Theory, principles, and practice*. New York: Wiley.

Gardiner, H. (1987). *The mind's new science: A history of the cognitive revolution*. New York: Basic Books.

Guba, E. G. The Alternative Paradigm Dialog. In Egon Guba, 17-30.

Guba, E. G. (Ed.) (1990). *The Paradigm Dialog. Newbury Park, CA: Sage*.

Guba, E. G., & Lincoln, Y. S. (1985). *Naturalistic inquiry*. Beverly Hills: Sage.

Hawisher, G. E., & LeBlanc, P. (Eds.) (1992). *Re-imagining computers and composition: Teaching and research in the virtual age*. National Council of Teachers of English: Urbana.

Hollandsworth, L. *A needs assessment model for college writing program evaluation*. Dissertation, Indiana University of Pennsylvania, 190.

Monroe, W. S. (1918). *Measuring the results of teaching*. New York: Houghton Mifflin.

Okawa, G. (1995). *Expanding perspectives of teacher knowledge: A descriptive study of autobiographical narratives of writing teachers of color*. Dissertation, Indiana University of Pennsylvania.

Popham, W. J. (1993). *Educational evaluation (2nd ed.)*. Boston: Allyn and Bacon.

Skinner, B. F. (1948). *Walden Two*. New York: Macmillan.

Taylor, P. Social epistemic rhetoric and chaotic discourse. In Gail E. Hawisher and Paul Leblanc, pp. 131–148.

Williamson, M. M. (1994). The worship of efficiency. *Journal of Assessing Writing,* *1*(2),

Williamson, M. M., & Huot, B.A. (Eds.) (1993). *Validating holistic scoring for writing assessment: Theoretical and empirical foundations.* Cresskill, NJ: Hampton.

Author Index

Subject Index